CONFESSIONS OF A BISHOP

A Guide to Augustine's Confessions

Kevin Dodge

Copyright ©2014 by Incarnation Classics Press
All Rights Reserved
ISBN: 0692266577
ISBN 13: 9780692266571
Library of Congress Control Number: 2014914547
Incarnation Classics Publishing, Dallas, TX

Cover Art:
St. Augustine's Vision of St. Jerome
By Benozzo Gozzoli
Apsidal Chapel, San Gimignano, Italy
Cover Design: Courtney Barrow

The truth is that to understand an author it is not enough merely to read him.

Henri de Lubac,
Augustinianism and Modern Theology

Each age has its own outlook. It is specially good at seeing certain truths and specially liable to make certain mistakes. We all, therefore, need the books that will correct the characteristic mistakes of our own period. And that means the old books.

C.S. Lewis, God in the Dock,
"On the Reading of Old Books"

ACKNOWLEDGEMENTS

Writing is mostly a solitary activity, but, in truth, no author ever really writes alone. This is certainly true in my case.

First, thanks go to Dr. Gregory Nagy of Harvard University, whose course "The Ancient Greek Hero" first provided the idea of employing "Focus Texts." The structure of this book is indebted to his insights on how to teach great literature.

I am also grateful to three teachers who enabled me read the *Confessions* with far more insight: Dr. Jeff Bingham, Dr. Michael Svigel and Dr. Barry Jones. This book would never have happened without their tutelage.

As someone who lives with Multiple Sclerosis, I am also grateful to those in the medical community who have invested their lives to looking after my health and well-being, especially Dr. Cinzia Levalds, Dr. Elliot Frohman and Diana Logan. This book hopefully shows good things can come from trials we would rather not endure.

Special thanks go as well to the community of Augustine scholars. My debts here are far too numerous to list as a perusal of my endnotes will show. Special mention goes to Dr. James O'Donnell, especially for his detailed philological work, Dr. Philip Cary, for his insights into the problem of evil, Dr. Michael Cameron, for his fine work in Augustine's exegesis, Dr. Frederick Crosson for his understanding of the structure of the *Confessions* and to Dr. Garry Wills for his interpretive insights.

My thanks also go to various Church leaders who have helped me along the way, especially John Gillette, who got me to read the *Confessions* for the first time, Dr. David Jeremiah, who taught me to love the Scriptures and Bishop Anthony Burton for his encouragement and gentle prodding to think bigger.

Thanks as well to those who read the manuscript and offered helpful comments, including David Baldwin, Matthew and Juliana Crownover, Leigh Fredrickson, Seth Hale, Mark Howell as well as Michael and Kristin Latham. Thanks especially to Ellora Hermerding for her tireless energy in editing the manuscript.

My most profuse thanks go to Father Joe Hermerding who hatched the original idea for this project, opened his home on multiple occasions to discuss it, spent hours helping to hone its message and managed to never fail in his enthusiasm. At many points when my confidence flagged, Father Joe was the friend I needed. I can say with confidence that this book would not have become a reality without his unflagging encouragement.

I am grateful as well to my wife Lorelee for her patience in enduring countless discussions about life in the fourth and fifth centuries. It takes a special woman to allow such an endeavor and I'm grateful for her love and partnership.

Despite all this help, all errors, omissions and other blunders are my responsibility alone. *Soli Deo Gloria*

A Note On Translations

This Guide employs many quotations throughout the vast corpus of Augustine's and others' writings. Out of necessity, this has required translating Augustine's fifth-century Latin into contemporary English. All translations, unless otherwise noted, are my own. My sources for these translations were primarily the critical texts found in in the Corpus Scriptorum Ecclesiasticorum Latinorum (CSEL) and Corpus Christianorum Series Latina (CCSL) volumes. My translations from the Greek of Plotinus are from the Loeb Classical Library Series. My translations from the Greek of Athanasius and John Cassian are from Sources Crétiennes (Editions du Cerf) volumes. Biblical quotations are from the Revised Standard Version (RSV). Of course, all translation errors are my responsibility alone.

TABLE OF CONTENTS

PREFACE

I have written this Guide to meet a need within the Church–[1] to help Christians interact with one of the greatest works of Christian literature, Augustine's *Confessions*. For those of us who appreciate the so-called "Great Tradition," Augustine was integral to the development and formation of that tradition. Thus we should try to understand what he was saying as he wrote.

As we'll see, Augustine wrote the *Confessions* for several reasons. I believe the primary importance of the *Confessions* lies in teaching us to read the Bible and to pray. Further, since the *Confessions* culminates in several mystical experiences, Augustine shows us that the apex of the Christian life is for the soul to turn inward, to rise up and participate in Christ.

The problem is that it has been 1,600 years since Augustine wrote. His life, assumptions, issues and controversies are largely different than ours. He knew little of our modern-day concerns. Yet he would have almost certainly been dismayed at the divisions which have occurred in the Church, as there is supposed to be One, Holy, Catholic, and Apostolic Church.

Augustine is endlessly fascinating once we understand what he is trying to communicate. On the surface, he is telling us the story of his life (which, in and of itself, is interesting), but below the surface there are deeper levels of meaning that unfold.

---

1   Throughout this Guide, I employ the word "Church" or "Catholic Church" to describe the universal Christian Church that existed in Augustine's day which confessed a common Creed, recognized a largely standardized Bible, had an authority structure with duly-constituted Bishops and observed a common set of sacramental rites. I do not deny that other groups existed calling themselves "Christian," but the "One, Holy, Catholic and Apostolic Church" is what Augustine means when he refers to the Church. With all Christians, I pray for the healing of the sad divisions which separate the visible Church in the present-day world.

My job is to be your guide for this story. Like travel to any foreign country, the language, the concepts and the assumptions all are jarring at first, but as we become acclimated, we often grow to love surroundings which were once foreign. My task is to lead you through a foreign land, interpreting Augustine without detracting from his remarkable message.

I have not written this Guide as a scholarly work, although it will make use of what scholars have observed through time. Perhaps like you, I am an interested reader, a Christian and one who struggled through the *Confessions* numerous times until wiser, more experienced guides came along to help me understand what Augustine was saying. This help was instrumental in my gaining a greater degree of understanding and my goal is to return the favor.

But how should we read Augustine? I invite you to use this book as a help while reading Augustine's *Confessions*. While you will get plenty out of just reading this Guide on its own, you'll maximize your efforts if you read the text of the *Confessions* along with this book. Any translation will do.

After an Introduction, each Chapter of the Guide corresponds to a Chapter of the *Confessions*. They all follow the same structure – (1) a summary of the Chapter, (2) a "Focus Text" section and, after some Chapters, (3) a background section which provides some theological, literary or historical aids for understanding. It's the Focus Text section that is especially important. I'd suggest reading the overview quickly, but then lingering on the Focus Texts with the commentary I've provided. You can then use the questions at the end of each Focus Text section for discussion or reflection.

One thing I want to emphasize is you do not have to agree with everything Augustine writes. Augustine forms the western consensus on Christian orthodoxy, so we should agree with him as much as we can. But most Christian traditions have found themselves troubled by something Augustine asserts. My suggestion is to approach this study with an open mind. You'll learn a lot if you do.

How to Use This Guide

But let's admit something. Augustine is not easy to read. He goes on long tangents that seem to have little to do with the story. He berates himself for things many consider normal. He doesn't even seem to be all that psychologically well at times. This has led to many misunderstandings of Augustine, particularly in the past century.

My first exposure to Augustine came as an adult. Having largely abandoned the Church for almost a decade in my twenties, I came back to it with vigor and an ardent desire to build a spiritual life. I wanted to understand the Scriptures since I was surprised to find out that Biblical language was all around me; I just didn't know it.

A friend suggested that if I really wanted to understand the Bible, I needed to read Augustine. This seemed odd – why did I need to read Augustine to understand the Bible? He pointed out that the Fathers of the Church provided a window into how the Bible was being read by those only a few generations removed from the Apostles. So the logical starting point seemed to be the *Confessions*. It was Augustine's story – how the great sinner became a saint, or so I thought. I was hooked on the *idea* of reading Augustine.

But then the reality came – it was really hard to read Augustine without help. Yes, people told me, Christians had been reading Augustine for centuries and the *Confessions* was the original Christian best seller. But that still didn't make it easier. I struggled through that first reading, often confused, because I had no one to help me. The point of this Guide is to give you the help you need to ask better questions of the text and, ultimately, of Augustine himself.

Please be sure to read the Introduction which follows this Preface because it is specifically designed to help with your exploration. To read Augustine well, we ought to understand something about his world, especially since it is so different from our own. We also ought to observe the societal issues that were swirling about him. Finally, we should understand why it was so important to Augustine that his readers understand the Bible well.

I believe Augustine meant for the *Confessions* to be read primarily within the Church since many of his original readers would have been under his care as their Bishop. To be sure, the Church was not his only intended audience. Particularly in the last three Chapters (11-13), Augustine seems to have some of his intellectual opponents in mind. Yet the *Confessions* has been read most profitably by those who can confess the Apostles and Nicene Creeds. As such, Augustine assumes the reader knows something about the Christian faith, about the triune God and about why that God is worthy of worship. I believe there are few better ways to deepen your faith than to read Augustine. He is just that helpful.

Yet this Guide is also trying to be realistic. I understand you probably don't have hours of spare time to devote to the study of the *Confessions*. I recognize that busy lives often press upon spiritual pursuits, however well-intentioned we might be. In short, I'm trying to make things easier for you, not harder.

After the Introduction which follows, the Guide is divided up into nine Chapters, representing Chapters One through Nine of the *Confessions*. My suggestion is to read a single Chapter of the *Confessions* at a time (the Chapters are fairly short). If, while reading, it confuses you, that's ok. Just read and don't worry if you haven't understood it all. The understanding will come as you use this Guide.

In each section, there will be a summary of the Chapter along with several Focus Texts. Please read the Focus Texts carefully. If you are short on time, I would rather you just linger on the Focus Texts than do anything else. After the Focus Texts, I have written some commentary to guide you. My hope is that these texts will then be the basis for a discussion or reflection prompted by some of the questions I have provided.

Focus Texts – An Example

Let me provide an example of how this works from the *Confessions*. We'll call this Focus Text A, and it is from the first paragraph of the *Confessions*:

Focus Text A

> You are great, O Lord, and greatly to be praised (Ps 48.1). Great is your power and, concerning your wisdom, there is no measure (Ps 147.5). Now man, a small piece of your creation, wants to praise you. But man bears about him his mortality (2 Cor 4.10), the witness of his sin and the testimony that God resists the proud (1 Pet 5.5). Yet, man, a small part of your creation, desires to praise you. You rouse him so that he might praise you because you have made us for yourself and our heart is restless until it finds rest in you (1.1.1).

The last sentence represents some of the best-known words from the *Confessions*. The first words of a work of ancient literature are important as they provide an introduction to the argument of the work. Augustine is reflecting the practice of classical literature with this technique, inviting us to pay close attention to the initial words, since most of them are from Scripture.

Notice the repeated words in the initial paragraph, especially the word "great" (which happens to be the first word of the *Confessions* in Latin), and "praise" (repeated four times). The impression we get from the initial paragraph is that God is great and worthy of praise, but we are weighed down by sin and pride and have difficulty doing what we were created to do. Human beings were created to praise God; and there is a pleasure in doing so. Yet sin, as pleasurable as it seems, gets in the way, causing us to turn away from what we were created to do. This is the fundamental dilemma that humankind faces – we were created to live in harmony with God and his creation, but sin fixes a great gulf between God and humankind. The result is human misery.

The last sentence sets the theme for the whole work: "You have made us for yourself, and our heart is restless until it rests in you." The key thought this famous sentence sets up is an essential contrast between "rest" (*requiescat*) and "restlessness" (*inquietum*). The notion of rest is important to Augustine; so important, in fact, that it not only begins the *Confessions*, but ends it. Focus Text B comes from the very end of the *Confessions*:

Focus Text B

> However, the seventh day is without evening and has no sunset, since you sanctified it to abide everlastingly, so that after your abundantly great works, which you did while remaining in repose, you rested on the seventh day. The voice of your book foretells us that after our works (which, because you have given them to us, are very good) we may rest in you on the Sabbath of eternal life. And then, you will rest in us, just as now you are working in us, and your rest will be through us, just as your works are through us. You, however, Lord, are always working and always at rest (John 5.7). Neither seeing for a time nor moving for a time nor resting for a time. Yet, you create our temporal vision and our temporal sight as well as time itself and our repose outside of time (13.36.51-52).

So what is it to rest? To Augustine, rest is not about relaxation and sleep, as important as these are. Rather, rest takes as a model what God did when he rested after creating the heavens and the earth (Gen 2.2). God did not "need" to rest. He does not get tired. In fact, Augustine notes twenty years later, in the *City of God*, that God is substituting an effect (rest) for a cause (God's creative activity) in this passage. As Augustine puts it, "Hence it is most fitting, when the sacred narrative says 'God rested,' it is signifying the resting place of those who are in him and whose rest he causes" (11.8).

So, again, what is it to rest? While rest looks back to what God did in the past during creation, it has both present and future connotations for us. The future rest that Augustine envisions in the *Confessions* transcends our experience on earth, and is something the Church eagerly awaits. In this sense, future rest for Augustine connotes a sharing in the presence of God. It looks forward to a world made right, not weighed down by sin and death. This is the rest that we all long for as Christians – the rest of redemption and resurrection.

But Augustine's point is that this rest is not just for the future! When we praise God in the context of worship and prayer (just as he is doing in the *Confessions*), we draw near to God and get a foretaste of that future rest. If rest in heaven is taken up in the form of endless praise, then when we praise God on earth, we taste a bit of heaven. Augustine wants us to experience this. Augustine is inviting us to contemplate Christ in a mystical way wherein we unite, however imperfectly, with the divine nature (2 Pet 1.4). This is what happens to Augustine several times toward the end of the story – he wants us to experience it as well.

By the way, this is why Augustine says the Lord is "always working and always at rest." In most cases, we are not at rest yet because we are focused on changeable, material, and temporal things. Augustine's statement is an allusion to something Jesus said in John's gospel: "My Father is working still and I am working" (John 5.7), a statement which almost got him killed perhaps because it was one of the most important statements of his deity in the Bible.

So God is now at rest in eternity, but somehow acts in time. Our task, even though we are finite creatures who exist in time, is to be in communion with the One who is changeless and, as an eternal being, is not bound by time. In short, we long for the rest of redemption. Our hearts are indeed restless until they find rest in God.

Questions for Reflection:
1. What does rest mean to you? How do you find rest in God?
2. What would it look like if you really were at rest right now? What would you have to change in your life to accomplish that?
3. How does your notion of rest now contrast with how rest will look in eternity? How can you get a taste of eternity today?
4. Do you ever feel overwhelmed with the tasks of life?

AUGUSTINE'S EARLY LIFE AND INFLUENCES

Childhood

Aurelius Augustinus ("Augustine") was born on November 13, 354.[1] He grew up in a small town called Thagaste (pronounced "*Tha-gas-tey*"), currently known as Souk Ahras, which is located in modern-day Algeria.[2] While only about sixty miles from more sophisticated coastal cities, Thagaste was quite provincial.

North Africa

One of the things most different from the modern perception of North Africa was its relative prosperity in Augustine's day. Given the insatiable demand for grain, wine and other commodities from Italy and other regions, North Africa became relatively wealthy as a supplier of basic staples to the Roman Empire. In fact, ancient records suggest that two-thirds of Rome's corn and almost all of its olive oil came from North Africa.[3]

North Africa, far from being a backwater region, had been a center of Christian activity for centuries. For example, Alexandria, Egypt was the home of the greatest library in the ancient world, where King Ptolemy I and his librarian, Demetrius, had acquired a copy of every known book, a collection which reportedly reached over two-hundred thousand volumes.[4] Alexandria was the place where the scholar Ammonius Saccas founded his influential philosophical school, which launched the significant advances within Plato's philosophical system known as Neoplatonism.[5] As we'll see, Ammonius' student, Plotinus, will play an extremely important role in Augustine's development, as Augustine synthesizes Plotinus into Christian thinking.

Augustine's Parents

Augustine, while observing prosperity around him, grew up with modest means. His father, Patricius ("*Pa-trish-us*"), owned enough land to be included on the town council and thus became known as a *curialis*.[6] This meant he was a member of the *curia*, a word derived from the Latin term for "care," most likely designating him as a land-owning citizen.[7] Augustine noted in a letter that he had "placed no value on the few small fields left to me by my father" (126.7), suggesting that the family's landholdings were small.

In all likelihood, Patricius' status as a middle class landowner was a burden on his family, given the frequent requirement for patronage. One of the jobs of the curial class was to collect taxes and make up for any shortages in revenue out of their own pockets.[8] Throughout the Roman Empire, when capital was needed for public works, projects were not always funded through taxation, as is the modern practice, but were often funded privately by a town's leading citizens.[9] Patricius, in certain years, did not have enough financial resources to fund his son's education, perhaps because of the ever-present need for capital required of him. Patricius' intermittent difficulty in funding Augustine's education will play an important role in the development of the story, especially in Chapter Two.

The popular understanding of Patricius is that he was a violent pagan.[10] Augustine strengthens this claim in Chapter One of the *Confessions* when he emphasizes that his father was not a believer (1.17) and in Chapter Nine when he notes that Patricius had a "quick temper" (9.9.19). Yet Patricius was baptized and received into the Church on his deathbed.[11] This seems suspicious. After all, what does it say that one waits until death to be received into the Church? Surely, this evidences grave doubts or indifference concerning the Christian faith. However, the practice of delaying baptism was common in the fourth century.

In Augustine's day, it was understood by most that baptism was essential for salvation. As Everett Ferguson, the greatest living scholar on the history of baptism attests, "The New Testament and early Christian literature are virtually unanimous in ascribing a saving significance to baptism…only a few (fringe) heretics of the ancient church tried to dehydrate the new birth."[12] Since baptism represented a one-time opportunity to wash away past sins, many waited as long as possible to be baptized.[13] This fact seems to be what is motivating Patricius to delay his baptism, not uncertainty over the Christian faith. Thus Patricius may not be the pagan of popular understanding. He died in communion, not in opposition, to the Church.

The opposite is true of Monica, his mother. The popular understanding of Monica is she was a faithful Christian and (literally) a saint. This is no doubt true. Yet Augustine is somewhat critical of his mother for delaying his baptism as a child when he clearly requested it while facing a life-threatening illness. Hence Augustine has a more complicated relationship with his mother, particularly in the early books of the *Confessions* than is popularly understood. We will need to unpack this further as we go through the work.

The praise of Monica is obvious in the *Confessions*. But there is a more complex back story. The problem is the evidence which suggests that Monica might have had a more complicated past from a religious perspective. For example, Monica's name appears to be derived from the pagan deity *Mon*.[14] Further, in her younger years, there was evidence that she was part of the separatist Donatist church. It also appears that the Catholic Church in Augustine's diocese of Hippo was quite a bit smaller than the Donatists.[15] If this is true, then it would have been embarrassing if his famous mother had had a Donatist past.

As such, Augustine's portrayal of Monica and Patricius might be a bit more involved than popular conceptions suggest. This demonstrates the importance of reading the *Confessions* with a critical eye. Like many great books, there is a more complicated aspect to the *Confessions* than a surface reading of the text presents. Of course, this is exactly Augustine's point as he is teaching us to handle the Scriptures. It will be important to evaluate the evidence when we read and one of the goals of this Guide is to help you do that.

Augustine's Vocation(s)

In its broadest sense, Augustine's vocation had three phases. During the first phase, he was a Professor of Rhetoric and one of the finest rhetoricians in the ancient world. During the second phase, he was an independent philosopher, writing philosophical dialogues and treatises. During the final phase, one which lasted for almost forty years, he was a leader in the Catholic Church, first as a presbyter and then as Bishop of Hippo.

Augustine the Rhetorician

Rhetoric was one of the most important skills in the ancient world. The ability to make a public speech was essential, since conflicts were usually adjudicated based on who made the best oral argument. Being a professional rhetorician was somewhat akin to our modern trial attorneys. In Augustine's day, the skill of rhetoric represented the ability to communicate beautifully, persuasively and clearly by making use of allusions to classical literature.[16]

When Augustine won a court rhetorician job in Milan, this was one of the most important positions in the Roman Empire because the Emperor Theodosius I was in residence there. To be asked to make speeches before the Emperor's court was somewhat akin to being Press Secretary or Solicitor General in the US government.

One finds evidence of professional rhetoricians all the way back to Socrates in the fourth century BC. Within the Platonic dialogues, Socrates complains bitterly about the sophists (roughly akin to the rhetoricians in Augustine's time) because they only cared about winning an argument, not about truth. Socrates found it abhorrent that these sophists took money to ply their trade since the life of wisdom is so far greater than anything material.[17] Augustine would make the same charge against his own teachers.

After Augustine's turn to Christianity, he resigned his professorship, for similar reasons as Socrates. Said differently, rhetoric without wisdom was simply empty words. As Augustine puts in his book *On Christian Teaching*,

> *Since the craft of rhetoric can stand behind what is true or what is false, who dares to say that the truth (veritatem) in its advocates ought to cease unarmed against the deceitful). Who would be so foolish to think this wise (sapiat)? (4.2)*

Augustine came to believe that while rhetorical skill was helpful, it was incomplete without the truths found in Scripture and the wisdom which was Christ.[18]

Philosopher

After resigning his professorship in Milan, Augustine moved to Cassiciacum ("*ka-sick-ia-cum*") to pursue philosophy with his friends. Later, after the death of his mother Monica in AD 387, he returned to North Africa to continue his philosophical activity. By all accounts, this was a very happy time for Augustine. The philosophical dialogues which he composed at Cassiciacum and Thagaste, while largely unread today outside the academy, provide great insight into who Augustine was and the things which concerned him. Yet his philosophical dialogues are works which Augustine himself would later criticize for their overtly secular tone.

Even after his baptism, Augustine considered his highest use – his "calling" as it were – to be a life of philosophy. He planned to live the quiet life of a scholar searching for wisdom. Thankfully, this would not be the end of the story. Had Augustine lived in seclusion, he might have been a footnote in the history of ideas. Instead, a fateful trip to the North African port city of Hippo to recruit a member for his philosophical community at Cassiciacum would take his life in a fundamentally different direction and lead him to have the outsized influence he would have in intellectual and church history.[19]

Priest and Bishop

The year was AD 391 when Augustine came to Hippo-Regius to recruit an interested member for his philosophical circle. Hippo was a coastal city in modern-day Algeria. Outside of its coastal position, a geographical quirk that made many wealthy, Hippo was not a particularly important city — that is, before Augustine got there. During this period, Augustine had taken pains to avoid the limelight. He did not want to be compelled into service for the Church, since this would likely end the life of peace he had found in Thagaste. He was happy; why would he do anything to threaten this? This is how Augustine describes it (I am quoting Edmund Hill's translation):

> I... came to this city as a young man; many of you know that. I was looking for a place to establish a monastery, and live there with my brothers. I had in fact left behind all worldly hopes, and I did not wish to be what I could have been, nor, however, was I seeking to be what I am now. I have chosen to be a nobody in the house of my God, rather than to dwell in the tents of sinners (Ps 84.10). I separated myself from those who love the world; but I did not put myself on an equal footing with those who preside over the Churches...so much, though did I dread the episcopate, that since I had already begun to acquire a reputation of some weight among the servants of God, I wouldn't go near a place where I knew there was no bishop (Sermon 355.2).[20]

Augustine made a fateful decision to go to Church one Sunday during his stay in Hippo, just when the Bishop, Valerius, was exhorting his congregants that he needed to hire a priest, one who could help him shoulder increasingly burdensome administrative tasks. By all accounts, Valerius was a good Bishop, one fluent in Greek, with roots in Southern Italy.[21] Yet Valerius was getting older and was not as vigorous as he had been formerly. He needed help.

Valerius made his plea for a priest during his Sunday sermon, during which he had acknowledged Augustine's presence as a visitor. Most knew about Augustine's famed reputation – he was the great rhetorician who had converted to Christianity. After the Bishop's exhortation, the laity literally rose up and demanded Augustine's ordination right then and there. No search committee; no hesitation. Augustine insisted he was not interested, but the laity, in ever louder tones, demanded his consecration. This is how Augustine came to be a presbyter in the Church – by compulsion. In truth, this is the last of Augustine's conversions. Against his will, he had found his vocation, his place in the Church. He would spend the rest of his life serving it. In the same sermon, Augustine notes the following (once again, I am quoting from Edmund Hill's translation):

> *I avoided this job and I did everything I could to assure my salvation*
> *in a lowly position, and not to incur the grave risks of a high one. But,*
> *as I said, a servant ought not to oppose his Lord. I came to this city*
> *to see a friend, whom I thought I could gain for God, to join us in the*
> *monastery. It seemed safe enough, because the place had a bishop. I*
> *was caught; I was made a priest, and by this grace I eventually came*
> *to the episcopate.*[22]

What was it like to be Bishop of Hippo? Augustine appears to have been a very busy man. Not only did he have to preach frequently and write scores of letters and theological works, but he appears to have spent a significant amount of time adjudicating disputes among his own flock. Since the Church in Hippo took very seriously Paul's admonition not to involve secular law courts when refereeing disputes among Christians, Augustine spent significant amounts of time as an arbitrator, a task he found difficult. One of the must unheralded parts of Augustine's legacy is that he came to be known as a fair and impartial mediator of disputes.[23]

It was his oratory skills that really won the day. Valerius, before his death, took the extraordinary step of having Augustine preach on a fairly regular basis. It was against the rules in North Africa to have a presbyter preach.[24] But Augustine was just that good and the people loved him. His surviving sermons are a rich treasure trove of interpretation, exhortation and application. Few in Christian history have bettered him.

Augustine and His Legacy

Princeton University's Peter Brown, the greatest modern biographer of St. Augustine, writes that "the study of Augustine is endless."[25] This is undoubtedly true. During his lifetime, Augustine wrote surviving works that totaled more than five million words, an unparalleled achievement for a writer who lived during the fourth and fifth centuries.[26] In addition to four hundred sermons and three hundred letters, almost one-hundred of Augustine's books have reached the modern world, a staggering total considering the painstaking, expensive and inherently fragile process of hand-copying manuscripts before the invention of the printing press. By comparison, Cicero (BC 106-43), who would play an outsized influence on Augustine's intellectual development and who was the most influential thinker of his day, has about nine of his rhetorical works and twelve of his philosophical writings still extant.[27]

Through time, Augustine has been alternatively discussed and demonized, revered and rejected, assaulted and admired. Apart perhaps from Jesus and the Apostle Paul, there is simply no other person who has had greater influence over Western Christianity. I think Jaraslov Pelikan is right when he describes theology after the fourth century as a "series of footnotes to Augustine."[28] Subsequent thinkers such as Thomas Aquinas, Anselm of Canterbury, Martin Luther and John Calvin are all directly indebted to Augustine's orthodox synthesis. Indeed, there are few areas of Christian theology where Augustine has not left his mark, even today.

Augustine's Broader Influence

Even more remarkable is Augustine's considerable influence on subjects outside Christian thought. For example, debates over the division of church and state find early consideration in Augustine's *City of God*, a work which did more to influence the operation of government than any other until Machiavelli's *The Prince* (1532) and Thomas Hobbes' *Leviathan* (1651).[29] Augustine's work *On Christian Teaching* was the most influential textbook on linguistics and Biblical interpretation for more than one-thousand years. Dante's *Divine Comedy*, perhaps the greatest work of medieval literature, is deeply indebted to Augustine's *Confessions;* so much so, that scholars believe Dante's own turn in the second part (*Purgatorio*) of the work is directly patterned after Augustine's.[30]

Additionally, Petrarch, a seminal figure in renaissance humanism, was meditating on Chapter Ten of the *Confessions* one day as he was climbing the highest peak in Provence, France, prompting him to self-examination and the subsequent writing of his *Ascent of Mount Ventroux*.[31] This letter, one his most famous, describes a kind of conversion experience that he had on the mountain. Petrarch's humanism would go on to have a profound effect on western thought and was shaped by the *Confessions.*

In more modern times, when Oxford University's Ludwig Wittgenstein, one of the twentieth century's greatest philosophers of language, wrote his best-known work *Philosophical Investigations* in the 1950s, he found it necessary to begin his discussion with a quotation from Augustine.[32] Moreover, the twentieth century atheist, polymath and chronicler of the history of philosophy, Bertrand Russell, pays Augustine a high compliment when he writes "I should go further, and say that [Augustine] is a great advance on anything to be found on the subject in Greek Philosophy."[33] This is high praise from Russell, one not naturally disposed to finding ancient Christian thinkers credible.

Augustine's Influence on the Church Today

Despite Augustine's great historical influence, he goes largely unread by many in the Church today. Augustine is still famous, his name recognized by many and his feast day celebrated on August 28th (the day of his death in AD 430). Yet his pervasive sway, his love for God and his indomitable spirit remain largely underappreciated by Christians. This is a pity because Augustine is so interesting, so passionate, and so incomparable.

Is Augustine a dry, sin-obsessed, sexually-repressed Christian? Some see him that way. But this is a gross distortion of who Augustine was and what he wrote. At the center of everything Augustinian is love. Although one discovers numerous examples of just how far short of this ideal he falls, Augustine believed the center of all thought – indeed, the center of life – was found in love, foremost for the triune God, but also for truth, for that which is eternal, for friendship and for family. Consider these words from the final Chapter of the *Confessions*:

> *My weight is my love. Wherever I am borne, there love brings me. By your gift, we are set aflame and lifted up. We catch fire and advance. We ascend by lifting up the heart and sing the songs of ascent (13.9.10).*

Augustine is many things, but dry and boring is simply not one of them, especially once one reads him with understanding. Indeed, as the above quote amply demonstrates, he is a lover. Once baptized, he became a celibate lover who answered the call to devote all his considerable talents to the love of God and his Church. As Augustine put it in a letter likely written in AD 411, "we come near to God not by walking, but by loving."[34] As such, while his voice has been muffled amidst the cacophony of distractions in our post-modern world, he will not go away quietly. His on-going influence resonates even sixteen hundred years after he lived.

As noted above, encountering Augustine is not an easy task. Not only did Augustine live in a world very unlike our own, not only do his immediate concerns seem foreign, but in many respects his assumptions are often meaningfully different than our own. Augustine knew little of the issues that face Christians today. For example, Christians in the Middle East – most notably in Egypt, Syria and Iraq – worry about the impact of sharia law on their ability to practice their faith openly. It would be another one hundred and forty years after Augustine's death before the prophet Muhammad was even born.[35] In some places, Christians worry about eroding free-speech protections. But there was no right to free speech in Augustine's day. In fact, Augustine was born twenty-six years before the emperor Theodosius I declared Nicene Christianity to be the official religion of the Roman Empire in AD 380.[36] Christians worry – or, at least, should worry – about the impact technology is having on their spiritual lives with the necessity of always being connected, always on and always entertained with news, sports and weather.

Augustine lived in a world where letters were routinely lost and communication was consistently disrupted. Most famously, Augustine's correspondence with Jerome, the greatest biblical scholar of the fourth century and the translator of the Bible into Latin, was undeniably shaped by several lost letters. Given Jerome's prickly inability to handle criticism, we can easily imagine the occasionally strained correspondence between Augustine and Jerome becoming worse had not misplaced mail intervened.[37] In other words, a wide cultural gulf separates Augustine and the modern reader of his works even before considering his language, his thought and his arguments.

Augustine's Times

There is a persistent temptation when encountering Augustine to treat him as a figure that transcends time. After all, his ideas have influenced the Christian Church to such an extent that he really does seem timeless. Augustine himself perpetuates this impression when, towards the end of the *Confessions* (in Chapter Eleven), he engages in a long excursus on time, which he sees as part of the fallen, created world and thus something to be transcended. Yet we should not forget the obvious – Augustine was working in the period of late antiquity.

The Roman Empire in the Late Fourth Century

One of the reasons that Augustine was such a pivotal figure was the "accident" of his birth. Augustine was born into a period in which the Roman Empire would fall to foreign invaders. Similar to Thomas Aquinas, the great medieval theologian, who happened to live at the moment Aristotle's philosophy was fully recovered in the West, or to Martin Luther, who happened to do his work of Reformation in a German region whose political leadership gave him protection, or to Karl Barth who happened to be working during the ascendency of Nazism, pivotal figures in Christian history often combine fortuitous timing with deep thinking. This combination of timing and thinking synthesizes what had come before and, in the end, often produces radically different perspectives.

Augustine is just such a figure. He was at the height of his influence as a Bishop when, under Alaric, the Visigoths brought about the fall of Rome. In fact, the sacking of Rome prompts Augustine to write *The City of God* in which he defends Christians against the charge that Rome fell because the monotheist Christians had abandoned the pantheon of Roman gods. On his deathbed, Augustine would also see the incursion of Vandal invaders into North Africa as his death occurred during the siege of the city of Hippo-Regius, the place where he had been Bishop for thirty-five years.[38]

The Confessions

Within Augustine's lifespan, the *Confessions* falls within the middle of his works. Likely started during his first year of being a Bishop in 397,[39] and finalized by 401, the *Confessions* is perhaps most notable for Augustine's copious use of Scripture, particularly the Psalms. Scripture pervades almost every page of the work.

The Purpose of the Confessions

Why did Augustine write the *Confessions*? Scholars are largely in disagreement about this. In his *Retractions*, a final review of all his written work produced three years before his death, Augustine noted the following about the *Confessions*:

The thirteen books of my Confessions extol the just and good [God] for my wicked and good [actions] and stir up human understanding and affection for Him. Now, as far as I am concerned, this is how they affected me while they were being written and they drive such a response while being read. How others feel, this is for them to consider. I know that they have given and are giving much pleasure to many of my brethren. The first ten Chapters were written about me, the last three on the Holy Scriptures, from the text, 'In the beginning God created heaven and earth,' up to the rest of the Sabbath (2.6.1).

Augustine says some interesting things in this paragraph. First, the content of the *Confessions* is contained in thirteen Chapters. One of the largest scholarly controversies to erupt over the *Confessions* in the past two-hundred years has been whether or not it is really a unified work. Some scholars in the early twentieth century came to believe that Augustine tacked the last three Chapters onto an existing autobiography since they seemingly have little to do with the story preceding it. We will give this perspective little attention in this Guide. It seems better to take Augustine at his word and treat the *Confessions* as a unity.[40] In fact, in this work, we will primarily be dealing with the first nine Chapters, which is the autobiographical portion. Nevertheless, Augustine writes the *Confessions* to culminate in a discussion of Holy Scripture concerning creation and rest.

Let me expand on Augustine's words briefly. The last three Chapters of the *Confessions* are a fascinating, yet highly technical, interpretation of the creation story in Genesis. Why would Augustine "tack on" a hard-to-understand section on Biblical interpretation to the story of his life? I believe that Augustine does this – and this point is critical to understanding Augustine's whole project – to demonstrate practically how to read the Bible. Of course, Augustine's first readers would more likely have heard the Bible read (or sung) since hand-copied Bibles were expensive and not commonly available.[41] Yet I think Augustine tells us his story, not to tell a good tale (although this is a very effective way to communicate), but to teach us how to read the Bible and how to pray. He wants us to put ourselves into the Biblical story.

Now, to be clear, these are not Augustine's only aims in writing. As one of the fourth century's greatest rhetoricians, little is ever simple or reducible to one thing with Augustine. Yet his main purpose in writing the *Confessions* is to demonstrate how we can know God in light of the Biblical story, an understanding that should result in praise to the God who made us. For Augustine, the Bible is not a story of how God worked with patriarchs, prophets and apostles thousands of years ago, but is a set of archetypes for how God works in readers' lives even today. As Michael Cameron, a noted modern interpreter of Augustine says:

> Christ supplies [sic] both a model and an authorization to read Scripture's words as his own words. Augustine doesn't storm the text with a claim to own it based on his personal intuitive identification with the writer and with the circumstances of the text's composition. Rather, when faith made him a participant in the salvation story, Christ mediated the Psalms to him. Christ's 'Action' earned him the right to speak the Psalms, not only as the Word who divinely authored them, but even more as the Just Man who humanely lived them.[42]

Although Cameron is writing about Augustine's understanding of the Psalms, the same words could apply to a discussion of the *Confessions* and its frequent use of the Psalms. Augustine again and again places himself within the Biblical story and encourages us to do the same.

Another important purpose in writing the *Confessions* was a defensive one. Augustine spent almost a decade of his life as a follower of the Manichees ("*Man-i-keys*"), a heretical splinter group. Although Augustine had thoroughly repudiated his Manichean past,[43] there were persistent questions that surrounded his very rapid ascent to being a Bishop of the Church and that questioned his orthodoxy. Those in Italy who had known Augustine as a Manichee must have particularly wondered how one with such a tainted past could have been consecrated a Bishop. Augustine also wrote the *Confessions* to counter these voices by telling his story.

Practically, the *Confessions* was likely written because a wealthy man, Paulinus of Nola, was curious about Augustine's conversion to Christianity. Paulinus himself had a spectacular conversion experience, forsaking his considerable wealth to form a monastic community and to fund a hospice.[44] When Paulinus was ordained a Bishop, Augustine would describe him has having reduced himself to poverty so that he could gain holiness.

When Alypius, Augustine's best friend, received a letter from Paulinus. he responded with copies of some of Augustine's anti-Manichaean works.[45]

As part of this exchange, Paulinus said that he had heard about Augustine and wanted to know more about him.[46] Alypius then told Augustine about the request, likely prompting him to write the *Confessions*, which included an extended treatment of Alypius' life in Chapter Six of the work.[47]

The Genre of the Confessions

What is the *Confessions*? This seemingly innocuous question has no easy answer and has puzzled readers for some time. The most popular answer to this question is that the *Confessions* is an autobiography, the first of its kind in the ancient world. Augustine wrote about himself in order to depict his spiritual journey to others.

Despite the obvious attractiveness of this option, it is almost certainly inadequate. First, a good 40% of the book is clearly not written in an autobiographical style.[48] Further, the *Confessions* cannot be an autobiography because the reader is never addressed in the *Confessions*.[49] How odd would it be for someone to write an autobiography and never address the reader? Moreover, if we consider the first words of the *Confessions* — "You are great, Lord, and greatly to be praised" – the first words of this so-called autobiography are not his![50] They are God's words, prayed back to him through the text of Scripture. Since Augustine is addressing God, who already knows who he is, the description of autobiography is clearly deficient.

Rather, it seems best to see the *Confessions* as a prayer.[51] Throughout this Guide, I will suggest that the entire *Confessions*, but certainly the first nine Chapters, is one long prayer to God. Having confessed his sins, Augustine is praying that he might be granted the grace to see God, something which ultimately occurs at the end of the story. Augustine thus demonstrates how to pray, how to read the Bible and how to grow in the spiritual life.

The Structure of the Confessions

There are as many opinions about the structure of the *Confessions* as there are scholars who have examined the subject. In short, there is no scholarly consensus on how Augustine structured the Book, except his own assertion that the first nine or ten books of the *Confessions* are autobiographical while the last three are about the exegesis of Genesis. On this subject, I have been influenced by James O'Donnell, the author of an important commentary on the *Confessions*.[52] O'Donnell believes that the *Confessions* centers around a text from 1 John 2.15-16:[53]

Do not love the world, nor the things in the world. If anyone loves the world, love for the Father is not in him. For all that is in the world, the lust of the flesh and the lust of the eyes and the pride of life, is not of the Father but is of the world.

The helpful thing about this structural theory is that it centers around Scripture and misplaced love, Augustine's favorite themes. It also has a textual basis since Augustine engages in an extended interpretation of 1 John 2.15-16 in Chapter Ten of the *Confessions*. Further, the theory is helpful because it is triadic, reflecting the triune God that Augustine serves. As human beings, many have a peculiar penchant for loving things which do not satisfy – the lust of the flesh, lust of the eyes and the pride of life. All three of these misplaced loves are represented in almost every early Chapter of the *Confessions*, but he emphasizes certain ones in different parts. For example, in Chapter Two, Augustine discusses his cravings for food and sex. He steals "forbidden" fruit, and discovers that it does not satisfy him. In Chapter Three, Augustine focuses on the lust of the eyes by falling in with the Manicheans who emphasized a physical understanding of God over the spiritual. In Chapter Four, Augustine experienced the pride of life as grief for a lost friend. The misplaced loves of 1 John 2.16 consistently assert themselves in the early sections of the *Confessions*.

There is a transition in Chapter Five when Augustine moves from Carthage to Rome and then, ultimately, settles in Milan. He realizes that none of these things are bringing satisfaction in his life. Having procured a prestigious job in Milan, Augustine then becomes disillusioned. After meeting Ambrose, the Bishop of Milan, he realizes that his rejection of Christianity might have been too hasty. He further realizes that sin is not making him happy.

Augustine spends Chapters six through eight undoing these misplaced loves. He sends his girlfriend, the mother of his child, back to North Africa in Chapter Six, taking a "proper" fiancée. He reads "the books of the Platonists" in Chapter Seven which causes his break with the Manichees to be complete. In Chapter Eight he has a profound experience in the middle of a garden, which we'll discuss at length later, an event which ultimately causes him to abandon his career. Chapter Nine "seals" the deal when he is baptized and has a vision of Christ. Thus the structure of the *Confessions* centers about the reversal of misplaced loves.

Misplaced Loves and Plato

One thing that is often missed is the interaction of the misplaced loves of 1 John 2.16 with Plato's *Republic*.[54] Although Augustine evinced significant familiarity with Plato's writings in some later works, there isn't much evidence that Augustine had actually read Plato directly when he wrote the *Confessions*, since his Greek ability was somewhat suspect.[55] While it's possible that Augustine may have read Plato in translation, it seems more likely that the later Neo-Platonist philosopher Plotinus had more influence on Augustine.[56] Mediated by Plotinus (and his student Porphyry), there is little doubt that Plato's teaching on the soul is something of which Augustine was aware.

Plato understood the soul to have a three-part structure, which just so happens to correspond to the three misplaced loves of 1 John 2.16. These three parts of the soul are often in conflict with one another.[57] For Plato, the three parts of the soul are (1) the animal, the location of appetite or desire, (2) reason and (3) spirit.

The misplaced loves of 1 John 2 match up very well with Plato's parts of the soul. For example, the "lust of the flesh" represents basic human appetites such as for food, sex and companionship. The "lust of the eyes" corresponds to the reasoning faculty of the soul. Usually, our animal desires are controlled by reason, but there are obvious exceptions when primal desires subsume reason, such as when someone has an outburst of anger or when a person cannot control his eating or drinking. The pride of life corresponds to Plato's third element which has many manifestations, but Augustine zeroes in on one, which is ambition. This ambition also often finds itself in conflict with reason.

Chiastic Structure of the Misplaced Loves

Eventually all of these misplaced loves start to come undone. Augustine does not reject all of them at once, but he starts to re-think why he has embraced the things he has. For example, Augustine starts to have grave doubts about the Manichees when one of their Bishops, Faustus, comes to town and cannot answer Augustine's probing questions. He starts to doubt his career since his students – both in Carthage and in Rome – annoy him. In short, his misplaced loves are not bringing him happiness or rest.

In fact, we will observe how Augustine removes each of the misplaced loves in reverse order from how they were initially presented. This means that there is a "chiastic" structure to the narrative portion of the *Confessions*. A chiasm was one of the most basic literary forms in the ancient world – we find it everywhere, even in the Bible. The word chiasm comes from the Greek Letter "χ" ("key"), which arranges ideas in a particular pattern. Since most ancient literature was written to be recited orally (because books were so expensive to copy), writers would use chiasms as memory aids. Such a structure can occur within a small unit like a sentence, a larger unit like a paragraph or in a something even larger like a book.

For example, the first seven chapters of Daniel in the Bible are an example of one giant Chiasm, where Chapter Seven recapitulates what happened in Chapter Two; Chapter Six recapitulates what happened in Chapter Three; and, Chapters Three and Four stand in the center with similar thematic content.[58] From an interpretation perspective, the center of a Chiasm is an important point of focus. This makes Chapter Five of the *Confessions* when Augustine starts to become disillusioned with his misplaced loves especially important. Since the Greek letter χ is the first letter in Christ's name, the chiastic structure could also be a subtle reference to Jesus.[59]

The Meaning of Sin

If O'Donnell's structural theory is correct, it means the *Confessions*, at least in part, is about the reversal of the effects of sin in Augustine's life. But we haven't yet nailed down just what Augustine means by sin. Given its importance to the *Confessions*, I want to be clear from the outset about what Augustine is asserting.

Sin, for Augustine, is not just some minor character flaw. It is about the corruption of our wills which, in turn, occurs because of the corruption of our natures in the fall. Humans are faced with a terrible problem – we desire happiness, but often act in ways that make happiness impossible. Augustine, along with most ancient thinkers, believed that living rightly (in accordance with virtue) is what would bring abiding happiness to life.

For Augustine, the virtuous life is about keeping the law of God, which was given to us for our happiness. I don't mean happy as something subjective and temporal, but as something which is objective and eternal. We are eternally happy, to Augustine, when we participate in eternal realities at the expense of temporal realities. Those who love eternal things (the one true God) are destined to be happy while those who fixate on temporal things (riches, honors and pleasures) will be unhappy.

Consider what Augustine writes in his work *On Free Will,* completed around the time the *Confessions* was written:

> *It is as you say and I agree that sins are all comprised by this one class, when one is diverted from sacred and truly enduring pursuits and is turned toward changing and inconstant pursuits. Although correctly located in its proper place and finding its own beauty, it is indicative of a corrupted and disordered soul to pursue that which he elevates and commands instead of that which corresponds to divine order and right (1.16.35.116).*

Thus we best understand sin as a preference for temporal things over eternal things.[60]

The Meaning of Confession

Finally, what about the title of the *Confessions?* Why does Augustine title the book this way? Many, when encountering the word "confession" think of the sacrament of reconciliation, whereby one confesses one's sins to a priest or to another mediator. This is certainly part of it. Augustine will leave the reader no doubt that he is a sinner, is fallen and is in need of redemption. His Adamic nature has influenced every area of his life. Yet, like most things in the *Confessions,* there is more to it than that. Consider, for example, the definition of "confession" as found in Webster's Dictionary:[61]

---

(1) The act of confessing, specifically: the disclosure of one's sins in the sacrament of penance.

(2) A statement of what is confessed: as

    a. A written acknowledgment of guilt by a party accused of an offense

    b. A formal statement of religious beliefs (creed)

(3) An organized religious body having a common creed.

To be clear, "confession" in the original Latin has an even broader sense to it since it also incorporates the idea of being a witness. In fact, the

Latin word "*confessio*" also carries the sense of being "a written or oral assertion against oneself made by a party regarding a matter under trial."[62] Augustine wants us to consider the concept of "confession" according to the full breadth of this understanding. This is important because Augustine also includes in his understanding the idea of confession as praise. Indeed, the *Confessions* will be a venue for Augustine to admit specific sins that he has committed, but will end up in praise for God because of his gracious work in Augustine's life.

However this is not the only thing that Augustine is doing. Equally important, Augustine is making a confession of faith, as the story centers about his turn towards orthodoxy and away from paganism. In the end, he also will join and serve an organized religious body, the Catholic Church, eventually rising to become a Bishop. By being reconciled to the Church, he is also engaging in praise, the result of having been forgiven. All of these understandings of confession are included in this work.

In a later sermon, Augustine admonishes his hearers that they should not make the mistake of understanding confession too narrowly. He says the following in the sermon:

> *Confession is either about praising or repenting. Now, there are some less learned people who, when they hear the word 'confession' in the Scriptures, immediately beat their breasts, and think it cannot be about anything other than sins. They think the Scriptures are strongly exhorting them to confess their sins. But so that we might acquaint ourselves with the idea that confession is not only about sin, let us listen to the one about whom there can be no doubt that he had no sin… you confess to the Lord because he is good. If you wish to praise, if you wish to make a confessions of praise, what can you do more securely, who can you praise more than the one who is good? If you wish to confess your sins, to whom can you more securely offer it than to the one who is good? If you confess to a man, you are discredited (damnaris) because he is evil. But if you confess to God, you are made clean because he is good (29.2.2,4).*

With that in mind, we should also notice that the word *Confessions* is not singular, but plural. This is a book not about a single confession. Rather, this is a story about the multiple confessions and conversions that Augustine makes during the course of his life. As we will see, these confessions result in conversions to philosophy, to paganism, to skepticism, to Neoplatonism, to Catholic Christianity, to celibacy and to the Church. Thus Augustine is not depicting a once-and-done conversion experience in the *Confessions*, but is describing the life-long process he undergoes, with the Spirit, to draw him ever-closer towards a spiritual vision of Christ. The description of this process culminates, both before and after his baptism, in several mystical visions wherein he encounters the presence of God directly.

Within the *Confessions*, Augustine is trying to get us to confess in the broadest sense. The *Confessions* demonstrates that all Christians have an innate need to confess their sins, but this is just the start. We also need to be a part of a believing community where we hear the Scriptures, pray and confess our faith. These are all on-going tasks involved in making a Confession.

To Augustine, the goal of the spiritual life is seeing God. Only a few experience this now, but union with Christ will be the experience of all believers after our resurrection. As we read the *Confessions*, Augustine is showing us how to see the invisible God. The goal of confession, and of the *Confessions*, is Christ himself.

CHAPTER ONE

AUGUSTINE CONFESSES

Introduction

For Augustine, the first Chapter of the *Confessions* introduces us to the concept of confession. In the Introduction, I noted that the word "Confession" has a broad range of meanings. Confession can refer to:

- A Confession of sins.
- A Confession of praise.
- A Confession of belief (as in a creed).
- A Confession of loyalty to a particular church body.

I also noted in the Introduction that the title "the *Confessions*" is rendered in the plural, not the singular. Augustine intends us to conceive of a confession in the broadest sense of the word. Thus the *Confessions* is about many confessions, not a single one.

In this Chapter, Augustine introduces us to the broad understanding of what confession entails. As we will see, the first three senses of confession are on display in this Chapter and Augustine builds anticipation for his eventual confession at his baptism, which will bring him into the Church.

This Chapter begins to follow the text of the *Confessions* itself. As a reminder, what is most important is reading the Focus Texts which follow a little later. You will get plenty from this Guide by simply doing that. The point of this Guide is to help you, so utilize it in whatever way is most beneficial to you.

Overview

On the surface, Chapter One seems to be about Augustine's infancy and childhood in Thagaste ("*Tha-gas-tey*"), a small town in North Africa. Augustine was born in AD 354 and this section carries his story through his pre-teen years.

Yet, as with most things in the *Confessions*, there is more going on than meets the eye. In particular, Augustine may start at the "beginning" of his life outside the womb, but he does this to set up a physical and spiritual journey – a journey that will take him far from Thagaste, his hometown.

This journey, which results in an eventual homecoming to Christ, is not ultimately about a physical location, but about his relationship with God. We get the sense that Augustine has never been without God, even when he may not have known him consciously. Augustine is setting up a journey wherein he searches for rest in God.

Summary of Chapter One

Augustine starts the *Confessions* with God in focus, praising Him, using the words of Scripture. We should notice that the first words of this work are not his own; rather, he uses Scripture to pray back God's own words to God. In this prayer, Augustine makes his first confession, praising the God who knew him intimately.

Augustine's prayer of praise to God surfaces a series of questions (1.2.2). Augustine wondered how we are supposed to praise God if we do not know him? Or this: how can we know God without knowing something about God? The answers to these key questions will unfold over the course of this Chapter and the book as a whole. To Augustine, we have to know God before we can understand ourselves since God gives the light for understanding.

God

But who is God? Augustine begins by describing God through his attributes (1.4.4). For example, God is omnipresent. If this is the case, how can Augustine call on God to come to him if God is everywhere? Moreover, God is the creator of everything, including Augustine's very existence. This leads Augustine to wonder how he can call on God if he is already in God in some way. God is simple (1.3.3),[1] meaning that he has no parts; God is also pure act (1.5.5),[2] meaning there is no potentiality for action in God. God is immutable, meaning that as a perfect being, God does not change. In fact, the way Augustine describes this incomprehensible being is by negating what is not true about God (He is im-mortal, in-visible, a-temporal, im-passible, immutable, etc.).

This causes Augustine (and some readers) to cry out in frustration, "Who then are you, my God" (1.4.4)? Augustine follows this with yet another question: "Who will grant me to find rest in you" (1.5.5)? This second question continues the key theme that Augustine set up in the first paragraph of the *Confessions:* how can Augustine find rest in God if he is so unlike God? We are left with the impression that God is a mystery beyond human comprehension.

Infancy

Only after confessing that God is beyond comprehension does Augustine start to recount his life. He does this to gain a greater understanding of who God is. If we cannot know God because he is incomprehensible, perhaps we can know him by observing his work in our lives. To this end, Augustine admits that he doesn't know "where he came from" (1.6.7), but he surmises that God formed him. Augustine may not remember his infancy, but his parents as well as his own experience with his son Adeodatus ("*Ah-deo-da-tus*") enable him to say something here. His memory has been activated by the testimony of others.

What Augustine surmises is that from the first day of his earthly life, his innate desire was for material, external things. He longed for milk. He wished "to suck and rest in pleasure and cry at what offended [his] flesh, nothing more" (1.6.7). He also had other desires, the ever-present need to satisfy his soul. He did not have to learn how to seek and satisfy what he desired. Rather, Augustine learned to manipulate others to get what he wanted. Although he had no memory of his actions, Augustine knew he did such things by learning "from the ones I have been able to watch" (1.6.8).

Augustine wondered what had preceded his infancy (1.6.9)? He was really wondering whether his soul preceded his bodily existence. No one, save God, could answer this, even if many philosophers had tried. This sets up a key question about time that he needed help to answer (this is also a major subject in Chapter Ten of the *Confessions*). After all, God, being eternal, was not made in time. For God, a day is an eternal day, not like the twenty-four hours it is for us (1.6.10). Thus, time and memory are key focuses for

Augustine both at the beginning and at the end of the *Confessions* since earth-bound creatures have a fundamentally different experience with time than God does. Here, Augustine confesses his ignorance unless he seeks understanding in light of God.

Having discussed time, Augustine then brings up the subject of original sin (1.7.11), paraphrasing Job 14.4-5 that "no one is free from sin before you, not even an infant whose life spans one day on the earth." He starts to consider his infant years in light of this. Augustine recalled that, he greedily clamored after food. Because he wasn't old enough, "neither custom nor reason allowed [him] to be reproved." In other words, it would have done no good to reprimand him. Babies, while cute, are often jealous and greedy, acting in ways that would bring strong rebuke if the child were older. Augustine saw this behavior as evidence that babies could not be innocent. The standards by which we judge infants are different. In this, Augustine confesses that he, at no point, has been without the taint of sin.

Young Childhood

Next, Augustine turned from infancy to boyhood (1.8.13), a period in his life where he began to remember. He recalled learning the letters of the alphabet and the importance of memory in that task. He improved his facility with language, but described his lot as miserable (1.9.14) since those around Augustine advised him "to obey in order to prosper and excel in this world." In other words, Augustine's parents and school teachers encouraged him to turn towards the world, not God. They prepared him for success in the world, not the pursuit of Christ. Augustine would come to see this as an example of misplaced love – he was focusing on winning the approval of those in authority over him instead of from God who knew him before he was born.

Augustine also described the beatings he received at school, the subject of the first prayer he remembers. Augustine recalled that "you did not hear me," which says something about his relationship with God at the time. Augustine distracted himself from his miseries through sporting events. He recounted that, during this season of life, he sinned by disobeying his parents and teachers. He even stole from his parents to participate in the sports and then turned on his friends and stole from them. Augustine "loved the pride of victory in [his] contests" (1.10.16) and was especially taken by "shows and games."

Augustine also had a desire for God, noting that while he was young, he was made a catechumen in the Church through "the sign of his cross" and the placing of salt on the tongue (1.11.17). Once, while gravely ill, he even begged for baptism, but this was deferred when he suddenly recovered. Most remarkably, Augustine recounted, "I was already a believer." He wondered how it was God's will that his baptism should have been deferred (1.11.18). Augustine wanted to join the Church through baptism, but was rebuffed by the decision of his mother.

Boyhood

As he became older, Augustine hated studying and learning (which is a remarkable admission, given his later contributions to Christian thought). He saw himself as "so small a boy, so great a sinner" (1.12.19). Apparently, Augustine's concept of his sinful nature did not improve as he got older.

Augustine next became highly critical of the education he received as a young boy. For example, he was forced to study Greek literature in school, which he hated (1.13.20). He read Virgil's *Aeneid,* the key text for teaching Latin to the young, which he claims he did not enjoy at all. We will see that Augustine gets over this dislike of Virgil, since references to the *Aeneid* appear throughout the *Confessions.* Yet Augustine's penchant for misplaced love caused him to miss the greatness of the work (1.13.21).

Moreover, the questions his teachers taught him to ask of Virgil caused him to give preference "to those empty fables instead of more profitable endeavors" (1.13.22). Augustine found the classical literature of his youth "shrill" (*amarus*). It was full of immorality and deceit. It also did nothing to point him toward the truth that he eventually found in Christ. Augustine had no love for either the Greek classics or for the Greek language.

So Augustine turned (briefly) back to prayer (1.15.24). He refused to cease his criticism of Greek literature, particularly because of the pervasive immorality among the Greek gods. He found that "Homer's fictions transferred human traits to gods" (1.16.25). Even worse, his teachers took money for introducing him to such depravity, meaning they had mixed motives and were no better than the sophists back in ancient Athens (1.16.26). In short, the role models Augustine was given in Greek and Latin literature were deeply problematic.

In fact, the climax of Augustine's criticisms comes when he combines an allusion to Homer's *Odyssey* with the story of the prodigal son. Augustine sees himself in the *Confessions* as the prodigal son about to go off and enjoy riotous living before making his way home. He was encouraged from his earliest days by his teachers to move away from a Christian understanding of the good life, a fact which caused him to wince in dismay (1.19.30).

Augustine refused to see all this as childish innocence. It was a sign that something was desperately wrong. Augustine summed it up this way: "This was my sin, that I was not seeking pleasures, sublimity and truth in God, but in myself and in his creatures. So I fell headlong into sorrows, confusions and errors" (1.20.31). According to Augustine's recounting, the sin of his childhood resulted in misery.

In the first Chapter, we observe that all four notions of what it is to make a confession are introduced. Augustine begins with a confession of praise; then, he confesses his sin. Even as an infant, Augustine makes a profession of faith to the Church and notes that he believed. He will spend the rest of the book developing these themes.

Focus Texts

We come now to the key part of the exercise. I have been suggesting that Augustine is introducing us to what it is to make a confession in the broadest sense. Here, I provide three short texts from Chapter One to show how he does this. My encouragement is to read these texts slowly. I then offer some brief commentary with reflection questions. My hope is that by reading the texts closely and thinking through the questions, you will build greater understanding.

Confession as Praise

Augustine starts with confession as praise. As we have seen, the Confessions itself is an elongated prayer. As a result, one of Augustine's goals in the *Confessions* is to teach us how to pray.

Thus the praise of the triune God through prayer is an obvious place to begin our discussion. Note this text from the prologue:

Focus Text 1A

Who then are you, my God? Who, I ask, but the Lord God? For who is Lord except the Lord? Or who else is God except our God? Most high. Most good. Most powerful. Most omnipotent. Most merciful and Most just. Most hidden, yet intimately present, most beautiful yet supremely mighty, stable yet inconceivable, immutable, yet changing all things; never new, never old, yet renewing all things and leading the proud though they are unaware. Always active, always at rest, gathering though needing nothing, supporting, filling and protecting, harvesting although you lack nothing; you love without agitation, you are jealous, yet secure, you repent without regret, you become angry while staying tranquil. You change, but never change your plan. You take back what you find, without ever losing it. Never in want, yet rejoicing in gain, never greedy yet demanding a return. You make us pay more than is owed which makes you our debtor, but who has anything which is not from you? You owe us nothing, yet you pay your debts. You forgive our debts to you, yet suffer no loss. And what have we said, O God, my life, my holy sweetness, or what does anyone say when he speaks of you? But woe to those who keep silent about you since, though windbags, they say nothing (1.4.4).

If there is a more powerful prayer which describes who God is in orthodox theological terms, I simply do not know it. It is important to note that Augustine begins the *Confessions* in prayer, thus setting up the idea that the *Confessions* is one big long prayer.

There is an important theme that runs through this prayer – the idea that God does not change, that he is immutable and thus is not affected by anything outside of himself. One of the bedrock beliefs of Christians is that God can't change and still be God. While a God who changes has become a popular view, it grates against the traditional Christian conception of God.

The reason God's immutability is so important is because if God changes, he cannot be perfect, since presumably he would change in a way that improves upon his previous state. It also imperils the preaching of the Gospel since our revised understanding might result in a God who is arbitrary. Ironically, the idea of a capricious God is closer to the gods of Greek and Latin literature, the ones explicitly rejected by Augustine in this Chapter, than to the one espoused by the Church. Augustine refuses to accept that this is right.

The idea of God's unchangeable nature sets up a difficult problem. If God doesn't change, then why bother praying? If our prayers do not affect God, if God does not change his mind when we pray, then what good does prayer do? Clearly, Augustine thinks prayer is useful since the whole *Confessions* is one long prayer. But why spend so much time upfront teaching us to pray to a God whose mind cannot be changed?

The answer that Augustine gives to resolve this dilemma is that believers pray because, in his sovereign will, God has determined that some things will only come about if we pray. In this understanding, God does not change. He always knew what he was going to do, since he could foresee the future. Yet he wills that some things will only come about if believers pray. For example, when the disciples wondered why it was that they were unable to cast out a particular demon, Jesus responded, "This kind cannot be driven out by anything but prayer" (Mark 9.29). In other words, some things will only take place if we do the hard work of praying. Augustine is thus demonstrating to us that the work of prayer – the central thing he is doing in the *Confessions* – is essential for Christians.

Questions for Reflection

1. What happens in prayer? How/when do you pray?
2. What is your experience in prayer? Has God answered any of your prayers recently?
3. How do you use the tools of the Church (liturgy, scripture, etc.) for your prayers?
4. Have you ever tried to "bargain" with God to get what you want? What happened?
5. How does it change your approach to prayer to know that you can't manipulate God?

Confession of Sin

Many readily associate the word confession in the context of the Church with the confession of sin. As we find in the James' epistle: "Therefore confess your sins to one another and pray for one another, that you may be healed" (Jas 5.16). The Bible is clear in the that believers ought to confess their sins. Yet our story takes a strange twist since Augustine finds it necessary to confess his sins as a baby. Consider the following text (1.7.11):

Focus Text 1B

> So the weakness of infant limbs is innocent but not the infant mind. I myself have seen and have known a jealous little child. He could not even speak yet he turned pale and bitterly watched another child nurse. Who is ignorant of this? Mothers and nurses will tell you that they charm such behavior away with some unknown remedy. Is that really innocence, if the source of milk flows freely and abundantly and the child attempts to stop it when another child needs it so badly and depends on that food alone for his very life? We put up with this not because it is nothing or a slight peccadillo but because as years go on, the behavior will disappear. Although tolerated now, the same behavior is not accepted when found in someone with riper years (1.7.11).

Augustine is telling us that babies are not born innocent. They are born greedy, jealous creatures, who have to be taught to follow a different standard. He points out that few would tolerate an older child exhibiting such behavior. This observation leads Augustine to conclude that all are born sinners with corrupt natures.

Original sin is one of Augustine's best-known observations of humankind. Interestingly, this concept proved to be controversial in Augustine's day. For example, the Pelagians, one of the groups Augustine would engage vociferously, took a more optimistic view of human nature, saying that the Fall did not really affect our ability to choose good or evil. Since Pelagianism got started when a British monk named Pelagius moved to Rome and started spreading his ideas among the upper class families, some have pointed out that those who had the biggest problem with Augustine's view of original sin in the late fourth century did not have children!

Augustine is well-known for his doctrine of original sin. With regard to infants, however, he never mentions his central argument for it in the *Confessions*. This is a pity since this concept is so central to his understanding of the Gospel. In the books which he writes against the Pelagians, Augustine composes an entire treatise, trying to prove to the Pelagians that babies are not born innocent, but sinful, called *A Treatise on the Punishment and Forgiveness of Sins and on the Baptism of Infants*. Augustine's great proof that babies are not born innocent is the very fact that some babies die. Essential for this idea is what Paul wrote in the book of Romans: "Therefore as sin came into the world through one man, and death through sin, and so death spread to all men because all men sinned" (Romans 5.12).

If death is connected with sin, then babies must be sinners since they die. Infants need grace like everyone else. Yet it is obvious that babies, not consciously being able to distinguish between right and wrong, have not sinned knowingly. Consider what Augustine writes concerning this (I am quoting Peter Holmes' translation):

> *As for [infants], however, who (as is manifest) never did an ungodly act in all their own life, if also they are not bound by any bond of sin in their original nature, how did [Christ] die for them who died for the ungodly? If they were hurt by no malady of original sin, how is it they are carried to the Physician Christ, for the express purpose of receiving the sacrament of eternal salvation by the pious anxiety of those who run to Him?...infants ought to be baptized because, although they are not sinners, they are yet not righteous.*[3]

What Augustine is attempting to teach us is that the starting point of the Gospel is the idea that we all have a problem – a sin problem. Yes, as humans, we are capable of great goodness and great beauty. Yes, the possibility of becoming more like Christ by the work of the Holy Spirit is real. Augustine understands that at our core is something rotten, something which we inherited from Adam and will not go away until our redemption is complete. Original sin is as true for infants as it is for adults. We know this with certainty because some babies perish. In short, we are mired with a corrupted nature and are in need of divine grace to save us. Only God can do what we cannot do ourselves.

Questions for Reflection

1. Recount your experiences with your children or those you know who have had children. What were they like as infants? Do you think Augustine is right or wrong?
2. How does Augustine's pessimistic outlook on human nature strike you? How have you seen sin affect your life and those around you?
3. The Apostle Paul insists that sin is linked with both spiritual and physical death. What would our lives have been like if sin were not present?

Confession of Faith and Baptism

The final aspect of confession we will consider is what it is to make a confession of faith. When we confess the Apostles Creed, this is a confession of faith. The Scriptures suggest that one not enlightened by the Spirit can't confess the Creeds with integrity. The Apostle Paul writes, "The unspiritual man does not receive the gifts of the Spirit of God, for they are folly to him and he is not able to understand them because they are spiritually discerned" (1 Cor 2.14). Thus grace is needed to make a genuine confession. Note what Augustine says in this next text about his state of belief as a child:

Focus Text 1C

> While I was still a boy, I had heard about the eternal life promised to us through the humility of our Lord God, who stooped down to our pride; and I was regularly signed with the sign of his cross and was seasoned with salt even from the womb of my mother, who steadfastly trusted in you. You have seen, Lord, how, while yet a boy, I was struck with stomach pains and a high fever which led nearly to death. You have seen, Lord, for you were my keeper, with what eagerness and with what faith I begged my pious mother and the mother of us all, your Church, to be baptized into your Christ, my God and Lord. The mother of my flesh trembled. With a pure heart and through faith in you she lovingly travailed in labor for my eternal salvation, hastily making arrangements for me to be washed in your saving sacraments, and confessing you, Lord Jesus, for the forgiveness of my sins. Yet I had already recovered so my cleansing was deferred under the theory that if I lived, I would likely pollute myself again, for it was understood that after the washing of baptism, sin incurred was graver and more perilous. Therefore, I was already a believer, as were my mother and her whole household with the exception only of my father (1.9.17).

Many, when approaching the *Confessions*, think that it is a story about a conversion, about a dramatic journey to a climactic scene in a garden at the end of the story. As I have already hinted, the *Confessions* is a story about many conversions, not simply a single one. What many miss is that Augustine says clearly in the text of the first Chapter that he was already a believer, albeit as a young boy. In fact, in one of his earliest works (*On the Usefulness of Belief*), written just prior to his baptism, Augustine claims that he was a Christian even during his nine-year sojourn with the Manicheans: "Why do I speak of myself, who was then a Catholic Christian, and who has now, nearly exhausted and parched after my long thirst, sought again with all eagerness the breasts which nourished me?"[4] A few sentences later, Augustine would question whether he was really a Christian at this point, since he walked away from the faith, but his identity as a believer was certainly there as a child.[5]

In fact, as the story of the *Confessions* unfolds, it is clear that Augustine would walk away from the Church for much of the story. But, in terms of a confession of faith, what more could we ask? Augustine says (1) that he believes, (2) that the Church initiated him (with the signing of the cross and the placing of salt on the tongue, which were the fourth century initiation rites for catechumens), (3) that he desired to be baptized, but that (4) others, namely his mother, prevented him from doing so.

The Church teaches that catechumens who die before baptism have received the sacrament "by desire." Consider the *Catechism of the Catholic Church* on this subject:

> *For catechumens who die before their Baptism, their explicit desire to receive it, together with repentance for their sins, and charity, assures them the salvation they were not able to receive through the sacrament.*[6]

By Augustine's own testimony in the *Confessions*, he has already believed. He has started the Christian life. As Augustine puts it in one of his sermons on John's Gospel, comparing those preparing to come into the church as catechumens with those already baptized:

> *Therefore, Jesus [only] entrusts himself to them, who are born again [by baptism]. Even if they had already believed in him and believe Jesus in the name of Christ, Jesus does not entrust himself to them [catechumens]…they do not understand what they are saying, since Jesus has not entrusted himself to them (11.3).*

What Augustine means is that since a catechumen has not yet been instructed in the mysteries of the Christian faith, he does not understand and is not fully a Christian. For Augustine, this understanding would come later. Indeed, Augustine's eventual baptism is critical to the story. Yet the *Confessions* cannot be about a climactic conversion because the way Augustine tells the story, he was initially converted as a child, even if his formation in Christian teaching was woefully incomplete.

But how do we then grapple with Augustine's fall away from the Church as he gets older? Augustine does not understand salvation the way some have come to interpret him. To Augustine, salvation is not about a "point-in-time" conversion experience, whereby one's conversion (or justification) is separated from one's growth in godliness (sanctification). To Augustine, salvation is about a long process of ascent whereby God calls his children to unite with him. To Augustine, salvation is a process that begins in baptism, goes through belief, but is finally assured by perseverance in the faith, all of which happens by grace. In a very real sense, Augustine has been saved, is being saved and will be saved at the final judgment. He is anticipating the journey God has in store for him, which will end with his being a Bishop of the Church.

One thing we can easily miss when we read the *Confessions* in translation is Augustine's verb choices. Scholars have noted for a long time that Augustine has a penchant for the imperfect verb tense (which usually suggests incompleteness) rather than present tense.[7] Through his writing, Augustine is emphasizing that our journeys are incomplete this side of resurrection.

We should conclude that baptism really meant something to Augustine. It was not just a symbolic ritual. Rather, as the Creed asserts and as the Apostle Peter preaches (Acts 2.28), baptism is "for the remission of sins." Even if we have to wait until the end of the story to observe Augustine's baptism, we already observe the stirrings of faith in the first Chapter.

Questions for Reflection
1. What has been your experience with Christian conversion? How have you seen God at work in your life both in the past and in the present?
2. What was it like to have children in the Church? Is the Christian faith still important to them? If not, why not?
3. Augustine describes baptism as a "sacrament of salvation." What do you observe when you see baptismal services?
4. Can you recount the baptismal vows you have taken and whether they matter to you?
5. Does it change anything for you to conceive of salvation as a process instead of a one-time event?

AUGUSTINE'S BIG FALL

Introduction

Chapter Two explores Augustine's "big fall." As we have seen from the previous Chapter, Augustine sees himself as fallen from birth. Within an Augustinian framework, we are not born in an innocent condition. What Augustine depicts in this Chapter is not an "original" fall from grace. Rather, Augustine demonstrates the implications of original sin for the will itself. If a corrupted nature is an inherited condition, the result is a corrupted will.

In the Introduction to this Guide, I noted that the autobiographical books of the *Confessions* are an extended discussion of the misplaced loves of 1 John 2.16-17. These misplaced loves are as follows:

- The lust of the flesh
- The lust of the eyes
- The pride of life

All three of these misplaced loves make an appearance in this Chapter, but the focus is on the lust of the flesh. Augustine, mired as he is in sin, would rather focus on his desires than the rest that God offers. Humanity, in its fallen state, follows readily in his footsteps.

In this Chapter, it will prove especially important to dig down beneath the surface of the text to ascertain what Augustine is trying to say. Those who do not dig deeper often find themselves frustrated with this part of the *Confessions*. For example, Augustine steals a pear in this Chapter and spends many pages decrying himself for what a wretched sinner he is. On a surface reading, it seems like an account blown completely out of proportion. I want you to see that there is more going on than meets the eye. In short, there's a reason. Augustine beats himself up over this (and other) incidents and we are going to have to unpack just what he is doing.

Another important feature of this Chapter is that Augustine starts introducing us to his method of Scriptural interpretation. What Augustine begins to do in this Chapter is to place himself within the Biblical story, thus providing a model of what he wants us to be doing when we hear or read the Biblical text. Augustine does not just recount the Parable of the Prodigal Son, for example, he *is* the Prodigal Son. Augustine's goal, of course, is to get us to read the Bible at a deeper and more thoughtful level.

Overview

Chapter Two takes place during Augustine's sixteenth year in AD 369-370. Augustine was away at grammar school in nearby Madauros, but returned to Thagaste likely because his father Patricius ran out of money.[1] As Augustine memorably put it (and Henry Chadwick brilliantly has translated it), his father had "more enthusiasm than cash" for his schooling (2.5).[2]

We encounter a situation where a sixteen-year-old boy has taken a break from school and has little to occupy his time. What could possibly go wrong with that? Anyone who has been sixteen knows that plenty can go wrong, and it does. Although the well-known aphorism, "an idle mind is the Devil's workshop," was coined in the nineteenth century, the idea is certainly found here.[3]

It is especially important to keep in mind that Augustine is providing us with an interpretation of events which had happened long ago. Augustine is forty-three years old as he is writing the *Confessions* and twenty-seven years have transpired since the events of Chapter Two had occurred. Given the detail Augustine employs to recount them, his sixteenth year was extremely consequential. He would by no means "bottom out" in AD 370, but we should get the sense that Augustine was recoiling in horror at what he remembers. It was a very, very bad year.

On a surface reading, we could be excused for wondering what all the fuss is about. In fact, this is what some modern readers find so odious about Augustine's writing – he's just (needlessly) hung up on sin and sex. Yet below the surface, Augustine has a surprise in store for us in this Chapter. It's a big one too. He will never be explicit about it; we have to read between the lines. But Augustine is trying to tell us that his self-condemnation is readily deserved (more on that below in the Focus Texts).

Summary of Chapter Two
A Scattered Soul

Augustine begins by reminding himself of his past foulnesses and carnal corruptions (2.1.1). Augustine places emphasis on his memory, which he indicates by making the Latin word for remember (*recordari*) the first word of the Chapter. Augustine desires to love God by remembering, even if the acts he describes bring back bitter memories. In confessing the sins of his youth in this Chapter, recollection becomes a key component of this confession.

Augustine was in a state of dispersion (*dispersione*), which is a reference to the state of his soul. The Latin word "*dispersio*" means to be "scattered," "confused" or "dispersed."[4] His soul, divided as it was between the desire to love God and the desire for pleasures, manifested itself in people pleasing. Augustine's warped will led to a misplaced love of temporal things over eternal things. As Augustine puts it, "I was torn piecemeal, while I turned away from your unity (*ab uno*) to disappear into multiplicity (*in multa*)."

Augustine "was wandering ever farther away" and God let him do it (2.2.2). This is the first of many references to the parable of the Prodigal Son in this Chapter. Just as the Prodigal Son wandered far away from home and his father did little to stop him, so too Augustine attempts to travel far away from God. The implication is that Augustine is traveling a great distance away from the rest he is seeking.

Augustine then wonders why no one tried to adjust his disordered life (2.2.3) by following the Apostle Paul's prescription for lust. Employing several allusions to 1 Corinthians 7, Augustine recalls that Paul urges those burning with lust to marry. In short, Augustine sees the sexual lust of his youth to be an important factor in his turn away from God and he wonders why his parents didn't step in to guide him.

We should recall from the previous Chapter that Augustine's teachers did little to encourage him to lead a morally upright life. In this Chapter, Augustine criticizes his parents for being more interested in his career than in the purity of his life (2.3.5). Had Augustine listened to the warnings of Scripture concerning lust, he thinks he would have been happier as "a eunuch for the kingdom of heaven" (Matt 19.12), thus implying the pursuit of pleasure brought little satisfaction. Augustine gave in to the "madness of lust" (2.2.4).

Lust of the Flesh

Augustine criticizes his father Patricius for his "perverse will," when, upon seeing Augustine naked in a bathhouse, showing "unstable manhood" (*inquieta indutum adulescentia*), he rejoices at the prospect of the fruit that would come from Augustine's loins in the form of grandchildren (2.3.6). Patricius cares little about Augustine's burgeoning immorality. Augustine is criticizing his father because he cares far more for earthly, temporal things than eternal ones.

In contrast to his father, Monica attempted to curb her son from his lustful impulses. She expressed concern that Augustine might "commit fornication or adultery with another's wife" (2.3.7). Augustine found Monica's counsel "womanish" (*muliebres*), and rejected her admonishment. It was only later that Augustine came to realize that God was speaking through Monica and thus he should have heeded her warnings.

Augustine had fallen in with a band of young ruffians. Augustine admits that they were more sexually active than he. They loved to boast of their exploits. Augustine found himself pretending he had done similar things in order to win the ruffians' approval. He desperately craved their acceptance. We observe here Augustine's deep need for friendship, albeit in a perverted form.[5] Augustine would surround himself with friends his whole life, but during this stage of life, his friendships proved to be destructive.

Augustine also implicitly criticizes his mother since she did little to restrain his sex drive "within the bounds of marriage" (2.3.8). Monica's motivation for this counsel was not particularly virtuous as she was worried that Augustine's career would be hindered if he were to marry at a young age. The Latin here is very strong, as Monica was suggesting a wife would have been a "chain" (*compede*) at this point in his life.[6]

In the fourth century, there was little upward mobility outside the Church, the military and the local municipal government. Augustine's towering intellect provided opportunities not available to others. If Augustine married young, he might cut himself off from a union that would bring him the power and wealth he would need to advance among the Roman aristocracy. While they were simply following the conventions of the day, his parents' obsession with success comes up for criticism here since it was so divorced from the life of the Spirit.[7]

Augustine is critical of both his parents because they did not discipline him. This situation led "various destructive affections" (2.3.8). As he reflects on his youth, Augustine is dismayed because no older, wiser guides came to help him stay on the straight and narrow.

You might be puzzled by all this. After all, Augustine's friends were clearly worse off than he was. Augustine was sixteen years old and desiring to be accepted by a peer group. His hormones were raging. Is this not a normal series of events for a teenager? Why does Augustine employ such overwrought language in this section? This will hopefully become clearer as we proceed to the Focus Texts.

The Dreaded Pears

Augustine then recounts how, having fallen in with the band of ruffians, he committed the sin of stealing some pears (2.4.9). After noting that this was a violation of the Ten Commandments (Ex 20.15), Augustine takes pains to confess that he had no need of what he stole. In other words, there were no extenuating circumstances to his crime. Then, in another allusion to the Parable of the Prodigal Son, Augustine and his friends threw the pears to pigs after they had stolen them. The joy of the theft came not from the consumption of the fruit, but simply from the pleasure of sinning itself. He also notes that the pears were attractive neither in color nor taste. As we'll see below, this small detail proves to be essential to the story.

It is here that Augustine literally falls.[8] Augustine writes the following: "It was foul and I loved it. I loved perishing. I loved my own fall (*defectum*), not that for which I was falling (*deficiebam*), but my fall (*defectum*) itself. I leapt down from your firmament to utter destruction" (2.4.9). This is an allusion to the fall of Satan from heaven (Isa 14.12). Just as Satan and his band of fallen angels did the unthinkable in rebelling against God and leaving the beauty, perfection and rest of heaven, Augustine did the same as he turned his back on God in his teenage years. Augustine decided to abandon the "better and higher good" for "things at the extreme other end of good" (2.5.10). The result of a disintegrated soul is a corrupted will.

The Motive

So what was the motive for his actions? As Augustine questions why he did these things (2.5.11), he finds no good reason save for the pleasure of sin itself (2.6.12). This realization horrifies Augustine. After all, shouldn't there be a good reason for sinning? One might covet to get something or murder to avenge being wronged, but the theft of the pears had no real motive attached to it.[9] This act brought no joy. It only made Augustine miserable.

Augustine then admits that the fruit he stole was beautiful (*pulchra*) since it was part of God's good creation (2.6.12). Augustine's statements might be confusing since he just stated a few paragraphs prior that there was nothing attractive about the fruit. The reason Augustine seemingly contradicts himself is that he has moved to interpret these events theologically. Augustine claims that the fruit was beautiful after all because God created all things good (Gen 1.12). In reality, the fruit was beautiful – he just could not see it given the state of his disintegrated soul at the time.

This leads Augustine to note it was from pride that he wanted to imitate what was lofty (2.6.13). In another allusion to the fall of Satan, Augustine contends that he was simply seeking "honors and glory." He then observes through an analysis of curiosity, luxury, pride, ambition, envy, anger, prodigality, and avarice that these are all simply corruptions of good things. To Augustine, sin takes what is beautiful and twists it.

The Result

The attempt to satisfy his bodily cravings led Augustine on a path which took him far from God. Augustine sees his disintegrated soul as having led him far from God's intentions for his life (2.6.14). The object of Augustine's love was no longer God; it was himself. He wanted to satisfy his fleshly cravings, even if it meant walking away from God. Augustine wanted to do what was wrong simply because it wasn't allowed.

What could Augustine offer to God in order to make restitution (2.7.15)? Augustine confesses his sin by noting that his life went horribly wrong during his sixteenth year. Indeed, it was only God's grace and mercy which could restore Augustine again (2.7.15).

Augustine loved his friends, but found himself even more miserable (*miserior*) (2.8.16). The result was fleeting pleasure in friendship (2.9.17). Overwhelmed by his disjointed soul, Augustine chose what was temporal over what was eternal. He took a good thing (friendship and fruit) and perverted it by living a life of moral license.

The whole situation leaves Augustine in a "twisted and entangled knot" (2.10.18). Augustine walked away from God and set off to lead a profligate life away from God's "unmoved stability."[10] The result was the same dejection the prodigal son experienced.

Focus Texts

As we turn to the Focus Texts, I am primarily trying to explain what is happening with the pear theft. Since the theft gets so much attention in Chapter Two, it makes sense to center our investigation here. To ensure we evaluate this scene well, I am going to present the story in several short sections and hold off on reflection questions until the end.

Admittedly, Augustine's reaction to the pear theft appears absurd since the condemnation doesn't seem to fit the crime. Of course, theft is a violation of the eighth commandment (Exodus 20.15). It's wrong. But how do we explain Augustine's rather extreme language? Further, Augustine spends much of the Chapter conflating his theft of the pear with the sin of lust. Why is this?

Breaking Bad... With Pears?

Augustine doesn't explain the importance of his stealing a pear. We're going to have to dig below the surface a bit. Augustine sees his theft as going against common sense. He spends the rest of the Chapter berating himself for it. Let's look at an example of Augustine's language in which he rebukes himself for his sin:

Focus Text 2A

But in misery I boiled, poor wretch that I was, and followed the rushing flood of my own nature and abandoned you. I exceeded all your limits, but did not escape your scourges. For what mortal can? You were always near, mercifully angry and harsh, sprinkling the bitterest displeasures over all my illicit pleasures so that I might seek pleasure without disappointment...Where was I in the sixteenth year of the age of my flesh when I accepted in myself the scepter of the madness of lust and gave myself completely to it? This lust was permitted according to shameful human nature, yet was illicit according to your laws. Nevertheless, my family took no care to save me from ruin by marriage. Their only concern was that I should learn to speak well and become a persuasive rhetorician (2.2.3).

This is very strange language if Augustine is simply concerning himself with the theft of a pear and the decision to run around with a band of ruffians. Augustine's language implies that what he has done is significantly outside the bounds of acceptable behavior. I do not mean to minimize the idea that theft is wrong. I am simply asking why Augustine uses such extreme language if petty theft is really all he is discussing.

Moreover, the above text has more to do with sexual lust than theft. Listen closely to Augustine's language in this text: "my misery boiled;" "madness of lust;" "illicit pleasures;" "age of my flesh;" "shameful human nature." Isn't it odd that if Augustine is about to beat himself up over the theft of a pear, the solution is marriage? He must be saying something else.

Was Augustine just scolding himself for the raging hormones of a sixteen-year-old? This is possible, although unlikely. Augustine's main concern with sin is the connection of our fallen nature to the will. To Augustine, we freely choose to sin even if our corrupted natures make it such that no one (save Christ) makes it through life without sin. In other words, Augustine concedes that it's possible that someone could make it through life without sin with the help of grace. It's just never happened.[11]

Yet there is no one that makes us sin. In fact, if God were to superimpose his will onto ours, then God would be the author of sin and man could justifiably be absolved from blame.[12] This is not Augustine's view.

Augustine seems to be berating himself for something else. It seems to me that he is scolding himself for an act of sexual sin. Consider, for example, how Augustine describes his own behavior and the lax reaction of his parents in the following text:

Focus Text 2B

> Indeed, with such companions I was roaming the streets of Babylon. I was wallowing in its muck as if enjoying a bed of spices and precious oils. And holding fast to its navel, the invisible enemy flattened me and seduced me (I was easy to seduce). The mother of my flesh had already fled out of the midst of Babylon, but she still tarried outside. She warned me to be chaste, but did not take care to act on what she had heard from her husband. She considered it to be to be a plague now and deadly for the future to restrain me within the bounds of marriage if that pestilence in me could not be not be cut away by the quick. My mother cared little for this out of a fear that my hope would be obstructed by a wife. This was not the hope of the world to come, but the hope of learning which both my parents wanted me to attain, my father since he thought almost nothing about you and only empty conceits about me, my mother because she considered the usual course of learning not only not to be a hindrance, but even of some considerable help in attaining you (2.6.8).

Augustine may not come right out and say it, but we have to admit that something more significant is going on. As we saw in Focus Text 2A, his language has more to do with sexual lust than with the theft of a pear. Augustine's parents pick up on it, although, out of sheer ambition for his future, they do little about it. What is Augustine doing?

Here's what I think is happening. In Chapter Two Augustine is reprimanding himself because he was sexually active with a hometown girl from Thagaste. In fact, it's worse than that. He got the girl pregnant. We know that Augustine has a child named Adeodatus with an unnamed girlfriend. However, he doesn't explicitly tell us about her until Chapter Four.

As a result, most readers think the pregnancy happens while Augustine is in Carthage, not Thagaste. Augustine even inserts language into Chapter Three which seems to imply this. There's just one problem. As James O'Donnell has pointed out, the math doesn't work very well.[13] Given the details Augustine presents in his writings, we can figure out that he got his girlfriend pregnant during his sixteenth year while he was in Thagaste. I work through the math in a short Appendix to this Chapter if you're interested.

What underlies the entire discussion in Chapter Two is something Augustine doesn't talk about overtly. He got a girl pregnant and this is why he's so adamant he has gravely sinned. In fact, it is this act which precipitates Augustine's great fall. Augustine falls because he gives into his lust and the consequences are dire.

Why doesn't he just tell us that? I'm speculating here, but I think there are two reasons. First, he is trying to protect the girl. Remember, he's writing the *Confessions* as a forty-three-year-old Bishop. He likely respected his former girlfriend enough to want to protect her identity. What better way to do that than to insert language to make it seem the illicit relationship started in Carthage, not in Thagaste? The second reason he doesn't tell us directly is he's trying to get us to read better, uncovering the symbolic meaning in the text.

How does Augustine tie together the theft of the pear and sexual sin? We've already discussed the most obvious way in Focus Text 2A. Augustine's own language in Chapter Two conflates the theft of the pear with notions of "lust." Yet let's think beyond the literal sense of the text for a minute. What does a pear look like? Perhaps I'm overreaching here, but doesn't a pear look something like a woman's body? In fact, in later artistic renderings of Mary, the pear is often used to depict the fruit of her womb.[14] Moreover, in Greek Mythology, the pear often shows up with the goddess Athena, who just happens to be the goddess of wisdom.[15] Isn't Augustine's embrace of "worldly" wisdom what has gotten him in trouble?

When Augustine approaches the interpretation of a narrative text, he is very interested in what he calls "signs," since he assumes that there is more going on in a text than meets the eye. Yet he is even more interested in where those signs point. This is how Augustine puts it in his book *On Christian Teaching*, his seminal work on biblical interpretation:

> *All teaching* (doctrina) *is either about things or about signs, but things* (res) *are learned through signs* (signa). *I now refer to a 'thing' specifically to indicate that it is not referring to something else such as wood, a stone, a flock or other such thing…Such things exist that they may be signs signifying other things. On the other hand, there are other kinds of signs, those which are never used except as signs. An example of this is words). No one uses words except as signs of something else* (gratia) *(1.2.2).*

To Augustine, words are only useful in as much as they point to something else. A word means nothing on its own – it's just a collection of letters. When both the sign and the thing signified are taken into account, a word starts to have meaning.

When it comes to Chapter Two, the character of Augustine's language regarding sexual sin seems so out of proportion that this serves as a clue that we're not supposed to be focusing on the literal theft of the pears. We're supposed to be digging for what lies below the surface, the thing signified. What's below the surface is an unexpected pregnancy.

To be clear, I'm not at all denying that the pear theft happened. Augustine is telling us a true (and paradigmatic) parable about his life. In fact, Augustine is adamant that the surface level of any text is essential. For the mature reader, however, there are many layers to unfold. Through his own story, he is trying to show us how to approach other stories that exist in the Biblical text. Let's turn now to the Bible and see how he employs a similar reading strategy.

Augustine and the Bible

The reason I'm convinced that there is more going on with the theft of the pears is how it nicely dovetails with his readings of the Bible in Chapter Two. The Biblical story is not just historical. It's the story of Augustine himself. Augustine spends much of Chapter Two putting himself into the Biblical story. He wants us to do the same as we come to the Scriptures. Michael Cameron, a noted expert on Augustine's exegesis, describes it like this:

> *Augustine transposes himself into [the Bible's] characters: he becomes Adam in Eden rebelling against God's command; he becomes the prodigal son of Jesus' parable seeking forgiveness after wandering... This is the hermeneutical aspect of Christ's 'astounding exchange' of redemption.*[16]

Chapter Two is important because it provides some of the best examples in the *Confessions* of Augustine's reading strategy. This is how the pear story and the Biblical text come together. Augustine is trying to teach us how to read well. Both in his use of the Biblical text and in his telling of the pear story, Augustine shows us what it is to read a text carefully.

Augustine as the Prodigal Son

Consider the following texts from Chapter Two, all of which allude to the Prodigal Son, depicting Augustine as the one in rebellion:

Focus Text 2C

I had become deaf from the rattling of my chain of mortality, my soul's penalty of pride, and I was wandering ever farther away from you and you let me (2.2.2).

Where was I in the sixteenth year of the age of my flesh when I accepted in myself the scepter of the madness of lust and gave myself completely to it? This lust was permitted according to shameful human nature, yet was illicit according to your law (2.2.4).

Woe is me! Dare I say you stayed silent, my God while I was marching ever farther from you? Did you really stay silent towards me then? (2.3.7)

We carried off huge loads, not to eat ourselves, but to throw to the pigs, although perhaps we did eat some. Therefore our pleasure came simply because it was not allowed (2.4.9).

The Parable of the Prodigal Son, located in Luke 15.11-32, is one of the most famous in the Bible. In it, Jesus tells the story of a man with two sons, one of whom demanded his inheritance and left his family to pursue "loose living." After the son had moved to "a far country" and had blown his inheritance, a famine arose, causing him to seek employment feeding pigs, a detestable vocation for a well-bred Jewish male. After coming to himself, the son realized that he should just return home, humble himself before his father and offer to be one of his slaves. He expected condemnation and expressions of disappointment upon returning home.

In one of the most poignant scenes in the Bible, when the father saw the son "from afar off," he ran (a most undignified thing for a well-bred patriarch to do) to embrace his son and welcomed him home. The father put his best robe on his son, shoes on his feet and ordered the servants to kill the fatted calf in celebration.

Augustine sees himself as the younger son in the story. He left God's fold as a youth to pursue "loose living." He eventually came back to the fold, but only after he had exhausted all his resources. The rest he was looking for would only be found in the Church in a life dedicated wholly to Christ. This is Augustine's point.

In Chapter Two, Augustine does not just recount the story of the Prodigal Son – he lives it. The Biblical narrative frames his telling of his own story.

Augustine and Adam's Fall

Augustine is not just the Prodigal Son. In Chapter Two, he also sees himself as Adam in the Garden of Eden. To Augustine, he is just like the first man who disobeyed God's command and thus becomes the archetype for the human race.

The inference is subtle, but when Augustine went off with his ruffian friends, he was making a similar decision as Adam when he took the forbidden fruit from Eve and ate it. Consider the following text from which describes the pear theft:

Focus Text 2D:

> There was a pear tree near our vineyard laden with fruit, though attractive in neither form nor taste. A gang of nasty adolescents went to shake down and rob the fruit from the tree and to carry it off in the dead of night. In our usual despicable way, we extended our games outside until the wee hours. We carried off huge loads, not to eat ourselves, but to throw to the pigs, although perhaps we did eat some. Therefore our pleasure in doing this came simply because it was not allowed (2.4.9).

While describing the theft of the pears, Augustine alludes to the story of the fall. He understands the fall in light of a key New Testament passage. The apostle Paul recounts the following in the New Testament concerning the fall:

And Adam was not deceived, but the woman was deceived and became a transgressor (1 Tim 2.14).

Augustine follows Paul in noting that Adam knew exactly what was happening when the serpent tempted Eve with the forbidden fruit. The serpent may have beguiled Eve, but it did not do so for Adam. Augustine's understanding of the fall was that Adam must have been after something else in taking the fruit from Eve. Augustine believes that Adam was after camaraderie with Eve.[17] As he writes in the *City of God*, "Eve received what the serpent spoke as conventional truth, while Adam was unwilling to be separated from his only partner, even if it meant participating in her sin" (14.11).

Augustine is subtly describing his behavior in parallel terms with Adam's behavior in the Bible. Augustine knew exactly what he was doing. He not only chose to sin, but he did it enthusiastically. He wanted the companion-ship of the ruffians so badly that he committed a crime with them. Augustine fell in Chapter Two just as the human race fell in Adam. He is therefore in need of redemption (and confession) like everyone else.

Not only does Augustine depict himself in terms of Adam, he also draws a parallel to the Garden of Eden itself with the story of the pear theft. These details are subtle and easy to miss. Yet they help to deepen Augustine's story.

When Augustine describes the theft of the pears, he mentions that there was only *one* pear tree. As Augustine puts it, "there was *a* pear tree near our vineyard laden with fruit..." (2.9).[18] Although there is no indefinite article (the word "a") in Latin, Augustine places the Latin word for tree (*arbor*) upfront in the original text to emphasize it. The focus is on one single tree, a detail critical for understanding this Chapter. We should recall that there was just one tree in the story of the fall in the Garden of Eden. As it says in the book of Genesis:

> But God said, "you shall not eat of the fruit of the tree which is in the midst of the garden, neither shall you touch it, lest you die (Gen 3.3).

Augustine also notes that there was nothing attractive about the fruit which he stole. As Augustine puts it regarding the fruit from the tree, it was "...attractive neither in color nor taste" (2.9). This small detail also proves important since Augustine intends the reader to recall a similar detail from Genesis Three which characterizes the fruit which Eve saw:

So when the woman saw that the tree was good for food, and that it was a delight to the eyes, and that the tree was to be desired to make one wise, she took of its fruit and ate; and she also gave some to her husband and he ate (Gen 3.6).

By reminding us that Eve found the fruit on the tree in the Garden of Eden a "delight to the eyes," Augustine is trying to indicate that the story of his fall echoes the Biblical story with a rather significant difference. Whereas Eve found the fruit attractive to the eyes, Augustine did not find it attractive at all. In so doing, Augustine indicates that, in his post-fall condition, the desire for sin itself was enough to make him turn away from God. In a sense, Augustine's sin was even more irrational than Eve's.

Thus, in Chapter Two, Augustine has shown us something important. Augustine's reaction to the theft of pears seems overwrought on the surface. But this is simply an indication that we are supposed to be digging below the surface of the text to uncover richer layers of meaning. As the *Confessions* progresses, we will discover that these lessons on how to read the Bible become ever-more subtle and intricate. For now, the simple lesson is that when we read the great stories of the Bible, we should picture ourselves with the narrative. If we do, we will gain much more from our reading.

Questions for Reflection
1. Do you have memories of mistakes you made during your teenage years? What lessons did you learn from them?
2. Augustine fathered a child out of wedlock and went on to be one of the great saints of the church. Do you think God can't forgive you because of something in your past?
3. Augustine spends a decent amount of time in Chapter Two placing himself within the Biblical story. Are there aspects of your life that match up with the stories of the Bible?
4. Augustine criticizes his parents in this Chapter for being more interested in his career success than his character. How do you define success both for yourself and your children?
5. Why is the Christian subculture so hung up on sex? Is confining sex to the bonds of marriage realistic? Old-fashioned? Biblical?

Appendix:

Chronology and Use of Scripture

Given the importance of Augustine's sexual sin and his use of Scripture in the *Confessions*, both subjects deserve some comment. The following fills in some details about the timing of the pregnancy and provides a primer on Augustine's handling of the Bible.

Pregnancy

In the Focus Text Section above, I recounted a theory about what was underneath Augustine's criticisms of himself in Chapter Two. Augustine got a girl pregnant and feels guilty about it. Here, I would like to work through why the math seems to necessitate this conclusion.

James O'Donnell noticed that in Chapter Nine of the *Confessions*, Augustine mentions that Adeodatus was about sixteen years old when he was baptized (9.6.14).[19] We know that Augustine's baptism was on Easter Sunday in AD 387. This would mean that Adeodatus was born in about AD 370 or 371. We also know from the beginning of Chapter Two that Augustine was born in AD 354 and was about sixteen years old when he came home to Thagaste during his hiatus from school (2.3.5).

If Adeodatus was sixteen when he was baptized, then he must have been born in AD 370 or 371. This means that Augustine's girlfriend must have gotten pregnant while Augustine was in Thagaste in AD 370. Thus the big sin behind Augustine's fall was not the theft of the pear, as serious as that may be. It was the sin of fornication. He got a girl pregnant during his sixteenth year. In other words, Augustine's language is ultimately about the illegitimate son he bore in AD 370. The theft is really about a girl's virginity, not a piece of fruit. The table on the next page lays out this chronology:

Event	Year
Augustine Born in Thagaste	AD 354
Augustine back in Thagaste from School	Age 16 (**AD 370**)
Adeodatus Baptized in Milan	Age 16 (AD 387)
Adeodatus' Birth Year	**AD 370/371**

In Chapter Three, we will observe that the situation only gets worse. Augustine moves to Carthage (the leading city in North Africa at the time) for his studies and presumably takes his girlfriend, now the mother of his child, with him. If this is the case, it would be mean that he ripped his girlfriend out of the Church. Not only does Augustine father a child out of wedlock, but given his Manichean ties in Carthage, it means that he likely forced the mother of his child to leave the Catholic Church. Or, as Gary Wills puts it, "he was not merely persuading [her] to live with him, but to make a break with her church (and, no doubt, her Catholic parents)."[20] To Augustine, there was no sin worse than this. It was grave.

Augustine and Scripture

One of the things that should have become clear by now is that Augustine is telling his own story via the Biblical story. We have seen him make allusions to the fall of Satan and to the Parable of the Prodigal Son among other literary allusions. In so doing, Augustine is teaching us how to read the Scriptures.

The implication for the *Confessions* is that the Biblical narratives are not just recounting events which transpired long ago, but were literally archetypes which are there to help Christians understand their own lives. Thus the story of the Prodigal Son is not just a good story – it is the story of every human being, past and present. We have all rebelled and willingly turned away from God (Rom 3.23). The Parable of the Prodigal Son is a story of grace which awaits anyone who is willing to turn from his rebellion and embrace the grace of God.

Chapter Two is a very important study in how Augustine uses the Scriptures to influence the lives of those who are in the Church. To Augustine, the point of the Scriptures, particularly the narrative sections, is to help believers understand themselves. This is important because, in the narrative sections of the *Confessions*, Augustine is not particularly interested in providing a rationalistic account of the Bible. Instead, Augustine wants his readers to *experience* the text.

We should also realize Augustine's strategy of teaching his readers to locate themselves within the Biblical narrative would have come very naturally to him because of his rhetorical training. Put simply, this is what a great orator did – adapt a well-known story for application to an audience in order to move it towards the speaker's point of view. Augustine likely learned this from the great Roman rhetorician Quintilian who wrote the following:

> *Let them [the students] learn, too, to take pieces of the verses of the poets, and then to express them in different words; and afterwards to represent them, somewhat boldly, in a paraphrase in which it is allowable to abbreviate or embellish certain parts, provided that the sense of the poet be preserved. He who shall successfully perform this exercise, which is difficult even for accomplished professors, will be able to learn anything.*[21]

As a boy, Augustine was taught to read literature by paraphrasing it in terms of his own life. In the *Confessions*, he is taking this rhetorical training and applying it to the Bible.

Augustine's Fall

Augustine, when he consorts with his ruffian friends, describes this experience like he was being dragged through the streets of Babylon. Not only was Babylon the place where the nation of Judah spent its years in exile, but Babylon was also the great, corrupt city which falls at the Lord's return in Revelation 18, where it is described as "a dwelling place of demons, a haunt of every foul spirit, a haunt of every foul and hateful bird" (Rev 18.2). In the Bible, Babylon is a symbol of fornication and sin, a city which would be "thrown down with violence" and ultimately destroyed at the end of time (Rev 18.21). Consider the following text from Chapter Two of the *Confessions*:

O my heart, O God, O my heart, upon which you took pity in the bot-
tommost part of the abyss. O my heart, let it now tell you what it was
seeking there, that I became gratuitously evil, having no motive for my
vice, but vice itself. It was foul and I loved it. I loved perishing. I loved
my own fall, not that for which I was falling, but my fall itself. I was
foul in soul, leaping down from your firmament to utter destruction
(2.4.9).

This text is a fairly evident allusion to the fall of Satan. Augustine is again telling the story of his own fall in light of the fall of the Devil.

One thing which is subtle, but that Augustine expects us to notice, is that Babylon is associated with the Devil. This is true not just in the book of Revelation where Satan is ultimately judged, but also in the Old Testament where his fall from grace is described. The following is a key passage which Augustine understood as describing the fall of Satan:

How you are fallen from heaven, O Day Star, son of Dawn! How you
are cut down to the ground, you who laid the nations low! But you
said in your heart, 'I will ascend to heaven; above the stars of God I
will set my throne on high; I will sit on the mount of assembly in the
far north; I will ascend above the heights of the clouds, I will make
myself like the Most High.' But you are brought down to Sheol, to the
depths of the Pit. Those who see you will stare at you, and ponder over
you (Isa 14.12-16).

Although many modern interpreters of the Bible find it difficult to understand this passage in light of the Devil, the Church Fathers had no such difficulties. Augustine interprets this passage as follows in his book *On Christian Teaching*:

The following is written by Isaiah: 'O How fallen is Lucifer, who rose
in the morning, he is fallen from heaven' (Isa 14.12), and so forth,
which, under the figure (figura) of the king of Babylon, refers to the
devil, as if one person (3.37.55).

In fact, Augustine believes it is Satan's own misguided will that caused him to rebel against God, and leave heaven to live at enmity with God. Augustine writes the following in the *City of God*:

*Here the suggestion is that the devil was at some point without sin...
Now, if such statements cannot be otherwise interpreted, then we must
understand the verse, 'he did not stand firm in the truth,' as meaning
that he was in the truth but did not remain there and that 'the devil
sinned from the beginning,' does not mean he sinned from the outset of
his creation, but must be considered from the beginning of his sin since
his sin started because of his pride (12.15).*

There is a connection throughout the Bible between the city of Babylon
and the fall of the Devil. Satan's pride and his desire to "ascend to heaven,"
caused his downfall.

This is precisely how Augustine understands his own fall in Chapter Two.
Augustine, in his youth, fell because he was attempting to imitate something
he thought was high and lofty. As Augustine puts it, "pride mimics what is
lofty" (2.5.13). Augustine puts the acceptance of his friends over the righteous demands of God, causing him to fall. Just as Satan fell from heaven
because of pride, so Augustine fell away from God because of pride. Once
again, Augustine sees himself within the biblical story itself.

Even before Satan's fall, Augustine admits that his immoral behavior did
not make him happy. In a letter written around AD 404, Augustine writes
the following:

*Moreover, if the holy and blessed angels not only have understanding
(scientia) of what sort of state each might be in now, but also the foreknowledge of what they will likely be in the future, I do not at all see
in what way was the devil happy (beatus) at any time, since while he
was still a good angel, he had knowledge of his future iniquity (iniquitatem) (73.7).*

Said differently, just as Satan had no chance at happiness while being
separated from Christ, Augustine would have no chance at happiness on the
path he was pursuing. Augustine is not just telling us the story of his life to
tell a story. He has a pedagogical aim in mind – getting us to read the Bible
with greater sensitivity and wisdom.

THE FIRST CONVERSION(S)

In Chapter Three, we observe Augustine's first conversions – not to Christianity, but to philosophy and to Manichaeism. Etymologically, the word philosophy means "the love of wisdom" and at the tender age of seventeen, Augustine starts to think about higher (and better) things. His loves may still be misplaced since they are not yet directed toward Christ, but Augustine decides to dedicate himself to the pursuit of truth, wherever that may lead. This pursuit would eventually bring him into the Catholic fold, and Chapter Three starts to foreshadow that outcome. We should not underestimate the importance of philosophy in bringing Augustine into the Church, as it plays a major role in the story.

I should briefly define what Augustine means by conversion. The Latin word *conversio* implies a "moral change."[1] In turn, this Latin word derives from a Greek term (*epistrepho*) which carries the idea of "changing direction, turning or changing one's mind."[2] In other words, the idea of conversion, as Augustine understands it, carries an association with movement in both a physical and spiritual sense.[3] While conversion is ultimately the return of the soul to participate in God, Augustine begins this process of return among the philosophers. In a very real sense, his turn to philosophy is a conversion experience.

Following the framework we have been using, the third Chapter centers around the lust of the eyes. Remember that Chapters One through Nine of the *Confessions* are structured along the lines of the three misplaced loves in 1 John 2.15-16 – the lust of the flesh, the lust of the eyes and the pride of life. While the implications of the lust of the flesh were obvious in the last Chapter, we are going to have to work a little harder to understand how the lust of the eyes works here. The short version is that Augustine connects with a heretical Christian group called the Manichees in Chapter Three. The Manichees, with their stark dualism between matter and spirit, could not conceive that God would ever take on human flesh in the Incarnation. They believed that Christ did not really die on the cross (he just appeared to) and that Jesus (and all of humankind) actually came from demons. I know this sounds bizarre, and I will explain as we go along what Augustine found appealing in this group. As it turns out, there was quite a bit that appealed to the young Augustine.

This is not the only important aspect of Chapter Three. Augustine's mother, Monica, has a vision at the end of the Chapter which seems to foreshadow Augustine's eventual embrace of Catholic Christianity. Monica plays a brief, but key, role in this Chapter, both in her rejection of Augustine's turn toward the Manichees and in her vision which portends a very different outcome. As we will see throughout Augustine's writings, dreams, visions and spiritual voices were important sources for discerning God's direction, just as they were for the Biblical characters. Once again, Augustine is teaching us to place ourselves within the Biblical story.

We should realize that Monica's vision was spiritual, while Augustine was focusing on that which was physical and temporal. Despite the Manicheans' abhorrence for the Incarnation of Jesus, even their notion of a spiritual reality ended up being physical since light was trapped in the flesh. Hence, we find that the lust of the eyes structures the Chapter.

Summary

Chapter Three takes place in the city of Carthage, which is in modern-day Tunisia. Augustine went to Carthage to complete his schooling, particularly in the subject of rhetoric, to which he found himself naturally drawn. Carthage was the leading city in North Africa at this point in history and must have been an exciting place to be for a young man who had grown up in a small town. This urban environment would bring more temptations for Augustine and we find that he has few guides to help him navigate the "frying pan of illicit loves" which he discovers there. In Latin, Augustine begins with a word play, noting that he came to Carthage (*Carthago*) and found himself in a frying pan (*Sartago*).

Following what we uncovered in Chapter Two that Augustine got a girl from Thagaste pregnant, we also need to realize that there is part of the story that Augustine does not tell us explicitly. If I am correct in my reading, Augustine would have brought this (unnamed) woman with him to Carthage, having ripped her out of the Catholic Church. We get some indications in the Chapter that this is the case, although Augustine is notably quiet about it. In short, there is once again a back story that only a close reading of the text will uncover.

One more thing we should realize is that Augustine is likely telling his story in light of Aeneas, the hero of Virgil's epic poem the *Aeneid*. One of the most memorable sections of the *Aeneid* occurs when Aeneas goes to Carthage, meets Dido and has a love affair with her. At the insistence of the gods, Aeneas makes plans to leave Carthage, thus breaking Dido's heart, and causing her to commit suicide. Hence, when Augustine characterizes Carthage as sin city, he has Virgil's famous story in mind as he is writing. This is why Augustine tells us upfront that he "fell in love with love" (*amans amare*). As we will see throughout the *Confessions*, Augustine is trying to present his story in a multi-layered fashion in order to get us to read beyond the literal sense of the text.

Illicit Loves

Augustine moves to Carthage to continue his studies. His attention was directed to external things, which were physical, soulless and corruptible, and that could not ultimately bring him satisfaction. Augustine wanted love, which, to him, meant "enjoying his lover's body" (3.1.1). On the surface, this is a subtle reference to his girlfriend, but perhaps also a future reference to the Church.

His first misplaced love was the theater, something that would be somewhat akin in our present-day lives to going to the movies. Augustine found himself titillated emotionally by representations of things that were not real (3.2.2). He notes that the theater might produce feelings of pity and even tears, but these were just imaginary (3.2.3). He wonders why he is so drawn to the sufferings of others. Augustine notes that he "loved grief" (*dolere amabam*) and even "sought opportunities for such grief" (3.2.4).

Yet God was never far from Augustine, even while Augustine was doing everything possible to turn his back on Him. For example, Augustine's "impious curiosity" (*sacrilega curiositate*, 3.3.5) was an attempt to live without God. Augustine even notes that he "dared, while the solemn rites were being celebrated within the walls of the Church to desire and conduct an activity that that would bring the fruit of death," a fairly obvious allusion to the affair he was carrying on with his girlfriend.

This would seem to argue against the theory that Augustine met his girl-friend and got her pregnant in Thagaste. Yet since catechumens were not allowed to see the sacramental mysteries before they were baptized, and since the sexes were usually separated (save for the occasional vigil), one could not just slip into a Church in the fourth century.[4] As a result, it's likely this refers to a previous event in Thagaste.[5] I'll explain a bit later why he's doing this.

Cicero and Philosophy

Next, Augustine provides some detail about his studies in Carthage. He was in Carthage to receive training in rhetoric, which is somewhat akin to being a trial lawyer (3.3.6). Here, Augustine takes up a friendship with a new band of ruffians, known in the Latin text as "*eversores*." This Latin word carries with it the connotation that his friends were "subverters" or "row-dies."[6] They clearly liked hazing freshmen and had fun doing wicked things. Just like the ruffians with whom Augustine stole the pears in the previous Chapter, he was perfectly happy to hang out with people of questionable character if it gave him the opportunity to belong.

In comparison to the other students in Carthage, Augustine distin-guished himself as an orator (3.4.7). Yet Augustine questions his own mo-tives, which he found vain. Augustine wanted to be noticed and liked, not an uncommon trait for those drawn to careers involving public speaking. "In the ordinary course of study," Augustine read a book by Cicero which was to change his life (3.4.8).

When Augustine read Cicero's *Hortensius*, he was transfixed by what he came across. The *Hortensius* was a call to pursue wisdom through the study of philosophy. Augustine "was on fire" to leave the earth and "fly back" (*revolare*) to God. It was Cicero's call to a life focused on reason and truth, which constitutes Augustine's first conversion.

In particular, Augustine became smitten with the idea that he could seek truth wherever it might reside. He was not bound to one system of thought, like his Christian mother was. He could branch out and explore many dif-ferent points of view. This caused Augustine to begin a decades-long search for what was true. As Augustine sees it, this search would take him far from God. Yet his intense longing to find truth never left him.

The first place Augustine turned to find truth was the Bible (3.5.9). He had likely grown up with his mother telling him that Holy Scripture was true. So he decided to check out the Bible for himself. Augustine was sorely

disappointed with what he discovered. He found the whole Bible, but especially the Old Testament, with its coarse style and its problematic morality, to
be "veiled in mysteries." After all, how could the patriarchs, exhibiting fornication, lust, polygamy, murder, rape and incest, possibly be people com-
mended by God? He quickly put the Bible down. The Old Testament was no
comparison to the majestic writing of classical authors like Cicero.

The Manichees

But, where should Augustine turn? Very soon after putting down the
Bible, he turned to the Manichees ("*Man-i-keys*") (3.6.10), a group outside
the Church who saw themselves as Christians. The Manichees had answers
to many of Augustine's questions. They rejected the Old Testament, finding it base and problematic. Plus, they claimed to be a more enlightened
religious system because they had incorporated all that was true from all the
other religions (including from Zoroastrianism in Persia where the sect had
started).[7]

Moreover, they claimed to focus on what was spiritual, not what was physical. Unlike the Old Testament which depicted God as having hands and feet,
eyes and nostrils, not to mention a temper, the Manichees had cogent answers to how the world was created, where man came from, what had gone
wrong with the world and what salvation entailed. It didn't hurt that they
were the fashionable sect for intellectuals at the time, either. To top it off,
they believed in Jesus, albeit with a very different understanding than what
his mother held. To Augustine, he was doing exactly what Cicero had exhorted him to do in the *Hortensius*, seeking truth wherever it might be found.

Augustine looks back on all this with dismay (3.6.11). According to the
Manichees, light and darkness were primordial substances that were once
separated, but because of a complex chain of events, had become mingled
within every human being. This mingling of light and darkness is what has
gone wrong in the world. In fact, everyone has two souls – one good and
one bad – in constant conflict. By associating with the Manichees, Augustine
adopted a worldview that caused him to intuit reality in "a carnal sense."

Among other things, Augustine was drawn to the Manichees because
they had plausible answers to the problem of the origin of evil (3.7.12). The
Manichean answer was that good and evil are locked together in a cosmic
battle (much like in the Star Wars movies). Evil was a real substance which
was fighting against the good. Augustine had not yet realized that evil exists
because it is not a "real thing" at all, but is an absence of good.

During this time, Augustine also wondered if God was limited by "bodily form" (*forma corporea*), especially since the Old Testament, which he had just read, implied it because of its frequent use of human body parts to describe God. Augustine had not yet realized that God is Spirit (John 4.24) who, in the person of Jesus, took on human flesh. In fact, Augustine had not begun to grapple with how man could be created in the image of God, especially if God is pure spirit and man has a body. This understanding would also come later for Augustine, but the Manichees gave him some initial (but erroneous) answers to these vexing problems.

Morality and the Law

Moreover, when Augustine read the Old Testament it seemed that there was no transcendent morality or justice among the Biblical characters. How could some acts be condemned in some places, but permitted in others (3.7.13)? For example, the Patriarchs in the Old Testament sacrificed animals, were circumcised, kept food laws and observed the Sabbath, while other groups (in the New Testament) were told these things were no longer valid. Didn't Augustine tell us that God does not change in the first Chapter? How could there be a universal moral law if such precepts could change from culture to culture and from generation to generation?

Further, in poetry, Augustine notes that different rules apply at different times (3.7.14). Some rules may apply in every situation the poet encounters, yet the poet applies other rules in differing contexts. What Augustine had not yet intuited was that there were some things which did not, and could not change, while other things should vary as customs, locations or times change (3.8.15). To Augustine, God's law is supreme because "God is over everything." But, why is the law still "on the books" if it is no longer valid?

Augustine next says there are three sources of iniquity: "the lust for ruling (*principandi*), feeling (*sentiendi*) and seeing (*spectandi*)" (3.8.16), roughly akin to the "lust of the flesh," the "pride of life" and the "lust of the eyes," of 1 John 2.16. As noted above, it is the misplaced loves of 1 John 2.16 that form the framework for how Augustine understands his fall away from God in the first four Chapters of the *Confessions*.

Those in the faith also sin and fall short of God's standards (3.9.17). To Augustine, God's standards (namely, the Ten Commandments) must always be kept, regardless of the community's wavering opinions. We should keep in mind that Augustine is commenting on the law in hindsight and freely admits that at this point in his life he was "ignorant" and "scoffed at your

holy servants and prophets" (3.10.18). At the time, Augustine did not realize that God does not act capriciously or contrary to reason and thus fell in
with the Manicheans because they purported to base all they did on reason
alone, not on faith.[8] In fact, the Manichean embrace of reason over faith was
central to his joining up with them.

Yet Manichean beliefs that a "fig weeps when plucked" or that one
would "exhale angels" or even "particles of God" as one "groaned in prayer"
or "belched," were also far from reason. These statements reflect the
Manichean belief that light was strongly present in fruits and vegetables,
which is one reason why upper-level Manicheans were strict vegetarians.[9]
Manichean leaders thought they were liberating light from fruit as they ate,
contributing to the redemption of the world. Augustine shutters to think
that the Manichean world view all seemed plausible at the time.

Monica's Vision

Monica's reaction to all this is telling (3.11.19). Augustine depicts Monica
throughout the *Confessions* as being loving and tender. She genuinely cared
for her son and prayed for him earnestly. But Augustine's Manichean phase
was just too much for her. She could put up with his fathering a child out of
wedlock, but she refused to let him in the house while Augustine was with
the Manichees because of her hatred of his "blasphemies."

Monica's refusal to let Augustine into the house is another example of
Augustine's conflating time periods within the narrative of the *Confessions*.
Given the difficulties of travel, it seems pretty clear that Augustine would
have been refused entry into the house while he was in Thagaste after his
studies were finished. This event likely occurs after he returns to Thagaste
after completing his studies in Carthage, which is the time period covered
in Chapter Four.

Monica's strong reaction caused some strain with Augustine until his
mother had a dream in which she perceived God encouraging her to live
and eat at the same table with her son. In the vision, Monica found herself
standing on a wooden rule (a *regula*), possibly "a leveling device used for
building aqueducts."[10] A "gleaming" young man (likely Jesus) came to her
in the dream and asked why she was so downcast. She responded that she
was in mourning because of her son's sin. The young man in the dream
then instructed her to not be anxious but exhorted her to notice that where
she standing, Augustine was there as well. In other words, Augustine was
standing on the same rule (*regula*) as Monica in the dream. I will reserve the

interpretation of the vision for the Focus Text section, but the short answer is that it is foreshadowing Augustine's eventual embrace of Christianity at the end of the *Confessions* when he discovers the truth of another *regula*, the Rule of Faith.

When Monica told him about the dream, Augustine attempted to twist its meaning, obviously annoyed that his mother would think he would ever stoop to becoming a Christian. He tried to convert his mother to become a Manichean, to no avail. Augustine would spend the next nine years with the Manicheans as a junior member. He makes it a point to note that his mother never ceased in her prayers for him during this time.

The Chapter ends with a memorable scene in which Monica asks a Bishop in the Church to confront Augustine about his ties to the Manichees. This Bishop had been with the Manichees at one point and thus Monica thought he would be a good witness to her son. Yet as the Bishop listened to her story, he refused to intervene, saying that Augustine was still "unteachable (*indocilem*)" (3.12.21). When Monica broke down in tears in a bid to manipulate him, the Bishop held firm. Augustine ends the Chapter with the Bishop saying, "Be on your way…it cannot happen that the son of these tears should be destroyed." This prophecy foreshadows the turn that Augustine would undertake towards the end of the story.

Focus Texts

In Chapter Three, we are primarily dealing with Augustine's initial conversion to philosophy, his initial rejection of the Bible and Monica's vision which foreshadows the future. The Focus Texts are designed to cover these issues and to provide insight on what Augustine was doing during this period. We should keep in mind that Augustine was only nineteen years old during Chapter Three and was just finishing up his schooling in Carthage. The mature Augustine is looking back on this time with dismay since it represents his turn away from God.

Conversion to Philosophy

As noted in the Chapter summary, Augustine's first conversion is to philosophy. After reading Cicero's *Hortensius*, he burns with a desire to "leave the earth and fly back to God." Hence Augustine is describing his conversion in very religious (and Platonic) terms. Augustine's intellectual conversion is very much tied to his spiritual conversion. Let's see how Augustine describes this:

Focus Text 3A

In the ordinary course of study, I now happened upon a certain book by Cicero, whose rhetoric almost all admire, but not his heart. This book of his contains an exhortation to philosophy and is called the *Hortensius*. But this book altered my affections, O Lord. It changed my prayers to be towards you. It caused me to have other purposes and desires. Every vain hope became worthless to me, and I had an incredibly burning desire in my heart for the immortality of wisdom, and I began to lift up to return to you (3.4.7).

It is notable that even as Augustine looks back on this conversion, he is struck how Cicero brought him closer to God. This might seem odd. After all, Cicero was no Christian. He was a great Roman orator, poet and statesman who had lived centuries before Augustine during the golden age of the Roman republic. How could reading a piece of pagan literature stir this kind of religious reaction in Augustine?

Augustine has this reaction because it incites a turn toward wisdom, the etymological basis of the word "philosophy." "Wisdom" is a loaded term. In Augustine's day, Christian readers would have understood it not only in intellectual terms, but also as a reference to Christ. Jesus was Wisdom personified. For example, the eighth Chapter of Proverbs is a call to join with Wisdom, which Christians in the fourth century would have understood as a reference to Jesus' status as God. Moreover, one of Augustine's favorite New Testament texts, 1 Cor 1.24, reads as follows: "but to those who are called, both Jews and Greeks, Christ, [is] the power of God and the wisdom of God." When we see references to Wisdom, we should remember that Augustine understands this, at least in part, as a reference to Jesus.

Augustine puts it this way in his work *On Christian Teaching*, likely not written long after the *Confessions*:

> *Christ, wanting not only to give possession to those who were finished, but himself also wanting to provide an approach to the start of the journey, was willing to take on human flesh, Hence the verse, 'the Lord created me in the beginning of his ways' (Prov 8.22) means that*

> *those who wanted to come would begin in him…from this starting*
> *point is a journey which ends in eternal life to all those who continue*
> *to desire to attain the truth* (veritatem) *(1.34.38).*

Thus the journey toward truth is found by joining with Wisdom, who is Christ. In short, truth participates in a real way in Christ.

As Augustine looks back on it from a later vantage point, this is the problem with the *Hortensius*: Cicero does not know, and does not mention, the name of Christ (3.8). Yet the work stirred in Augustine a strong desire to search for, and seek after God, wherever He might be found. As Augustine writes, "Any book not having that name [Christ], no matter how learned or refined or truthful, could not seize me completely" (3.4.8).

This ardent search for Christ sounds very pious. However, it actually expresses Augustine's naiveté at this point in his life. From Augustine's youthful perspective, any book or group which mentioned the name of Jesus a lot must be worth pursuing. He did not yet have the maturity to evaluate critically groups like the Manichees. They mentioned the name of Christ and were constantly claiming to be aligned with truth, but with an understanding that was far from Catholic Christianity. In other words, code words like "Jesus" or Christ" could be inviting, but deceiving. Augustine describes his turn to philosophy in his book, *On the Happy Life*:

> *From my nineteenth year of my life, after encountering in rhetoric*
> *school that book of Cicero which is called 'Hortensius,' I was set on*
> *fire, having received a great love of philosophy, such that at once I*
> *wanted to give myself to it. But I was not wanting for confusion,*
> *which confounded my forward movement. I also acknowledge that for*
> *some time I was led into error, sinking in the ocean while looking up at*
> *the stars. A boyhood superstition deterred me from real searching and,*
> *when I was more bold, I dispersed the fog, having been persuaded by*
> *better teachings over that which is decreed for submission (1.4).*

In other words, Augustine's embrace of philosophy led him toward Christ. But, because he did not have the Church to guide him in his understanding of who Christ was, Augustine embraced "a boyhood superstition." Augustine is demonstrating the powerful need for catechesis in the Church, a central purpose of his writing.

Questions for Reflection

1. Augustine describes the *Hortensius* as having "changed his feelings" and "his prayers." What book has been the most life-changing for you? Why did it have that effect?
2. What impact (if any) has Christian catechesis had on you?
3. Do you agree with Augustine that one needs to know Christ to know truth? What about those who don't know Jesus?
4. What does the word "philosophy" connote for you? A dry academic subject? Something to be avoided? Why is philosophy so important for Augustine in the *Confessions*?

The Scriptures

We have seen that one of Augustine's purposes in writing was to teach the flock under his care to read the Bible and to pray. His teaching on prayer happens throughout the *Confessions* because it is one extended prayer. His instruction on the Scriptures comes up in a brief, but significant way in Chapter Three because Augustine rejected them. When read outside the Church, the Bible can be a very confusing (and offensive!) book. The following is Augustine's description of his first attempt to read the Bible:

Focus Text 3B

Therefore I resolved to apply my mind to the Holy Scriptures and to see what they were like. And this is what I saw: something not understood by the proud, nor open to babes, a book lowly to the novice, but to the lofty heights of the advanced, veiled in mystery. I was not able to enter into it, nor could I bow my head to advance in its steps. It is different now as I speak than how I felt when I attentively read these Scriptures back then. But the Scriptures seemed unbecoming to me compared to the majestic authority of Cicero (3.5.9).

In this text, Augustine is describing the difficulties he had with the Bible when he tried to read it in light of his secular training and apart from the Church. He found the text "lowly" and "enveloped in mysteries." As we will see, this was one of his chief attractions to the Manichees. Outside of Paul's epistles, the Manichees did not care much for the Bible, either.

What were Augustine's problems at this point? They were numerous enough to fill a book-length treatment on the subject. But, here are just a few to mention:

- In the Old Testament, God is often depicted with human characteristics such as hands, feet, eyes and breath as well as human emotions such as anger, jealousy and disappointment. How could this be if God is spirit, can't be seen and doesn't change?
- Israel is often called the "apple of God's eye" (Deut 32.10, Ps 17.8, Zech 2.8). Yet Israel is also faithless, rebellious, idolatrous and constantly walking away from God. Isn't this an obvious contradiction?
- Genesis 1.26 says that humankind was created in the image of God. Doesn't this mean that we have to picture God as having a body like humans do?
- The creation story in Genesis One makes no sense. To take just one example, how exactly did God create light before he created the sun on day four?

I should note that these are not new questions. Almost all of these questions had been previously lodged at the Church by those trying to show that Christianity was nothing but a superstition. By the way, many of the questions posed by the Manichees, which Augustine eventually refuted, form the basis of the critique of the New Atheists today. Despite centuries of distance between Augustine and us, these questions have not gone away.

Augustine would eventually produce satisfactory answers to these difficulties. But the key to his understanding the Old Testament was that it contained all sorts of types and figures which pointed forward to Christ. In other words, we must not read the Bible, especially the Old Testament, in a woodenly literal fashion. The literal sense of the text is essential, but not all there is. Most importantly, without Christ, we cannot properly understand the Old Testament. Had not Jesus, right before his ascension, said "Everything written about me in the Law of Moses and the Prophets and the Psalms must be fulfilled?" (Luke 24.44) In other words, the Old Testament was Scripture because it pointed forward to Christ and thus must be understood in light of Christ. To refuse to read the Old Testament in light of Jesus was to miss the point.

Further, Augustine urged his readers not to take the so-called anthropomorphisms (human characteristics ascribed to God) in the Bible literally. These were merely figurative expressions used to describe the indescribable God to finite human beings. When the infinite God speaks to us, he has to use common language to communicate, even if, upon further reflection, it proves inadequate to describe God in all his glory.

As for Israel, she was punished for her idolatry in the exile, and thus symbolically becomes the story of all who have sinned. Augustine does not at all deny that the stories about Israel and the Patriarchs really happened, but their importance is that they are archetypes which point forward to something greater. Israel is a model for our own rebellion from God.

Lastly, when God creates the heavens and the earth in Genesis One, the creation story is not to be taken as a scientific account of how the world began. Today, Augustine would be opposed to both young-earth creationists, who say the world was created in six literal days, as much as to those who deny the validity of Biblical revelation. He would point out that neither group is employing helpful assumptions in their interpretations of the Bible.

In fact, as we come to the end of the *Confessions* (in the second half of Chapter Twelve), Augustine presents many plausible interpretations of the creation story, but chooses to describe the creation story in spiritual, not physical terms.

To Augustine, Genesis One is not about physical creation at all, but the creation of "forms" in the mind of God, the invisible, incorporeal, spiritual "stuff" out of which the world was made. This enables the created order to participate in the uncreated, unchanging, perfect nature of God. The bigger point is that Augustine is trying to tell us the Bible is understandable if it is read within the Church in light of the Rule of Faith. Yet read apart from the Church and the Rule of Faith, the Bible just produces more problems than it solves.

Questions for Reflection

1. Describe your practice of reading the Bible. Do you read it?
2. What do you do if you do not understand something in the Bible?
3. Have you ever been in conversations with friends, family or neighbors when someone brought up a difficulty in the Bible? Were you able to answer the objection?

4. If Genesis One is not about seven literal days of creation, does that re-solve any issues for you? Does it create new ones?
5. How should we engage with others who think differently than we do with regard to interpreting what the Scriptures mean?

Monica's Vision

The vision that Monica has in Chapter Three is an important part of the unfolding story. The vision takes seriously the concerns that Monica has over her son's ties to the Manichees and looks forward to his eventual turn to the Church. This foreshadowing is significant, as it suggests that Augustine's spiritual darkness will not be the end of the story. It also signifies confidence that God will not cast off someone who earnestly seeks Him.[11]

Focus Text 3C

> How else can I interpret the dream she had by which you encouraged her to live and eat at the same table with me in the house (early on, she was unwilling because of her abhorrence and loathing for the blasphe-mies of my error). She saw herself standing on a certain wooden rule and a gleaming young man, cheerful and smiling, came towards her laughing while she was mourning and overwhelmed with grief. When he asked her why she was grieving and in tears, it was, as usual, to teach, not to acquire knowledge. So when she answered by bewailing my ruin, he admonished her to look and observe that where she was standing, there I was too. And when she looked, she saw me standing next to her on the same rule (3.11.19).

In the Summary Section above, I noted that Augustine makes a refer-ence to a rule (*regula*), which is likely an allusion to the Rule of Faith which Augustine will ultimately adopt and defend when he becomes a Bishop of the Church. As usual, there is more here than a surface reading of the text uncovers.

The Rule of Faith is a phrase which refers to the "sum content of the ap-ostolic teaching."[12] In the first few centuries of the Church, after the apostles had died, it became increasingly important to be able to recognize what was true teaching. After all, there were groups such as the Gnostics, the

Manichees and the Ebionites running around teaching aberrant interpretations of the Scriptures that departed from the apostolic teaching. The Rule of Faith, revealed to Christians at their baptism, became an important interpretive key for understanding the Bible.[13] Ultimately, the Rule of Faith was put into creedal form and became the basic Christian understanding through which one was to read the Scriptures. In a very real sense, when we confess the Nicene Creed, we are confessing the Rule of Faith.

The *regula* also has a subtle association with baptism. A *regula* was a "leveling device used in building aqueducts."[14] Thus one way to interpret the Rule of Faith is to see it as a baptismal creed.[15] Given that an aqueduct holds water and the Rule of Faith indicates a confession of faith, this connotation is also likely in view. The vision's rule, in other words, looks forward to Augustine's baptism and his eventual embrace of Christian orthodoxy.

The rule is also an allusion to the idea of justice which Augustine has been exploring in Chapter Three. Augustine goes on a long excursus regarding the law in which he tries to figure out how to interpret changing moral standards in the Bible. After all, outside of sins against nature, which are always wrong (Augustine cites sodomy in this regard), there seems to be changing views of sin in society. Thus, if God's commands are always authoritative, how can there be a change in standards between the Old and New Testaments?

The answer to this dilemma is that there are some things which never change (like the Ten Commandments), while other things do. Some scholars believe that many of the laws in the Old Testament were case laws, meaning that they were specific applications of the Ten Commandments to a particular society at a particular time.[16] Thus much of the Old Testament law does not have on-going validity for Christians, not because it wasn't good, but because times have changed. This is often Jesus' point in the New Testament when he is arguing with the Pharisees over the law. If the Law becomes a burden on the people and is not a guide to find righteousness, the law is not helpful. It is the principles that stay the same (i.e. the Ten Commandments), not always the codification of those commandments in law.

What does this have to do with Monica's vision? Augustine, looking back, realizes that once he comes into the Church, his dilemmas regarding the law will start to melt away. Christians have the Holy Spirit to guide them, to chasten them and to comfort them. Monica's vision shows that one day

Augustine and his mother would be on the same page. As we will discover in Chapter Nine, this is exactly what happens at the end of the story.

But what about Patricius? When Augustine makes an oblique reference to his father's death earlier in Chapter Three, it is the last time we will hear about him until Chapter Nine. I have waited until now to comment on this because we ought to consider Augustine's reaction in light of Monica's vision. Augustine writes, "I was in my nineteenth year, my father having died two years prior" (3.4.7). Augustine never claimed to be close to his father, but this seems really cold. It is as if his father's passing meant little to him.

Yet if we read Augustine's work *Against the Academics*, we get a different picture. Writing to Romanianus, his patron from Thagaste, Augustine says the following: "When I was bereaved (*orbatum*), you consoled me with friendship, refreshed me with encouragement, and helped me with your influence. (2.2.3)" Augustine did mourn his father, even if it doesn't sound like it.

Despite this, many readers of the *Confessions* have taken Augustine's silence to mean that he hated his father. Some have even turned Patricius into a "hot-tempered," "habitual adulterer."[17] While there is evidence in the *Confessions* itself that Patricius had a temper (9.9.19), Augustine's overall perspective toward his father would change once we get to the end of the story. If his goal is to find rest in God, Augustine would find peace with his parents as well.

It is worth remembering that Augustine was critical of Monica in Chapters One and Two for refusing to have him baptized as a child and for not doing more to curb his sexual appetites. But Augustine finds peace with her here, largely thanks to her vision. We will have to wait until Chapter Nine to see how Augustine makes peace with Patricius. Patricius may not have been a helpful spiritual influence in Augustine's life, but he is ultimately baptized into the Church, just as Augustine will be. Chapter Three anticipates this well.

Questions for Reflection

1. Have you ever made an important decision based on a dream? What was the outcome?
2. Have you had any vivid dreams recently? What happened? How did you interpret it?
3. Some Christians are critical of those who purport to hear the voice of God or to have visions. What is your opinion?

4. Characterize your relationship with your parents. If they are living, what is your relationship like? If not, how did their parenting affect your life?
5. The issue of changing norms is ever-present in our world in issues such as abortion and gay marriage. How do you draw the line between what never changes and what must change?

Appendix: Manicheanism

To read Chapter Three well, we ought to know something about Manichaeism. At the time of Augustine's association with the Manichees, they were a global religion which saw themselves as Christian. The following Appendix provides some background information on the religion of the Manichees which captivated Augustine's attention for close to ten years.

Manichaeism

Manichaeism is so named because of its founder, Mani, an Iranian who was martyred by the king of Persia in about AD 276, or almost one hundred and twenty years before Augustine wrote the *Confessions*.[18] Manichaeism was a "smorgasbord religion," wherein adherents took elements from Gnosticism, Zoroastrianism, Buddhism and Christianity to produce a synthesis that purported to be the "one true religion." Based on some Manichean manuscripts discovered in the twentieth century, it appears that Christianity was the most powerful influence for the Manichees.[19] This is likely why the Manichees claimed to be Christian even though they rejected both the Incarnation and the sacraments.[20]

As a teenager, Mani claimed to have received a revelation from the Paraclete (the "comforter" or "Holy Spirit") of John's Gospel.[21] Although Mani kept this revelation secret for some time, he opened up as a young adult and started to refer to *himself* as the Paraclete.[22] Seeing himself as an apostle or demi-god, Mani then proceeded to build a complete religious system from this revelation. Ironically, the key attraction for Augustine was that the Manichees claimed they could defend their system using nothing but reason.[23]

Cosmology

Manichaeism is based on the dualistic premise that from all eternity there were two primordial substances that were completely separate. Because of their separation, there was no likeness between them. The kingdom of light was characterized by rest and peace; the kingdom of darkness by a lust for power, turmoil and war. At some point before the creation of the world, the kingdom of darkness attacked the kingdom of light since its defenses were non-existent. The kingdom of darkness pierced the kingdom of light and thus light and darkness were co-mingled.[24]

The response from the leadership of the kingdom of light was to produce three so-called emanations to ward off the attack, which represents the beginning, middle and end of salvation history.[25] The first emanation produced a being known as "primal man." When Augustine mentions "the Five Elements which take on different colors" (3.6.11), this is a reference to the five "bright" elements produced by primal man (air, wind, light, water and fire) which form the soul of the kingdom of light.[26] Primal man was defeated by the kingdom of darkness and the five elements were subsumed. This constitutes the fall of the world.

Primal man then fell into an eternal abyss. In response, the kingdom of light created another emanation, the Living Spirit, which descended into darkness and issued a call for salvation. The Living Sprit then descended and rescued primal man out of the abyss and brought him up to heaven, making him the first martyr and the "first of the redeemed."[27]

This led to the third emanation, the creation of the twelve virgins of light (the signs of the Zodiac), which created the world to restore the captured light to its proper place in the heavens.[28] Note that everything prior to this third emanation occurred before the creation of the world. In order to expunge the light from the darkness, the world was created, enabling the Living Spirit to liberate the light by dividing it into three entities – the sun, moon and stars.[29]

A bi-sexual messenger next appeared to entice male and female demons to give up their captured light particles.[30] Unfortunately, the female demons enflamed the males' sexual desire, provoking an emission of seed in which light and darkness were again co-mingled (no, I'm not making this up).[31] Some light went to the moon and sun while the darkness fell back to earth. This gave rise to vegetation, then the animal kingdom. Two demons produced by the kingdom of darkness to counter the messenger were then sent into the world to frustrate the powers of light.[32] They united to create the first human beings – Adam and Eve.

To the Manichees, humans come from demons, not God. The existence of decaying bodies proves this.[33] Because of the presence of light, man has some good in him, but this is intermixed with a great propensity for evil because the light is trapped in lustful flesh.[34]

Jesus

Man is clearly in a problematic condition within the Manichean system. What can humans do about this? Well, this is where Jesus comes in. Since Adam was weighed down because of his flesh, Jesus came to help

him. To the Manichees, Jesus came from the same demons who had pro-
duced man in the first place. In fact, it is Jesus who beguiled Adam and
Eve in the form of a serpent in Genesis.[35] He is not good, but simply the
Devil in disguise.[36]

When Adam became aware of what happened, he resolved to live free
from sexual relations with Eve. Thus, at its core, sex is a problem for the
Manichees since every human spreads the problem of trapped light. This is
why the Manichean leadership refused to have sex and discouraged anyone
from having children. It simply continues the problem.

Moreover, Jesus becomes symbolic of the anguish of the human soul
weighed down as it is by matter.[37] In fact, there is a big difference between
Jesus and the Christ. Jesus, who came in the flesh and beguiled Adam, was
not good. Christ, on the other hand, was purely spiritual and was very good.
Faustus, a leader of the Manichees, describes their beliefs this way:

> We worship one and the same God under the three-fold designation
> of our Father, who is God Almighty, and Christ, his Son, and the
> Holy Spirit. But we believe the Father himself dwells in the highest or
> principal light which Paul in another place calls 'unapproachable' (1
> Tim 6.16). The Son, however, stands fast in this second or 'visible'
> light. Since, according to Paul, the Son himself is twofold, he speaks
> of Christ as 'the power and wisdom of God' (1 Cor 1.24). Thus we
> believe that his power dwells in the sun and his wisdom in the moon.
> We also believe that the Holy Spirit, who is the third sovereignty, makes
> his seat and his lodging throughout the entire extent of the atmosphere.
> Through his influence and spiritual profusion, the earth conceives
> and gives birth to the suffering Jesus, suspended from every tree, who
> is the life and salvation of mankind (20.2).

Thus the Manichees claim to be Trinitarian Christians. Yet even a cur-
sory reading of their writings would uncover that they were very far away
from Christian orthodoxy.

In fact, the above passage explains why Augustine says in the *Confessions*
that "a fig weeps when it is picked" (3.10.18). This is so because, to the
Manichees, Jesus is hanging from every tree in the form of fruit. This is also
why the Manichean leadership ("the elect") ate only vegetables. In so doing,
they believed they were releasing the light trapped therein.

Eschatology

The Manichean story does not end on a downbeat tone. The kingdom of light, battered, bruised and trapped in matter, will eventually win out at the last judgment. Light and Darkness will again be separated and all will be well in the world.

At the last judgment, the world will discover that it was the Manichean church that was right all along. The elect will live in the kingdom of light and be restored to a situation of peace and tranquility while the damned and the demons will be buried in a deep pit.[38] In other words, the Manichees win and everyone else loses. Thus you should want to be a Manichee.

Augustine's Place with the Manichees

It is perfectly justified to wonder what could possibly attract the bright, young Augustine to such a group. Their story seems far-fetched and like something out of a science-fiction novel. Augustine was likely drawn to the excitement and adventure the group provided.[39] Indeed, they were probably fun to be around, especially with their extravagant claims of ecstatic experiences and prophetic utterances. It is also true that by refraining from sex, eating vegetables, fasting regularly and not killing animals, they appeared to live morally upright lives.

The key to Augustine's attraction to the Manichees was that they purported to arrive at their beliefs through reason.[40] Making use of what Augustine thought was the best science of the day, they could show that their beliefs matched up to current understandings surrounding the Zodiac, the moon, the sun and the stars. They were merely taking what was in front of them, combining it with the best of secular learning and presenting it as a fully-integrated system. They did not need faith or the authority of a superstitious Church; they had reason on their side. Augustine describes the appeal of the Manichees in his book *On the Usefulness of Belief*:

> *Now, you know, Honoratus, the cause of my falling in with such men was none other than they asserted they would separate from terrible authority and by their simple reason alone would introduce those who wanted to listen to them to God and would thus liberate them from all error. For what else restrained me for almost nine years from despising the religion which was implanted in me from my childhood by my parents and to follow those men and to listen carefully to them? Nothing*

restrained me, except being frightened by superstition and being compelled to believe contrary to reason…Now, I was a 'hearer,' meaning I did not have to resign the hopes and business of this world (1.2).

However, Augustine was never fully convinced.[41] In fact, in his book, *On the Happy Life*, Augustine admits that he had trouble buying Manichee beliefs, but just assumed they would eventually produce someone who would convince him (1.4). As the years went on, however, Augustine found increasingly greater problems with the system. As we will see in Chapter Five, Augustine rejects the Manichees primarily because their greatest leader, Faustus, was not aware that late fourth-century science poked significant holes in the whole story. In short, the Manichees had stopped thinking. They liked their story and were sticking to it no matter what the facts were.

Augustine was drawn to their ascetic lives, their reason and their wit. He was a junior member (a hearer) for almost ten years. Yet the Manichean system eventually fell apart under the weight of the very reason they purported to value. Augustine looked back in disgust at his naiveté at falling in with this group.

AUGUSTINE GRIEVES

Let's remember what Augustine is trying to do in the *Confessions*. He is searching for rest for his troubled soul. As he memorably puts it in the first paragraph of the *Confessions*, "Our heart is restless until it finds rest in you" (1.1.1). To Augustine, the only way to find true rest is to find it in God. Since Augustine has rejected an orthodox view of God for a fashionable, but heretical, sect like the Manichees, he has found no rest.

Far from resolving this tension, Chapter Four sees it grow worse. For the most part, we encounter Augustine back in his hometown of Thagaste. He is twenty years old, done with his schooling, and has turned his attention to teaching, possibly as a tutor for his friend Romanianus' children. Having made peace with his mother, he is likely living with her.

In the Chapter, we observe that Augustine is a good evangelist. As always, he has friends around him. Augustine has convinced each friend we meet to join the Manichees. Using his massive intellect and powerful rhetorical skills, he spreads Manichean beliefs and ascetical living standards to those around him. This will cause some real problems for Augustine in the Chapter.

We also find Augustine being open for the first time about his living with his girlfriend, who is also the mother of his child, Adeodatus (meaning given by God). If it is the case that Augustine moves back to Thagaste to teach and moves in with his mother, it is entirely possible that Monica and Augustine's girlfriend lived under the same roof during this period. However, this is speculative because Augustine does not tell us what the living arrangements were.

Chapter Four also continues the structural framework we have been employing throughout the *Confessions* with reference to the misplaced loves of 1 John 2.16. In Chapter Two, we observed how the "lust of the flesh" controlled the discussion; in Chapter Three, the "lust of the eyes" structured the argument. In Chapter Four, we observe that the "pride of life" controls the account, sometimes in surprising ways. Pride, in this sense, is giving the "impression of substance" but really only being "filled with air."[1] In this Chapter, Augustine attaches himself to things that simply will not last, and thus finds himself ever-further away from God. As we will see, his embrace of the pride of life also makes him miserable.

Overview

From a chronological and geographical standpoint, Chapter Four can be confusing. Augustine is not attempting to tell his story in a straight chronological fashion. Rather, he goes back and forth between Thagaste and memories that he had from Carthage. At one point, Augustine tells us that one of those Carthage memories occurs when he is twenty-six years old, or about six years after the events taking place in Thagaste. [2] He sees the nine years between finishing his schooling and his transition to Rome as one big block.

Chapter Four can also be a bit depressing. After all, Augustine is morose much of the time. He grieves the loss of a friend for much of the Chapter. He is trying to show us that the logical conclusion of the life he was leading apart from God is not joy, but misery. Some might take umbrage at this perspective. Do we not all know perfectly "happy" people who live apart from Christ? Yet Augustine cannot conceive of happiness apart from truth.[3] Truth, for Augustine, is not intellectual knowledge, but Wisdom. This Wisdom finds its source in Christ who is Wisdom personified. We should not forget that Augustine considers the grace of spiritually seeing Christ as the apex of the Spiritual life and the goal toward which he is heading. As Augustine looks back from his perspective as a Bishop, he was very far away from true happiness during this period of his life.

Chapter Overview

Augustine opens the Chapter by claiming that over a nine year period (between his nineteenth and his twenty-eighth year) he was "led astray (*seducebamur*) and led others astray (*seducebamus*)...in a diversity of desires."[4] What he means is he was seduced by the Manichees and, influenced by their unorthodox beliefs, he, in turn, led others astray, both his students and his friends. He admits the driving force for all this was popularity and ambition for success.

We also observe Augustine as faithful, both to the Manichean elite ("the elect") whom he cared for and fed, as well as to his girlfriend (4.2.2). Augustine's girlfriend is the subject of only five sentences in Chapter Four, but he makes it a point of telling us that "in those years I had one woman… and I remained faithful to her" (4.2.2). Augustine is hardly the roving philanderer of popular imagination. Yes, he fathered a child (Adeodatus) out of wedlock, and lived with a woman who was not his wife. But, by all accounts, he was faithful to her.

Occult Practices

Augustine also makes it a point to tell us that he rejected sorcery (4.2.3). This occurs when Augustine entered an important poetry contest in Carthage and a psychic reader offered to intervene with the "*daemons*" (divine spirits) by offering up animal sacrifices to them. Augustine stoutly rejects the sorcerer's offer, but for questionable reasons. Augustine cared little about offending God; he was simply following Manichean practice by rejecting sorcery.

In fact, Augustine was entirely inconsistent in his rejection of sorcery since he openly embraced astrology (which, by contrast, was an acceptable Manichean practice). He embraced astrology against the counsel of Vindicianus (*"Vin-dic-ee-ahn-us"*), one of the leading medical doctors in the Roman Empire and someone who would play an important role in Augustine's later advancement. All Augustine could surmise was that the astrologers had a track record of correctly predicting the future. Vindicianus, who crowned Augustine as the winner of the aforementioned poetry contest, reasoned that this track record came from luck, not skill. Augustine remained unconvinced and continued to consult the astrologers, a decision he will re-think later in the book.

Chapter Four also introduces one of Augustine's best friends, Nebridius (*"Neb-rid-ee-us"*), a man who would join his philosophical community later in the story. He is also the person who would do much to question the intellectual claims of the Manichees. Like Vindicianus, Nebridius was dead-set against astrology, "ridiculing every kind of divination" (4.3.6). However, even after hearing Nebridius' arguments, Augustine was still not convinced.

Yet we start to see the seeds of doubt in Manichean belief being sown. These seeds would bear fruit in the future.

Grieving Loss

Augustine next engages in an extended discussion about the loss of an unnamed friend. From this discussion, it is clear that Augustine and his friend had been very close from childhood. Augustine and he "had grown up" together, "were in school together and played together" while growing up in Thagaste (4.4.7).

Looking back, Augustine notes that they didn't have a true friendship since they did not share the love which is found only in God. I'll have more to say about this later, since we'll have to unpack just what it is that Augustine means. The reality is that Augustine did not think that true friendship could happen apart from God.

Augustine had convinced his friend to join with the Manichees and thus had "diverted him from the true faith." This fact clearly embarrasses Augustine since his friend was not one naturally given to such "superstitious and destructive fables."

Augustine's friend came down with a fever which rendered him unconscious. Fearing for his life (and soul), his family had the friend baptized while he was unconscious. Unexpectedly, the friend regained consciousness and the fever broke. Augustine, who had not left his friend's side, joked with him about the ridiculousness of his baptism once he awoke. After all, the Manichees did not at all believe in the practice of water baptism and found such "fables" to be repugnant and "absent from mind and understanding" (4.4.8).[5] Augustine must have thought his friend would feel the same.

The friend, in very strong language, rebuked Augustine for his mockery of the Christian sacrament, saying if Augustine "wanted to be his friend, he had to abandon such talk" (4.4.8). Augustine was shocked, but kept his feelings to himself.

Given that his friend was a Manichee, we should note that Augustine is showing us that something really tangible happened to the friend after he was baptized. No longer was his friend's view that baptism was just a bunch of hocus-pocus. Rather, Augustine is showing us that his friend had been enlightened by the Spirit and was no longer swayed by Augustine's intellectual skepticism towards Christian rites. Shortly after this exchange, the friend fell back into his fever and died while Augustine was absent.

This plunges Augustine into a terrible state of grief. He describes his home town as bringing "suffering" and that he "hated every place" because it "did not contain him" (4.4.9). Further, Augustine says, "I became a great enigma to myself and I examined my soul, demanding to know why it was so sad and why it was disquieted within me." This is a subtle allusion to the story of Cain and Abel in Genesis Four, which we will unpack further in the Focus Text Section. Augustine, by identifying himself with Cain, is demonstrating how to put ourselves in the Biblical story with a bit more sophistication.

After the friend's death, he could do little except to "grieve and cry" (4.5.10). Thus Augustine found himself in a state of misery. Given that Augustine's raw descriptions of his grief go on for some time, he is obviously trying to tell us that the friend's death affected him deeply. But, why so much focus on this? After all, the death of Augustine's father received barely a sentence.

Augustine writes that he is telling us about these matters in order to describe how his attachment to "mortal things" caused his grief (4.6.11). In mourning, Augustine had become more attached to his "misery" (*miseriam*) than he had ever been to his friend. There was pleasure in all the emotional pain he was feeling. In other words, the idea that "it hurts so good," is not a modern concept, but one well-depicted by Augustine.

Augustine's grief ceased to be about the friend and came to be about Augustine's "dread of dying." Augustine comes face to face with death and has no intellectual or emotional categories to answer the threat of "non-being." He knows how to be a friend to the living, but he cannot handle the death of someone, especially someone close. The pride of life is all he knows since he cannot answer the question of what happens after death.

To be fair, the Manichees also had no good answer for what happens after death, which meant that Augustine had no way to process his friend's passing. How does one come to grips with death?[6] Finding no rest, Augustine picked up, fled Thagaste, and returned to Carthage (4.7.12).

Mortal Friendship
Augustine moves past the telling of the story of his friend's death to discussing friendship in abstract terms. Once again, we observe the idea of the pride of life at work. Augustine notes that his grief was raw because he had split open his soul "by loving a person who would die as if he would never die" (4.8.13). Augustine realizes he is in love with external, temporal things

which disappoint him. It is the love of God (*agape*) which lasts, not mortal bodies.

To Augustine, it is impossible to love a friend well apart from the love of God. As Augustine looks back on it, he realizes that it is only with God where we experience no loss since God is eternal. The only way to experience loss with God is to abandon him. Since this is precisely what Augustine had done, the predictable result is misery. In Augustine's abandonment of God, he has found neither rest nor a safe harbor for his soul (4.9.14).

Moreover, since "everything grows old and everything perishes," all things "hasten out of existence" (4.10.15). Hence misery is the natural result of focusing solely on perishing things. Since Augustine defines "evil" as the absence of being, he is trying to tell us that not only is a focus on material things distressing, but it is evil because it excludes God from the picture. Once again, Augustine simply has no categories to deal with this, as there can be no rest or repose among changeable things. Augustine has met the logical conclusion of his worldview – misery.

Christ

Looking back on this, Augustine analyzes the reasons for his misery. As Augustine puts it, the Word himself (Christ) "is the place of undisturbed quiet (*quietis*) where love is not forsaken if it does not give up" (4.11.16). This statement is important because the idea of quietness will play an important role at the end of the *Confessions*.

The only real answer for Augustine's grief is Christ. But, when he was twenty-years old, struck down by the loss of a friend, Augustine was a long way from seeing this. With the benefit of hindsight, Augustine now knows that he needed to turn from "following the flesh" (4.11.17) since only God, who made all things, "does not pass away." The soul acquires stability only in God as it rests in that which does not change (4.12.18). Augustine was seeking "the happy life in the land of death." Yet, it was evidently not there.

Augustine then engages in one of the most explicitly Christological discussions of the *Confessions*. In our bid to find happiness, Jesus "thunders" that we should "return to him" (4.12.19). In being born of a virgin, Jesus truly became a man in the Incarnation. In so doing, Jesus experienced what it was like to be human. As Augustine puts it, "he did not tarry, but ran, shouting by his words, deeds, death, life, descent and ascent – shouting out to return to him." To Augustine, to escape the misery of life where death is inevitable, we must descend in confession so that we can turn inward, ascend and capture a vision of Christ. This is the goal of the Christian life it-self. At the time, Augustine admits, he "was not cognizant (*noveram*) of this" (4.13.20). He had descended into misery, but had not yet discovered the joy of ascending to Christ.

Beauty

Next, Augustine discusses the first book he wrote called *On the Beautiful and the Proper* (*De Pulchro et Apto*). Augustine admits that he wrote this work in order to get noticed. He was an up-and-comer in the world of professional rhetoricians, a highly prized position. But, living in North Africa, he was away from the center of the action which happened in Rome and Milan. He needed to do something to get the leading lights of his field to notice him.

Augustine dedicated his book to a man named Hierius, who was a famous orator in Rome at the time (4.14.21). Augustine had never met Hierius, but was impressed with him nevertheless, both by his reputation and his speech-es. Although he was Syrian, Hierius had such command of both Greek and Latin that he could dazzle his students or his listeners in either language. This impressed Augustine enough to dedicate the work to him.

The praise he was heaping on Hierius was something Augustine really wanted to receive himself. Augustine wanted to be just like him (4.14.23). He wanted the admiration and professional approbation of a clever peer. However, this was not to be. Augustine's book was soon lost and it received no attention.

In the book itself, which was written six years later, when he was twenty-six, Augustine takes up three key questions (4.13.20):

- "Do we love anything but the beautiful"?
- "What is the beautiful"?
- "What is beauty"?

In the book, Augustine presents beauty as a philosophical concept.[7] He distinguished between beauty as an end in itself contrasted with beauty as serving something else, a means to an end. (4.13.20). In other words, either beauty is intrinsic or it is peripheral.

What is Augustine really talking about? He is using the book to discuss the beauty of friendship. He admits that "he loved people based on human opinion (*iudicio*)," (4.14.22) suggesting that God's judgment was wholly for-eign to him. The key question that Augustine asks is how are such "diverse loves distributed in a single soul with varying weights?" Augustine is saying there are different kinds of love. For example, we might willingly die for our children, but might hesitate to do so for a stranger. Augustine's love was not the self-giving love which comes from God (*agape*); it was simply love that he hoped to have returned through career success (*eros*, 4.14.23). He was passionate, but was also giving to get something in return.

To Augustine, one cannot understand beauty apart from God's act of creation (4.15.24). Thus Augustine's understanding of beauty necessitated a distinction between that which was intrinsic versus that which becomes apt when applied to something else. This was all Augustine could conceive at the time since he was thinking about beauty in light of "corporeal things." Lacking any substantial notion of the love of God and thinking about things only in material terms, Augustine looks back and admits, "I had no idea what I was talking about" (*loquerer*).

Illumination

In criticizing his own youthful thinking, Augustine then suggests that one of the main things he missed was that his "soul needed to be illuminated by another light" in order to discern whether something was true (4.15.25). The need for illumination is one of Augustine's most innovative ideas and would be essential to the way western Christians conceived of reality throughout the Middle Ages. We'll explore this in detail below.

God was not yet ready to illumine Augustine's mind (4.15.26) because, as he notes, "God resists the proud" (1 Pet 5.5). At the time, Augustine was mixing his conception of God with his understanding of the human soul, leading him to believe that God could change.[8] Augustine was still weighed down by his Manichean worldview which had taken him far from the truth of Christ. In a preview of some twentieth-century theologians, Augustine even thought that God was "compelled toward error" (*coactam errare*). Augustine erred since he did not know the true God. This caused him to "sink into the deepest pit" (4.15.27).

Aristotle

Augustine ends the Chapter by picking up the theme of the "pride of life" again, recounting how he was able to read any work and understand it without the help of commentaries or teachers (4.16.28). Yes, Augustine was just that smart. The example he gives for this is his reading of Aristotle's *Categories*.

Augustine mentions his reading of Aristotle because the book is a discussion of "substances," a technical term which describes true reality. Man, for example, as a human being, is a substance. However, details about a particular man, such as his height, weight, color or even actions a man takes like being active or passive, sitting or standing, walking or running, are different. These are called "accidents" because they are not essential to his being, but characteristic of a particular being (4.16.28).

Aristotle was able to place the interrelation of these substances and accidents into ten categories which, when taken together, describe all being. In this way, Aristotle created a highly influential framework within which mutually-exclusive things could interrelate.[9]

When it comes to the unchangeable, eternal, omnipotent God, Aristotle's categories were useless. This is so because God's being is so unlike that of a created being (4.16.29). In a sense, because God does not change, God is pure being. God's essence and his existence are the same thing. Thus what seemed like the pinnacle of learning with Aristotle turned out to be yet another obstacle for Augustine. The categories simply did not hold true for God. This blew Augustine's mind since he could not yet conceive of God in incorporeal terms (4.16.31).

In the end, Augustine returns to the idea of illumination and realizes he had none. He not only was in error in his thinking; but, as a teacher, he was imparting error to his students (4.16.30). Once again, Augustine conceives of himself as the Prodigal Son, having travelled to "a far country" only to realize the things which had looked so pleasurable from afar, were bringing him no rest. The brightest man of his age was ignorant while living apart from God.

Focus Texts

Throughout Chapter Four, we have observed Augustine in grief. Much of the Chapter takes place with the underlying assumption that true friendship, knowledge and even happiness is impossible apart from God. We will take special care to unpack these themes in the Focus Texts below. Augustine's use of the story of Cain to describe his disordered soul also needs to be unpacked since it is not obvious what he is trying to accomplish. Finally, Augustine's theory of divine illumination has proved very influential through the centuries. This also deserves some attention in this Chapter, given its influence on western society in the middle ages.

Augustine and Friendship

As we have already seen through the first four Chapters of the *Confessions*, Augustine has a deep-seated need and desire for friendship. He is rarely alone, but is almost always in the company of friends, some of whom are positive influences and some of whom are not. Generally, in Chapter Four, with references to Nebridius, Vindicianus, and Romanianus as well as to his unnamed friend who passes away, these are all positive influences. Yet Augustine still struggles to figure out how to carry on a true friendship when he knows little about self-giving (*agape*) love. Consider the following text which describes Augustine's unnamed friend who dies:

Focus Text 4A

> During this time, I had begun to teach in the city of my birth. I connected with a very dear friend, of a similar age, who shared my zeal for certain things. He was flourishing in the flower of his youth. He had grown up with me and we were in school together and had played together. But he was not yet a true friend, nor even later would he be, since it is not a true friendship unless both bind together, cleaving to [God] 'by the love which is poured out in our hearts by the Holy Spirit which was given to us' (Rom 5.5)…you took this fellow out of this life, after only a year of friendship. He was sweeter to me than all the sweetness of my life (4.4.7).

This text is important because it describes Augustine's mature view of friendship. Augustine was the first Christian author to tackle the subject of friendship in a systematic way.[10] At first glance, Augustine's view of friendship might seem a bit strange. After all, is it not a bit odd that Augustine claims that this boyhood friend was "not a true friend, nor even later would he be"? This seems to suggest that, to Augustine, true friendship is impossible between believers and unbelievers. For those (like me) who have non-Christian friends, this might be disconcerting.

The first thing we should realize is that friendship was one of the favorite subjects for ancient writers. For example, very early philosophers saw friendship as the cosmic principle of attraction which held the world together.[11] In Plato's dialogue *Lysis*, for example, Socrates is unable to come up with an adequate definition for friendship, but thinks it is probably based on his concept of "the good."[12] To Plato, "the good" was the key to harmony in the world.[13]

Drawing on this idea, Aristotle argues in his *Nicomachean Ethics* that friendship is really brotherly love (*philia*) based on another's character. For Aristotle, friendship can be found in "the good, the useful or the pleasant," but only friendships based on "the good" are true.[14] If you find someone who is upright and moral, you can forge a friendship.

Cicero also wrote at length about friendship, believing that friendship could be defined as "agreement on human and divine matters combined with charity and good will."[15] Cicero's view of friendship, based as it is on shared values and views, influences Augustine's early understanding of it.

In a letter to Maurianus, a "true friend," Augustine starts to modify his earlier views by introducing the role of grace in friendship. Augustine writes the following in the letter (I am quoting the Roland Teske's translation):

> *Thus it turns out that between friends who do not agree on things divine there cannot be a full and true agreement on things human either. For one who holds things divine in contempt necessarily evaluates things human otherwise than he should, nor can anyone correctly love a human being who does not love the maker of that human being. Hence, I do not say that you who had been partly my friend are not more fully my friend. Rather, as reason shows, you were not even partly my friend, since even with respect to things human you did not possess a true friendship with me. You were certainly not a companion of mine in things divine, by which things humans are correctly weighed...But when the goodness and grace of our savior shed its light upon me, not in accord with my merits, but in accord with his mercy, how could you be my friend when you had no part in this...thanks be to God, then, that he has finally been so gracious as to make you my friend (258.2-3).[16]*

Augustine's views are clear. One cannot be true friends with someone who does not know the grace of God since grace is an integral component of friendship.

While there are obvious similarities between the letter quoted above and Focus Text 4A, one difference stands out. Whereas Augustine retains the idea of agreement in friendship in the letter to Maurianus quoted above, the Focus Text's emphasis is that the grace of God is in the very bond of friendship. Because friendship is based on the grace poured out by the Holy Spirit, to Augustine, there is no true friendship apart from it.

To Augustine, true friendship comes about because of the grace of God. In asserting this, Augustine transforms classical notions of friendship beyond Cicero's agreement "on all things human and divine" into the idea that true friendship can only take place 6with God's grace.

What does Augustine really mean by grace? In our day, many understand grace to be the "unmerited favor of God." This is true, but I think Augustine had a more robust view of grace than this. Grace is not passive to Augustine. Rather, grace is a power of God whereby "men and angels are moved to know and love God."[17] Said more simply, grace really does something.

In viewing grace as a power, we must be careful to avoid thinking of it as something merely external. God is intimately involved in his creation and thus his grace is at work in everything he made. Said differently, we must not separate the natural and the supernatural, as they exist and co-inhere with together.[18] The supernatural enables the participation of the natural in a reality beyond itself. If we reduce grace to a power which merely works on the natural extrinsically, we potentially miss the utter gratuitousness of the gifts of God.[19] This reduction has, in part, led to the desacralized world in which we live.

How does this impact friendship? Friendship is about love for another. To Augustine, without the love of God, we simply cannot fulfill the commandment which Jesus gave to love both God and neighbor. Grace, working within our natures, transforms our very being, enabling us to participate in something greater.

Thus we find ourselves back in familiar territory. The apex of the Christian life is turning inward, ascending and capturing a vision of Christ with the eyes of the mind. It's about participation in a greater reality, a mystical experience of "pure love." Whereas Cicero and Aristotle had set forth a detached view of friendship wherein one sought friendships based on "likeness in virtue," Augustine is after something fundamentally more robust.[20] To Augustine, and the Christian tradition which follows him, true love is self-giving, not self-loving. However, the ability to give oneself fully is a gift given by God through his grace shed abroad in our hearts (Rom 5.5).

Friendship, then, is not ultimately about agreement or moral improvement in this life, as good as this is, but about union with the divine nature in the next. True friendship becomes a model for how we are supposed to love God, something which can only occur in cooperation with God's grace.

Questions for Reflection

1. What is your reaction to Augustine's mature view of friendship? Helpful? Ridiculous?
2. Describe the friendships in your life. How have they changed?
3. What constitutes a "true" friend to you? What do you expect from friendship? Loyalty? Shared Values?
4. Do you agree that friendships are difficult for those of differing belief systems? What are the downsides of this view?
5. If God's grace penetrates his whole creation, what does this mean for the prospect of friendships with unbelievers?

Augustine, Cain and Grief

We turn next to a Biblical allusion which Augustine makes in Chapter Four. Augustine again places himself within the Biblical narrative in order to tell his own story. This time, he does it through the story of Cain and Abel. Once we unpack this allusion, it might shed some light on Augustine's tortured grief. The text from the *Confessions* is as follows:

Focus Text 4B

> Grief cast a dark shadow over my heart and everything I beheld was death. The town of my birth brought suffering and my father's house entailed extraordinary misery. Everything I had shared with [my friend] was now without him, and became a distracting torture. My eyes sought him everywhere, but such was not granted. I hated every place since it did not contain him, nor could they now tell me, "look, here he comes," as happened when he was alive and when he was away from me. I became a great enigma to myself and I examined my soul, demanding to know why it was so cast down and why it was so disquieted within me (Ps 42.5), but it never responded to me. And if I said, 'hope in God,' it justly did not comply. For that beloved man I lost was a better and truer man that that phantasm which I embraced as my hope. Only tears were sweet to me, as they followed my friend as the ornament of my soul (4.4.9).

Augustine is in the midst of mourning the loss of his boyhood friend and finds unhappiness wherever he turns. Every place he goes in Thagaste becomes an opportunity for another memory to well up within him of his dear friend. But, how does this text have anything to do with the story of Cain and Abel?

Frankly, Augustine is asking a lot of us here in Focus Text 4B. This is the case because he is asking us to notice that an allusion to Psalm 42 is itself making a reference to the story of Cain and Abel. One of the most remarkable things about Augustine (and most of the Church Fathers) is that they are so thoroughly conversant with the Scriptures that they could make such textual associations. Augustine can do this because he has much of the Bible memorized.

The problem is that, even today, the story of Cain and Abel can be difficult to interpret. The underlying text is not all that clear which makes the overall meaning of the narrative ambiguous. This was equally true in Augustine's day. In reading the story of Cain through Augustine, we will hopefully gain some clarity on the point he is trying to get across to us.

The Story of Cain and Abel

The story of Cain and Abel goes like this: Cain and Abel were the first sons of Adam and Eve. Cain was a farmer, while Abel was a shepherd. Both brought out sacrifices to God. Abel brought out the firstborn of his sheep, while Cain brought an offering "from the fruits of the ground." Yet the Lord did not regard Cain's offering (for some unstated reason). This causes Cain to become sad and for his countenance to fall.

Next, the Lord comes to Cain and asks what the problem is. Enigmatically, God continues (I'm translating here from the Greek text of the Septuagint in this verse which is likely closer to what Augustine was reading), "If you brought it out rightly then you have not sinned, have you? Be at rest. Its submission will be towards you and you will rule over it." Now, let me admit, most would translate the text this way: "*His* submission will be towards you and you will rule over *him*." Either translation is possible. Yet it's really hard to explain what God does next if he was telling Cain that eventually he would rule over his brother. We'll come back to this text in a minute. But, first, let's finish the story.

What does Cain do in response? He goes and murders his brother, the first murder recorded in human history. When the Lord comes and asks where his brother is, Cain famously responds, "Am I my brother's keeper?"

This causes God to curse the ground under Cain's feet, meaning that from then on, the ground "would not give its strength" to Cain.

Eventually, Cain would go on to found a city, which he named after his son Enoch (Gen 4.17). Cain's city plays a significant role in Augustine's great work the *City of God*, because Augustine writes that there are two cities in conflict with each other. There's the "earthly city" (founded by Cain) which sets itself against God and which stands in opposition to the so-called City of God. Both cities are mixed together in this life, but eventually, they will be separated at the judgment of the righteous and the unrighteous.

The Allusion to Cain and Abel

I have to admit that I missed the point of all this for a long time. It was Garry Wills, a Pulitzer-prize winning author, and translator of the *Confessions* for Penguin who has written about it most recently.[21] What Wills noticed was that in the Old Latin Text, the language of Ps 42.5 and Gen 4.6 were very similar. Notice what happens when we put the text of the two verses close to each other: (I'm quoting from Wills' translation): [22]

> Ps 42.5: "*Why are you sad and why are you very distressed?*"[23]
> Gen 4.6: *Why [have you] become sad and why is your face struck down?*

This is all to say that Augustine expects the more advanced reader to catch the allusion to Cain as he grieves. Just as Cain's face "was struck down" Augustine was also "very distressed."

Augustine's Interpretation

But, what does Augustine mean by all this? In the *City of God*, Augustine engages in a lengthy discussion about the above text. We should keep in mind that the parts of the *City of God* where Augustine gives this interpretation were probably written over twenty years after he wrote the *Confessions* (AD 418).[24] Yet Augustine seems to have something similar in mind here.

Augustine first tries to answer the problem of why it was that Cain's gift wasn't accepted by God. Augustine notices that there is a New Testament text (1 John 3.12) which explains it:

> *And do not be like Cain who was of the evil one and murdered his brother. And why did he murder him? Because his own deeds were evil and his brother's righteous.*

This leads Augustine to note that Cain's offering was not accepted by God because "it was wrongly divided." Augustine continues,

> *He gave to God something belonging to him, but gave himself to himself. This is what is done by all those who follow their own will and not the will of God; that is, those who live with a perverted instead of an upright heart, and yet offer a gift to God.*

Said differently, Cain's heart wasn't right. He was focused on himself at the expense of his brother. God knew it and thus did not "regard" his offering.

So far so good. But what caused Cain's countenance to fall? Augustine thinks it was because Cain envied his brother.[25] Let me again quote the Greek text of Gen 4.6 which we discussed above since it is likely the basis of Augustine's interpretation:

> *If you brought it out rightly then you have not sinned, have you? Be at rest. Its submission will be towards you and you will rule over it.*

I noted above that this text should be translated with the pronoun "it" instead of the pronoun "he." Augustine believes that the text should be translated "it" because God is telling Cain to get mastery over his own sin, not his brother. Further, the Greek word (*esuxadzo*) which I have translated "be at rest," carries the idea of "refraining from something" or "remaining undisturbed."[26] When Cain gives into his sin and kills his brother, he has done the opposite of what God instructed him. Cain certainly should have known that "his sin ought to be attributed to himself, not another" (15.7).

Implications for the Story

It shouldn't surprise us that in the *Confessions* Augustine is pointing the finger at himself. He also has sinned. Yet isn't Augustine's grief a normal reaction to a friend's death? The problem here is not grief, which is very much a normal human emotion. To Augustine, what was horrifying was his utter disregard for his friend's spiritual well-being. This is the big point. When Augustine mocks his baptism and makes light of his mortality, he imperiled his friend's soul. Augustine could not have been less of a friend.

Had his friend listened to Augustine and repudiated his baptism as some silly superstition, Augustine fears (looking back on it) that his friend's eternal destiny might have been imperiled. Augustine realizes that, even though he stood by his friend's bedside during his illness, he was not a true friend at all.

Even worse, Augustine's grief was really about his own guilt rather than the loss of his friend. Given Augustine's Manichean beliefs, he had nothing to offer his friend in the throes of death. Bereft of any substance, Augustine realizes that in the midst of it all, he loved himself immeasurably more than he loved his friend. God commanded Cain to "be at rest," but Augustine was as far from rest as he could imagine.

In losing his friend, Augustine is playing the role of Cain. Spiritually, he attempted to kill his brother by tempting him to deny his baptism. Only by the grace of God did things turn out differently. His friend found faith while Augustine held onto a worldview that was incoherent. In the midst of his turmoil, Augustine's only recourse was to run – run as fast as he could back to Carthage (the earthly city) to teach half-truths to his eager students. The logical implication of Augustine's worldview was deep-seated grief.

Questions for Reflection

1. Has anyone died recently with whom you were close? How are you processing your grief?
2. Does baptism do anything objectively real? Why do we make such a big deal about it?
3. Do you identify more with Cain or Abel? How is it just that a murderer lived?
4. Have you ever acted selfishly toward someone close to you? What happened?

Illumination

Throughout the *Confessions*, Augustine is on a journey to find God. In Chapter Four, we find that Augustine has managed to walk farther and farther away from God in his search. As we saw in the previous Focus Text, Augustine is starting to get indications that his association with the Manichees is not leading him towards the truth. They may talk about Christ a lot, but their understanding perverts the Biblical teaching.

Towards the end of Chapter Four, Augustine makes some comments that are very interesting in light of the theory of knowledge which he develops during his lifetime known as "divine illumination." In short, Augustine believes that humans can know very little with certainty apart from God. It is God's grace which enables the intellect to understand the sensory data which it receives. To stand apart from God, as Augustine is doing during Chapter Four, is to commit intellectual suicide.

We must not see illumination as something merely extrinsic to our natures. It would be easy to conceive of God's work of illumination as something which merely comes in from the outside. This is partly, but not wholly, true. What divine illumination does is enable us to participate in a greater reality, one that we cannot perceive on our own.

Augustine's theory of divine illumination would essentially influence how Christians during the Middle Ages understand the acquisition of knowledge, a division of philosophy called epistemology. Despite modern advances, we are still encountering this problem. Modern thinkers, together with medical science, usually reject Augustine's ideas as un-scientific. As a consequence, they continue to stand in the midst of the same dilemma since they have difficulty explaining consciousness. The reality of modern thought is that having rejected God, or anything transcendent as an essential input to knowledge, there is relatively little that moderns can know with certainty. By contrast, the whole modern project has been forced to concede great skepticism about whether it can know anything at all. Postmodernity, despite its helpful correctives to modernity's overreach, has only made the firmness of knowledge worse.

I should admit that those who study Augustine's theory of divine illumination do not usually use this section of the *Confessions* as an important source. Although Augustine would touch on these ideas with more detail in Chapters Twelve and Thirteen of the *Confessions*, the so-called narrative sections are not usually central to this subject. Yet Augustine's take on how we know shines brightly in Chapter Four. If Augustine's goal is to know God, how we can know becomes central to his project. Consider what Augustine writes next:

Focus Text 4C

> For just as evil deeds are done if the stirred-up soul, impetuously act-
> ing, is full of vice, and is tossed about insolently and frantically, and just
> as disgraceful acts occur if the affective part of the soul is disorderly be-
> ing swallowed up by carnal pleasures, so errors and erroneous opinions
> defile a life if the rational part of the soul is itself corrupted. Such was
> the state of my soul then. I was unaware that my soul needed to be il-
> luminated by another light so that I might participate in truth since it is
> not itself the essence of truth. 'For you will light my lamp, my God, you
> will lighten my darkness' (Ps 18.28). And 'of your fullness we have all
> received' (John 1.16). 'You are the true light who illumines everyone
> coming into this world' (John 1.9), for 'in you there is no change nor
> shadow of turning' (James 1.17) (4.15.25).

What is Augustine trying to tell us here? He is saying that he could not
access the truth because he had not yet been enlightened by the light which
only comes from God. Augustine thought the Manichees had intellectual
rigor and sophistication. In grieving his friend's death, however, he starts to
realize that this might not be the case. Mind you, it's just a start. Even bigger
intellectual problems with the Manichean system will surface later.

Augustine's theory of illumination introduces us to the idea that truth is
inherently sacramental. What I mean by that is Christian truth "participates"
in a divine reality. This is how we can assert that Christian teachings are really true. It's not that human statements are infallible. The history of the
Church demonstrates this clearly. Yet when human ideas participate in the
divine (especially in association with the Scriptures), we are able to catch
glimpses of realities which are beyond our usual human abilities to understand. God may be incomprehensible and mysterious, but his truth is really
present.[27]

Augustine comes to the realization (of course, in hindsight) that he
was not in a position to discern what was true apart from God. He needed
light, which, following from the prologue of John's Gospel, is a reference to
Christ. The pride of life, which causes Augustine to focus solely on what is
right in front of him, leads him away from what is eternal, unchanging and
true. This is at least part of the reason why he grieves so deeply in Chapter
Four. In the face of death, he literally has nothing useful to say to his friend.

I have to admit I find parallels to our modern situation especially intriguing. The modern project is inherently one of reductionism.[28] We reduce things – whether ideas, categories or matter – to ever smaller pieces so we can manipulate and control them. Clearly, the modern project has been great for technology, medical advances and gadgets. But it's been a disaster for certainty.

Notice the Biblical texts that Augustine employs in Focus Text 4C. For example, he includes two texts from the prologue to John's Gospel where Christ is described as the light which brings light into the world by means of the Incarnation. Years later, when Augustine preaches on the text of John 1, he points out that light illumines things that are in the world. If anyone looks at the sun, the source of the light, she will find herself blinded by it. Without God's help, we cannot even catch a glimpse of God and we cannot observe things illumined in this world. If Adam had not sinned, this situation might be different. But, in our post-fall condition, we cannot know God without help. There is no genuine knowledge of God without grace. Consider what Augustine says in a sermon on John's Gospel:

> Therefore, that light is the light of all men. But maybe foolish hearts cannot yet join with that light, since they are so aggravated by their sins that they are not able to see it. Just because they cannot see it does not imply the absence of light. It is this way on account of the darkness of sins. 'And the light shines in the darkness and the darkness did not comprehend it' (John 1.5). Therefore, brothers, this is just like a blind man who is put in the path of the sun – the sun is present to him, but he is absent from it. Thus, every fool, as well as every unjust and impious man, is blind in heart. Wisdom is present, but even though present to the blind man, it is absent to his eyes – not since Wisdom is absent, but because it is absent from him (1.18-19).

We cannot see God without God's help. Augustine desperately wants to find God, wants to be present with God and wants to know God. But having rejected the God who exists in favor of the Manichees, Augustine's embrace of reason without faith has made him ignorant.

Augustine is not trying to convince us to abandon reason – far from it. His is not a call to stop doing science, to stop investigating our world or to just wait for God to illumine our intellects. Rather, Augustine is encouraging us to start with faith. To Augustine, true faith is reasonable faith. His great statement, "faith seeking understanding," would be the guiding principle for all his work and would set the agenda for Christian investigation for centuries.

His broader point is that true understanding cannot come apart from participation in the truth itself, which is Christ himself. He would want us to remember this the next time someone intimates that Christian beliefs are "naïve," "backwards," or "outmoded." It's actually the quite the opposite. The pursuit of reason is essential. Yet done apart from the light of God, the results can be disastrous. This is what Augustine has experienced in his own life and will continue to experience as long as he embraces "the pride of life."

Questions for Reflection

1. Throughout history, Christians have often found themselves outside the cultural consensus on important issues. Are there any current debates which are affecting you?

2. Most of us have some expertise in something (parenting, work, relationships). Can you think of any areas of your life where revelation has been integral to that expertise?

3. As a Christian in an increasingly intolerant society, how can you have civil conversations with those who think differently than you? Do you avoid such situations? Why?

4. Augustine seems to think that God's truth is unchanging. But, then, how do we account for changing societal standards (race relations, gender roles, usury, divorce, sexual norms)? How do we decide what shouldn't change and what must?

5. What does Augustine's statement that we should pursue "faith" by "seeking understanding" mean to you practically?

AUGUSTINE FLEES

Introduction

Chapter Five marks the half-way point in the narrative portion of the *Confessions*. There are several tangible indications that Augustine is well aware of this fact as he writes. As one of the finest rhetoricians of his day, it is simply inconceivable that the literary structure of the *Confessions* came together in a haphazard way. Thus Chapter Five marks an important transition not only in the structure of the book, but in the story as well. It's no accident that the first half, which has taken place in Africa, now transitions to the second half which takes place in Italy.[1]

I have entitled this Chapter "Augustine Flees" because that is what he is doing most of the time. Augustine flees from the Manichean leadership, from Carthage, from Rome, from his students, even from his mother. Of course, as the Prodigal Son, he has also been fleeing God throughout the whole of the first half of the book. We might say his flight culminates in Chapter Five, as Augustine hits an important speed bump when none of the things in his life seem to bring him any lasting satisfaction. We also observe a transition in geography from North Africa to Italy where we will be until the end of the book.

Misplaced Loves and the Structure of the Confessions

In the Introduction Section to this Guide, I noted that there is a Chiastic structure to the narrative portions of the *Confessions*. A Chiasm ("*key-asm*") is a fancy word for a very common literary strategy employed in the ancient world which introduces several themes, but then undoes them in reverse order from how they were presented. Chapter Five represents the center point of the narrative and thus the center part of the Chiasm. It is the place where the misplaced loves Augustine developed in the early Chapters of the book start to become unwound.

We have been using the misplaced loves of 1 John 2.16 – the lust of the flesh, the lust of the eyes and the pride of life – to guide our reading thus far. Augustine, who is now twenty-nine years old, starts to become disillusioned with all of these misplaced loves. In fact, all three of them make appearances in the Chapter. In the face of his disappointment, Augustine's only recourse is to flee – first to Rome and then to Milan.

We should note that this is exactly how Augustine reacted in the previous Chapter when he came face to face with his unnamed friend's death. When Augustine realized that he had nothing useful to say in the face of death and could not process the idea of "non-being," he ran away to Carthage. This idea of "running away" has been a significant theme throughout the first half of the book. Augustine runs away from God to find answers to his difficulties, but finds no answers on his own. This, of course, is also what the Prodigal Son did, a theme Augustine is still tracking. We observe here that his running away causes significant grief, especially for his mother.

Names as Structural Markers

We should observe another transition which occurs in Chapter Five – Augustine begins to name people. Up to this point, the only close friend that Augustine has outright named is Nebridius. All of a sudden, in Chapter Five we start encountering people like Faustus, Elpidius, Ambrose and Symmachus. For some reason, the restraint comes off. As Fredrick Crosson has noticed, everyone who is named becomes instrumental (either positively or negatively) in his eventual embrace of Christianity.[2] This is also likely not a coincidence.

Philosophies as Structural Markers

Finally, Chapter Five is interesting because it stands in the middle of another structural subtlety.[3] Have you noticed that starting with Chapter Three, every Chapter has ended with Augustine's embracing some sort of thought system? For example, Augustine embraced Cicero in Chapter Three; he read Aristotle's *Categories* at the end of Chapter Four. Augustine will embrace Academic Skepticism at the end of this Chapter. This continues on in both Chapters Six and Seven when he embraces Epicureanism and the "books of the Platonists." Only in Chapter Eight and the famous garden scene does Augustine embrace Paul and the Scriptures, finally breaking this pattern.[4]

Overview

Augustine begins Chapter Five by reminding us of the first paragraph of the *Confessions*. He reiterates that he is writing to make a confession to God. Yet unlike the confession of sin which we saw early on, here we are treated to a confession of praise. Augustine repeats the word "confession" (*confiteatur*) four times in either its verb or noun forms in the first paragraph. He marries this together with praise ("*laudo*") which he repeats three times in the text. In other words, Augustine is offering up a sacrifice of praise to start, his way of showing us how to begin our own prayers.

Of special note in the first paragraph is that Augustine reiterates the idea of "ascent" towards God. Augustine's idea of the apex of the spiritual life is an ascent to see Christ with the mind's eye. It's a participation in divine reality. At this point, he understands that participation in distinctly Platonic terms – namely, that the soul needs to rise up, leave the confines of the material world and join with that which is unchanging and divine. While Augustine will come to a richer understanding of ascent later in the story, he understands the highest spiritual good as contemplation, which enables him to participate in that which is eternal and spiritual.

Augustine continues his recapitulation of the beginning of the *Confessions* by returning to God's attributes. God is omnipresent and "no space encompasses him" (5.2.2). If God is everywhere, including in believers' hearts, then the logical thing to do is to turn inward to find him in contemplation, for it is God who will readily "wipe away [our] tears" (Isa 25.8; Rev 21.4). The problem is that, while God was near him, Augustine "had withdrawn" from himself. The things Augustine was chasing had taken him father away from God.

Disillusionment in Carthage

Augustine next recounts how he began to be disillusioned with the Manichees. It's important to keep in mind that Augustine makes a significant effort to describe how he understood the Manichaean thought system in Chapter Five and his objections to it. The most significant detail from this description is the Manichaean discomfort with physical matter, which leads to their rejection of the Incarnation. As we'll see in subsequent Chapters, the Incarnation becomes the central Christian doctrine which Augustine will come to embrace. Since I described Manichean beliefs in the Appendix to Chapter Three, I am deliberately not including a detailed summary of Augustine's descriptions here.

Rather, we should focus on knowing something about Faustus, the Manichaean Bishop who came to town in AD 383 when Augustine was twenty-nine. Faustus was the greatest Manichaean apologist and was a skilled public speaker, precisely the kind of person who should have been able to impress Augustine. Even though Augustine appreciated his understated teaching methods, he "discerned" that Faustus' teachings were not true (5.3.3). This was a very significant step towards his eventual rejection of the Manichaean religious system.

Faustus had a reputation for being learned. But he turned out to be a big disappointment to Augustine who "had read much in the philosophers" (5.3.3). Augustine is not against learning; he readily admits that non-Christians have "discovered many things, and "have predicted solar and lunar eclipses, forecasting the exact day, the exact hour and the extent to which it would be total or partial" (5.3.4).

The problem is that he finds the "haughtiness" (*exaltationes*) of the philosophers and their penchant for "curiosity" (*curiositates*) to be bothersome. Augustine was taken in by the "lust of the eyes," represented by the *curiositas* of his intellectual pursuits. He specifically mentions his "indulgent behavior" which he compares to the "beasts of the field," which is likely a reference to the sexuality of the "animal appetites" in Plato's writings. Referencing Romans One, Augustine becomes disillusioned by the philosophers' penchant for "assigning" to God qualities which are their own (5.3.5).[5] They have exchanged the creator for the creature (Rom 1.25).

This does not mean that the philosophers have not been good observers of the created order. They know much about "mathematical calculations," the "arrangement of seasons," and the "visible testimony of the constellations" (5.3.6). In fact, this is Augustine's central problem with the Manichees. Although they profess to be dedicated to the pursuit of truth through reason alone, the sayings of Mani did not match up well to the most up-to-date science of Augustine's day. Despite this, Augustine "was commanded to believe" what Mani taught. The problem was that Mani's teachings were divergent from Augustine's "calculations" and the "testimony of his own eyes." In short, the Manichees did not care very much about truth, and were protecting dogma that was verifiably wrong. To Augustine, people who think they know all sorts of mysteries, but miss the God who really exists, are bound to be unhappy (5.4.7).

For Augustine, scientific knowledge of the created order is inferior to revealed knowledge about the Creator. Mani was simply ignorant about the created order. Yet it was worse than that because Mani claimed to have the Holy Spirit "with full authority personally resident in himself" (5.5.8). Augustine exposes Mani as a fraud when he finds out that his sayings were not true. As Augustine puts it, "He was not only asserting things of which he was ignorant (*ignorata*), but also saying things which were false (*falsa*) with so insane prideful futility that he assigned them to himself as a divine person."

Looking back on it, Augustine claims that he has no need to correct error in everyone he encounters. If he finds an ignorant Christian who is in error, he holds his tongue unless he says something "unworthy" (*indigna*) of God (5.5.9). This all gets a bit complicated for Augustine when someone ignorant claims his beliefs to be "sound doctrine" (*doctrinae pietatis*). Mani was the personification of this problem. Augustine quickly ascertains that Mani's teaching would not hold up to critical scrutiny.

This was all terribly disappointing for Augustine since he had been looking forward to Faustus' visit. He had had concerns for a long time, but the Manichaean leadership told him to be patient and Faustus would answer all his objections. Augustine found Faustus to be "agreeable and well-spoken" (not an insignificant complement), but eloquence is not the same thing as truth (5.5.10), a subtle dig at Augustine's own profession of rhetoric. As it turns out, Faustus was not very well read and not very learned (5.6.11). He was hardly the man of massive erudition that his reputation claimed.

One interesting detail is that Augustine found Faustus was refreshingly humble, an ironic twist for a Chapter expressing disillusionment with the "pride of life." As Augustine puts it, "the self-control of the mind which acknowledges its limitations is more beautiful than the things I longed to know" (5.7.12).

The result was that the enthusiasm Augustine had for the Manichees declined (5.7.13). Augustine liked Faustus personally, but could not abide his false teaching. The Manichees had been the prime mover in Augustine's fall from truth – yet he finds himself disillusioned over his association with them.

Disillusionment in Rome

Having discussed Augustine's disillusionment in Carthage, we find the same as he moves to Rome. Augustine interprets this move as being driven by God's providence. Augustine claims his main motivation for going to Rome was to find better students, as he was fed up with the "disgusting and licentious" behavior of the students in Carthage (5.8.14). Augustine explicitly denies that money or fame were motivators in his move. But this is somewhat difficult to believe given how eager Augustine was for career advancement. Whatever the truth may be, money and fame may not be explicitly spiritual goals, but God used them to great spiritual effect.

Although Augustine claims he never stooped to the level of his students who engaged in vandalism and criminal activity, he seems to be overlooking his ties with the young ruffians with whom he stole the pears in Chapter Two, as well as his friends, the "wreckers" in Carthage whom he described in Chapter Three. Nevertheless, Augustine was sick of the poor behavior of his students and resolved to use his Manichean connections to secure a better position in Rome.

Monica was terribly upset about Augustine's decision to depart. She wanted to go with him. But Augustine had no interest in letting his mother hold him back. So he lied to her, saying that he had to go see a friend when in reality he got on a ship to Rome, leaving her behind. As Augustine puts it, "So I lied to my mother – and oh such a mother – and managed to escape from her" (5.8.15). I'll have more to say about this in the Focus Text Section below.

Once in Rome, Augustine immediately became physically ill and was "on the way to perdition" (*inferos*). He was "shouldering many serious sins he had incurred against God, against himself (5.9.16), and against others, over and above the fetter of original sin (*orginalis peccati*), whereby we all die in Adam" (1 Cor 15.22). This sentence is the first specific mention of original sin in the *Confessions*, even if the concept has been frequently discussed. Notice how different Augustine's reaction to his illness is here compared to his childhood when he requested baptism, but was denied it. He is so lost spiritually that he doesn't even consider requesting baptism (an action which would have been directly against Manichaean teaching). Augustine realizes that had he died he would have gone "into the fire and torments which my misdeeds deserved in the truth of your decree."

Augustine associates his not dying primarily with his mother's prayers. While Augustine sees his own actions in moving to Rome as prideful, he has nothing but praise for his mother, a change from just a few paragraphs prior. Monica had a "broken and humble heart," was "chaste and sober" and "never missed a day of offering oblations at the altar" (5.9.17). Augustine believes God heard Monica's prayers and was "following the predestined order" of his plan.

Augustine got better physically, but still was waiting on spiritual healing. As Augustine reflects on this, he realizes that he had no real concept of sin. Influenced by his Manichaean beliefs, he did not "judge himself a sinner" (*peccatorem*), but thought there was some foreign nature in him that caused him to sin (5.10.18). This, Augustine admits, stemmed from his inability to conceive of God in anything but corporeal terms, leading him to conceive of evil as a "substance" with an "ugly and shapeless mass" (5.10.20). One of Augustine's central problems with Christian teaching was Jesus' Incarnation since Augustine could not understand how this did not leave Jesus open to "be polluted by the flesh," an objection Augustine finds laughable in hindsight.

Augustine started meeting people that had answers to some of his Manichaean objections. For example, he remembers encountering Elpidius (*El-pid-ius*") in Carthage who actually had answers to his objections to the Old Testament (5.14.21). The Manichees had claimed that the Old Testament was corrupted, but Elpidius pointed out that they had never actually managed to produce an uncorrupted copy which would support their allegations.

Not only was Augustine starting to doubt whether the Manichees were right, he rapidly became disillusioned with his students in Rome (5.12.22). Augustine was incensed that his students had perfected the art of skipping out on their tuition by switching tutors right before the bill came due. Even in this period of his life, Augustine could not abide dishonesty. Augustine disliked these students since "they esteem a world passing into exile." Augustine was sick of his students' dishonesty and became unwilling to suffer their wicked habits (*malos*).

Signs of Hope in Milan

In what is becoming a well-worn pattern, Augustine then picked up, left and moved to Milan. He had only been in Rome for about a year.

However, given the state of his students, he found little satisfaction there. Outwardly, his move to Milan made sense because of the important job he procured. He had reached the pinnacle of his career since he had won the position of head Rhetorician at the royal court, a prestigious job in the Roman Empire. Augustine had impressed Symmachus, the head governmental official in Rome, who put Augustine up for the position (5.14.23).

When Augustine came to Milan, he met Ambrose, the Bishop of Milan who greeted Augustine warmly. We'll have more to say about Ambrose in the next Chapter. He will turn out to be extremely consequential in Augustine's life. It was Ambrose who gave Augustine an intellectually-defensible way of understanding the Old Testament. He was a terrific preacher, was better informed than Faustus and taught salvation "soundly" (5.13.23).

Augustine was drawn to the outward forms of Ambrose's style rather than his message. At first, Augustine did not "busy himself, trying to understand what Ambrose was saying" (5.14.24). He was merely drawn to Ambrose's eloquence as a speaker. Yet the more he listened, the more Augustine realized Christian beliefs were, in fact, defensible against objections. The key, for Augustine, was the spiritual interpretation of the Old Testament which Ambrose offered. Although Augustine still could not accept the Christian faith, his encounter with Ambrose made him "question his hopelessness, stemming from the belief that the law and the prophets could not be upheld against those who loathed and ridiculed them." Augustine, while not fully convinced, was on his way.

This led Augustine to investigate the Christian faith once again to see if the Manichees were wrong. Instead of accepting Christianity, he embraced the skepticism of the Academics, an important philosophical school. As a result, Augustine started "doubting everything" (5.14.25). At this point, Augustine also "decided to become a catechumen in the Catholic Church" (*catholica ecclesia*). It's just a small little detail, but Augustine's turn toward orthodox faith had begun.

Focus Texts

Chapter Five takes place in three different locations – Carthage, Rome and Milan. I have chosen texts from two of those locations – Carthage and

Rome. It might seem odd not to discuss Milan, but I want to wait until the next Chapter when Augustine fills out the picture of Bishop Ambrose. Ambrose is a pivotal figure for Augustine, but, as usual, it's a more complicated story than the surface level of the text in the *Confessions* reveals.

In Chapter Five, Augustine has become disillusioned with each of the misplaced loves that had been driving him in the first half of the book. As a result, we will be paying particular attention to his disillusionment in his career (the pride of life) and with the Manichees (lust of the eyes). We should not miss the irony that by ending up in Academic Skepticism, Augustine signifies that he is becoming disillusioned with his misplaced loves. The trajectory he is on will ultimately lead him to Christ and to the Church.

Augustine and Prayer

I have been claiming from the beginning of this Guide that Augustine writes the *Confessions* as a newly-minted Catholic Bishop, in part, to teach those under his care in Hippo to pray and to read the Scriptures. Thus far, we have frequently discussed Augustine's handling of the Bible. As we have seen, Augustine is consistently telling his story in light of the Biblical narrative, thus putting himself into the stories of Adam, Cain and the Prodigal Son, among others. The text of the *Confessions* is saturated with quotes or allusions to the Bible. We simply cannot get away from it.

Up to this point, however, we have not talked as much about Augustine's commitment to prayer. If the entire *Confessions* is one long prayer, then, in a sense, there is less to say. Augustine "prays without ceasing" in the *Confessions* (1 Thes 5.17) and uses this as a model of what he would like us to do. In a sense, having read the Bible, Augustine is emulating its authors, particularly in the Psalms, by discussing his life within the context of a prayer.

Although we discussed in the First Chapter why the omniscient God commands us to pray – because he has ordained that certain things will only come about if we pray – we have not talked very systematically about what prayer is for Augustine. The first paragraph of Chapter Five, which recapitulates the first paragraph of the *Confessions,* is a good place to begin.

Focus Text 5A

Receive the offering of my confessions (*confessionum*), offered by the 'power of my tongue' (Prov 18.21) which you have fashioned and stirred up in order to confess (*confiteatur*) your name. 'Heal all my bones' (Ps 6.2) and let them cry out, 'Lord, who is like you' (Ps 35.10)? The one confessing (*confitetur*) to you is not informing you what is happening within himself. The closed heart does not hinder your eye, nor is your hand repelled by human hardness, but you release it when you want, with either mercy or punishment, and nothing can hide itself 'from your heat' (Ps 19.6). But let my soul praise (*laudet*) you that it might love you, and make confession (*confiteatur*) to you and your tender mercies that it might praise (*laudet*) you. Your whole creation does not cease praising (*laudes*) you nor is it silent, neither is the spirit of anyone who converses with you, nor any corporeal being who contemplates you. The result is that our soul ascends to you away from its weariness, resting on that which you have made and then crossing over to yourself who marvelously made this. And here there is refreshment and true fortitude (5.1.1).

I pointed out in the Summary Section that the words "confession" and "praise" are repeated several times in the above paragraph. As we discussed early on in our study, praise is one of the senses of confession which is central to his writing. Just as he began the book with a confession of praise, he starts the middle part of our story in the same way. Augustine wants us to realize how far we've come. We've gone through about thirty years, three cities, many crises and much soul searching in the first five Chapters of the *Confessions*. Augustine has risen in his career to a place of prominence. Everything looks good on the outside, but, inwardly, Augustine is seriously ill because his embrace of paganism has taken him away from the truth.

The first thing we should notice in the text is just how often the Psalms are alluded to or quoted. By now, this shouldn't be a surprise. Augustine literally lives and breathes the Psalms as he writes. Since Augustine likely recited the Psalms at specific intervals throughout the day, he would probably have had the Psalter memorized. The Psalms are the language which guides his life. In fact, to Augustine, Christ is usually speaking in the Psalms. When Christians use the words of the Psalms, they are using Christ's own language. Commenting on Psalm 30, Augustine wrote the following:

> *So let us hear the voice of the Lord, who said on the cross, 'into your hands, I commend my spirit' (Ps 31.5, Luk 23.46). Certainly, we are aware that his words in the gospel come from this Psalm. We do not doubt that he himself was speaking in this place... not without reason, he wanted these words to be his. He admonishes you that he has spoken in this Psalm. Search for him there. Reflect on how in that Psalm he took it upon himself to be found... so that he might admonish you that his utterance was fulfilled in himself, he put in his own mouth the heading of that same Psalm, 'My God, My God, why have you forsaken me?' (Ps 22.1, Matt 15.34). However, it was the voice of his body which was transfigured in him, never did the Father forsake his only-begotten son (2nd discourse, 30.11).*

We should note that Augustine employs a different strategy in the Focus Text 5A than he did in the prologue to the *Confessions*. In the prologue, he quoted from Ps 48 to begin, but then was much more intent on employing New Testament texts. At the start to Chapter Five, Augustine is subtly signaling that he is coming around to the acceptance of the Old Testament as Christian Scripture as he exclusively employs Old Testament texts, mostly quoting from the Psalms. As he does this, the Psalms just roll off his tongue.

Further, the prayer which he offers is focused almost entirely on praise. To Augustine, "Praise is both the beginning and the end of prayer."[6] Prayer transforms the heart and converts it to praise.[7] In other words, done right, our prayers should result in praise to God since there is nothing about which God is unaware and nothing in existence which God did not create. This is why Augustine notes in Focus Text 5A that he is not setting out to instruct God. God already knows exactly what is happening to Augustine.

Augustine is not against offering up petitions for things we need, but he observes that in the end, we really aren't aware what our petitions should be as we pray (Rom 8.26). Augustine understands the troubles that exist in life "are generally useful either to heal the swelling of pride or to exercise patience for which a rich reward is secured." We often pray for the things we need in ignorance, not knowing what God is doing.

In fact, Augustine notes that words are often unnecessary as we pray. As Augustine puts it in a later letter written to the widow Proba on the subject of prayer:

> *Now, most times, this business is more about sighing than convers-*
> *ing, more about weeping* (fletu) *than uttering* (affatu). *However, he*
> *places our tears in his sight and our sighing is not hidden from him,*
> *who has created all things through his word and does not demand hu-*
> *man words (130.10.20).*

If our hearts are right, using our own words is almost unnecessary. To Augustine, it was far better to use the words of God found in Scripture for prayer, especially the words of the Lord's Prayer.

To Augustine, the point of prayer was a "happy life," which he under-stands as the fulfillment of the Great Commandment of love for God and neighbor. Prayer is working well when it is comes out of the overflow of our love. This is why praise is so natural when it comes to prayer. Prayer should increase our love for others and for God. As such, when we pray we are really praying for a happy life.

This is why Augustine concludes his prayer with language of "ascent." If Augustine's goal is to experience Christ, the way this is accomplished is through the ascent of the soul. Here, the problem is not that Augustine's soul is trapped in his body. The problem is that the sin of his flesh has weighed down his soul, preventing it from rising up and joining with Christ.[8]

This is why one of Augustine's most famous statements from the *Confessions* is the phrase, "My weight is my love" (13.9.10) (*pondus meum amor meus*). Sin has weighed down Augustine's soul, but when he replaces sin with love, this enables ascent.

Practically, this moves Augustine into a mode of contemplation wherein he saturates his mind with thoughts of eternal things. In short, it's his ulti-mate embrace of Christianity, understood through the lens of Neoplatonic thought, which enables him to make that ascent and join with God. Augustine describes the process of ascent in *On True Religion* written just before the *Confessions*:

> *However, the soul, buried and confused by its sins, cannot by itself see*
> *and comprehend this. In human and divine things no man can attain*
> *an intermediate state to which he might ascend from an earthly life to*

the likeness of God. God, in his unspeakable mercy, through a temporal dispensation, has employed the changeable creation, while serving eternal laws, to commemorate its first and perfect state. Thus He has come to assist individual men and, truly, the entire human race. That is our Christian religion in our times. To inquire after it and to follow it is the most secure and most certain way of salvation (10.19).

By referencing ascent and contemplation, Augustine is indicating that he is heading toward the Christian faith. Thus, Chapter Five marks a major transition. Augustine reiterates his confession of praise to indicate that he is heading in a different direction.

Questions for Reflection
1. What might it look like if you prayed without words?
2. Have you ever used meditation as part of your prayer life?
3. *Lectio Divina*, or prayer using the Scriptures to allow thoughts and feelings to rise up which one then offers to God is an ancient practice. Have you ever tried this?
4. If the goal of the spiritual life is union with Christ, how do we attain this? (Consider the sacraments).

Faustus and the Problem of Curiosity

Faustus was a very senior Manichean intellectual. His visit to Carthage was something Augustine had been eagerly awaiting for a long time. Augustine had built up many issues with the Manichaean religion. But the local leadership could not answer Augustine's questions. He was told to wait for Faustus, a Manichean Bishop, who would provide the answers.

Structurally, Faustus' visit is important because three paragraphs into the Chapter, Augustine meets the Manichaean Bishop, who disappoints him. Yet three paragraphs before the end of the Chapter, Augustine meets Ambrose, a Christian Bishop, who utterly impresses him.[9] The reversal, placed at similar points in the Chapter, is intentional. Once again, we are getting an indication that Augustine is about to start heading towards Christianity, not away from it.

But, why have I entitled this Section "the Problem of Curiosity"? I am playing on the Latin word *curiositas* which means "inquisitive," but which ultimately derives from the word *curiosus*, which adds a second sense, that of being "wasted by cares." When Augustine discusses the "lust of the eyes," he is talking about both being "inquisitive" and being "wasted by cares." In other words, Augustine's pursuit of rational knowledge with the Manichees weighs him down. These cares play an important role in the disillusionment of Chapter Five.

Focus Text 5B

> You are not reached by the proud, not even by those who by their curiosity (*curiosa*) and practical knowledge are able to number the stars and the [grains of] sand, measure the starry heavens and track the orbits of the planets. With their intellect and cleverness, which you have given them, they have discovered many things. Many years prior to the event, they have predicted solar and lunar eclipses, forecasting the exact day, the exact hour, and the extent to which it would be total or partial. Their calculations have not disappointed them...now, people not in the know, marvel and are astounded by such things while those in the know prance about and are extolled. In their impious pride, they retreat from you. Fading from your intense light, they foresee a solar eclipse long ahead of time, but do not see their own eclipse right before them. They don't religiously strive to discover from whom they received their natural talent in the first place. Further, when they find out you have made them, they do not give themselves to you, so that you might watch over what you have made...they do not crucify their own haughtiness like the predatory birds, or their own curiosities (*curiositates*) like the fish of the sea or their indulgent behavior like the beasts of the field. They walk about over secret paths to the abyss. But you, O God, are a consuming fire, let their lifeless desires be consumed and recreate them for immortality (5.3.3-4).

This is a very interesting text because Augustine really admires the learning of these intelligent scholars. They have investigated many things and discovered much. The big problem is they have done it without any sense of God. As a result, their learning is mere "curiosity," which is focused on earthly and temporal things.

We should remember that this admiration for secular learning comes after Chapter Four in which we explored the topic of divine illumination. Looking back on it, Augustine made the point that we can't know very much unless God's illumination points the way.

Why should we care about this? The problem of learning in Augustine's day is simply a foretaste of what would happen on a much grander scale during the Enlightenment in the eighteenth and nineteenth centuries. Many marvelous advances came as a result of the Enlightenment. Beethoven is just one example. Human rights and liberal democracy are another. The widespread ownership of private property is a third. These are all good things which, despite their shortcomings, have resulted in greater human flourishing, at least in some parts of the world.

Yet when the basis for knowledge loses any sense of ultimate reality, the pursuit of truth gets reduced to things which humans can manipulate and control. Today, people get paid enormous sums of money to manipulate material things – be it in the form of a microchip that goes into a cell phone, a switch which transmits terabytes of information from one place to another at the speed of light, or in a financial institution which is able to move billions of dollars at the push of a button. All of these things are remarkable innovations. They enthrall our eyes and dazzle our minds; they make us financially richer. These inventions quickly become indispensable for our lives. Yet such things have little to do with transcendence or with ultimate reality. Said differently, they have little to do with what is true or eternal.

The whole point of the scientific method is to explain reality through rigorous, repeatable testing of a hypothesis. But, just because something can be repeated over and over again does not necessarily make it true. It simply describes reality as we know it, see it and experience it *at this time*. But truth transcends time and place. The scientific method does a marvelous job of making conclusions based on the best fit for the data at hand, but does not necessarily tell us what is true. The method is helpless when the issues in question are either not repeatable or not readily observable.

Augustine's point is why would you spend your life loving things that aren't, or ultimately might not be, true? One of the most pervasive misunderstandings in our culture is that Science alone produces truth, whereas religion, based as it is on faith, produces mere conjecture. Augustine would flat out reject this distinction.

But we also need to bring some balance to this discussion. There is nothing wrong with science and there should be no conflict between science and religion. Both science and religion need each other and ought to be pursuing the same thing – the truth.

Hence, Augustine would never dissuade someone from pursuing science as a vocation. We should recall that Augustine's primary objection to the

Manichees developed because their beliefs did not match up well to the best science of his day (which he knew well). Science helped Augustine see that the Manichaean belief system did not comport to reality and helped him understand reality better. The problem is not with science, but with our lust for knowledge, which, apart from God, is mere curiosity.

To Augustine, knowledge acquired by faith is far surer than that which comes from the senses. Why is this? It's because, in Augustine's worldview, the creation is a mere shadow of what is ultimately true. More specifically, knowledge acquired by reason is meaningless unless it is first purified by the virtues of faith, hope and love.[10] As Augustine puts it in the *City of God*, "Without true piety, no one can have genuine godliness, that is, without the true worship of the true God, and there is no true virtue, when virtue serves human glory" (5.19). Knowledge without God is mere *curiositas*, a contributor to pride, which separates us from the God our souls are seeking. The great Medievalist Etienne Gilson describes this well:

> *Once our science has been transformed by faith, it is subject to the workings of wisdom and benefits from the help of grace; what was once but vain curiosity lacking both beginning and end becomes now a legitimate desire to understand revealed truth. This is the genesis of Augustinian knowledge in the proper sense of the term, with the characteristics it will retain for thinkers of the Middle Ages.[11]*

This does not at all mean that Augustine was against the acquisition of knowledge. He is not advocating that Christians climb into a hole and hope the world ends. After all, Augustine was one of the most learned men of his day. He set the standard for scholarship for over one thousand years. Yet, what Augustine understood is that scientific knowledge was useful, but ultimately incomplete. In other words, there are things that are useful to know (scientific knowledge), but far more important are the things that we must know, namely who God is and what he expects from us.[12] The things we must know come to us by faith, not by the scientific method.

But there's one more aspect which is important to Augustine as well. Not only is true knowledge impossible without God, it's also impossible without love. Knowledge isn't just about thinking; it's about the heart as well. Paula Fredrickson says it well,

'Knowing' for Augustine is never solely a function of thinking. Knowing immediately implies loving. People seek truth because they love truth, and their love directs their path. Love is the motor of the will.[13]

The ability to predict that an eclipse is going to happen is amazing. It wows people. It stirs up pride in those who were able to do it. In fact, today, the ability to predict a hurricane is even more amazing because it saves lives by providing early warnings. We are ever-wowed by the technological capabilities of the modern world. We live longer, healthier lives. But, are we happier? Augustine would take us back to the words of Jesus: "For what will it profit a man if he gains the whole world and forfeits his life?" (Matt 16.26) The pursuit of knowledge as *curiositas* is to sell one's soul cheaply. This has been the story of Augustine's life in the first part of the book.

Questions for Reflection
1. Does the admiration given to scientific enquiry remind you of how clergy used to be revered? What are the pitfalls of this?
2. Discuss the ways science and technology have improved your life. Do we want to go back to a world where disease was untreatable, communication difficult and air-conditioning non-existent?
3. Have any of the above advancements brought lasting happiness?
4. Do you find "faith" to be less certain than "scientific knowledge"?

Fleeing To Rome

When Augustine runs away to Rome, he leaves his mother, Monica, behind. This scene is important for a number of reasons. First, it shows that he is not yet the dutiful son that he will become. But, more importantly, it provides another example of how Augustine's relationship with his mother is a bit more complicated than popular imagination usually understands it. There is a reason for Augustine's harshness. Looking back on it, Augustine is not particularly pleased with his actions, but he doesn't berate himself for it either. Not only does he go to Rome in search of better students, more prestige and more money, he also turns away from his mother because she is holding him back. Consider the following text:

Focus Text 5C

You knew, O God, why I went away from Carthage and went to Rome, yet you revealed it neither to me nor to my mother, who bitterly lamented my departure and sought me down at the sea. She latched on to me ferociously, wanting me to go back with her or to come with me. But I deceived her by pretending to have a friend I did not want to leave until the winds were favorable for him to set sail. So I lied to my mother—and oh such a mother—and managed to escape from her. You have forgiven me for this as well. I was full of detestable defilements, but you saved me from the waters of the sea by the waters of your grace. Being purified by this, the river of my mother's eyes dried up, which, on my behalf, she watered the ground under her face daily in prayer to you. Yet refusing to return without me, I barely persuaded her to spend the night close to our ship, near the blessed shrine of St. Cyprian. But that night, I secretly stole away without her. She stayed up weeping and praying. And what, O God, was she petitioning with those tears? Was it that you would not permit my sailing away? But in your profound counsel, you heard the crux of her longing. While not providing for what she asked at that time, you would make me into what she was always praying for. The wind blew and filled our sails and the coastline withdrew from our sight. In the morning, she was insane with grief and her complaints and groans filled your ears, but you disregarded them. You seized me, using my desires to finish off those same desires and beating out her carnal desires by the flogging of grief. In truth, she loved my presence with her, which is typical of mothers, but her much more than most. Little did she know what great delight you were about to bring about as a result of my absence. Yet she wept and wailed and by this suffering she was convicted of the vestiges of Eve within her. With groans, she sought the one she had given birth to with groans (Gen 3.16). And, then, after accusing me of treachery and cruelty, she changed course and interceded on my behalf again. She departed for home and I for Rome (5.8.15).

Augustine's Relationship with Monica

The first thing we should notice is how harsh the language of Focus Text 5C is towards Monica. Augustine actually says that he sees remnants of Eve in his mother. That's right, Augustine sees his mother in the same light as the woman who tempted Adam in the Garden of Eden and precipitated the fall of God's good creation. Is this a fair depiction of pious Monica?

I have been trying to express that Monica is not quite as innocent as we sometimes picture her. This text is a good example of why I think this is so. With the perspective of hindsight, Augustine sees his mother here as a hindrance to his spiritual development, not a help. I'll admit this perspective cuts across the grain of popular imagination about Monica, but I think it's the right way to read it. This follows from texts in Chapters One and Two where we saw Monica refuse Augustine baptism as a child and where she did little to curb his sexual lusts after he reached puberty. In hindsight, Augustine sees Monica as an obstruction to the work that God was doing in his life.

Now, to be fair, Monica was doing this without any awareness of being an obstacle. She simply wanted to be with her son. Is that so bad? Yet Augustine had to deceive his mother so that a greater good might come later; a good he, too, is unaware of at this point. In other words, God does not answer Monica's heart-felt prayers and does not impede Augustine's departure from Carthage. Put simply, she is praying for something God was not prepared to grant.

There is a very interesting letter which Augustine wrote years later to a young man named Laetus who had left a monastery because he was so attached to his mother. In the letter, Augustine invokes a text from Luke 14 in which Jesus says the following:

> *If anyone comes to me and does not hate his father, mother, wife, children, brothers and sisters, and even his own soul, he cannot be my disciple (Luk 14.26).*

Augustine then implores Laetus to return to his monastic vocation by writing the following (I am quoting Roland Teske's translation):

> *You can easily recognize this in your own mother. For why does she hold you like someone trapped in a net and, after you have been impeded, why does she turn and divert you from the course you have undertaken except because she is your own mother? For, because she is the sister of everyone whose father is God and whose mother is the Church, she holds back neither you nor me nor any of our brothers who love her not with a private love as you do in your house but with a public love in the house of God…But what I said about one's mother should be understood of any other relationship of the sort. This is what*

everyone should think concerning his own soul, so that he may hate
it in a private love, which is undoubtedly temporal...[parents should
not] be angry that the Lord commanded we hate them, since the same
thing is commanded us regarding our own soul (243.4-5).[14]

Contemporary commentators who handle this text from Luke often soft-
en the "hate" language, saying (rightly) that the word in Greek carries the
connotation of "preference." Jesus is saying that God is to come first in our
lives. But Augustine cares little for this nuance. He is suggesting that we are
not in any way to impede the work of God. Although her motives were not
bad, Monica was doing just that. We observe that Augustine's relationship
with his mother is more textured and nuanced than popular imagination
usually allows. Generally, Monica is an excellent model for mothers, but
Augustine finds her actions worthy of criticism here.

Augustine and Virgil

The second thing we should notice in Focus Text 5C is that it betrays a
fairly obvious allusion to Virgil's great epic the *Aeneid*. Put simply, the story
of Augustine's wanderings in the first half of the *Confessions* loosely tracks
the story of Aeneas and his quest to found the city of Rome. I mentioned
this literary parallel very briefly in Chapter Three, but I want to describe it
a little more here. Despite Augustine's professed antipathy for classical literature in the first Chapter, Augustine refers to Virgil in the *City of God* as "a
great poet, bettering all others in renown" (1.3). Augustine apparently got
over his dislike of Virgil. As the greatest Latin epic poet, this shouldn't be
too much of a surprise.

Virgil's epic the *Aeneid* takes place after the Trojan War and represents
a great journey, not unlike the journey which Augustine is describing from
his own life. The *Aeneid*, written not long before the birth of Christ, is a
story about the founding of the city of Rome. The brilliance of the *Aeneid* is
Virgil's ability to combine the two founding myths of the city of Rome into
one epic poem. In it, Virgil conflates the story of Aeneas, which probably
took place in the tenth century BC, with that of Romulus, which probably
took place in the late sixth century BC, into one big story.

Aeneas, an important fighter on the Trojan side during the Trojan War,
leads a group away from Troy after the city's fall to the Greeks. Along the
way, Aeneas meets Dido, a princess of the Phoenicians, who founded the
city of Carthage in North Africa. Dido and Aeneas fall in love, but Aeneas,

his destiny bound elsewhere, leaves Dido and sails away at the behest of the gods. Dido kills herself out of grief. The story ends with a series of epic battles, which enable the founding of the city of Rome along the Tiber River.

The goddess, Juno, plays an important role as Aeneas' chief antagonist in this story. She is constantly resisting Aeneas' efforts to reach the end of his journey because she was on the side of the Greeks in the Trojan War (and thus against Aeneas and the Trojans). To make matters worse, she loves the city of Carthage which Aeneas injures when he leaves Dido and she kills herself. In this story, the gods make human progress very difficult.

You might be wondering why any of this matters. One of the things Augustine wants us to notice is that the language he uses in the above text is very similar to the language Virgil uses when Aeneas leaves Dido for Italy. Augustine could have assumed that almost all his original readers could have picked up on the allusion since the *Aeneid* was the standard text for teaching Latin in grammar school.

There are similarities to the story of the *Confessions* in many places. First, in the *Aeneid*, Aeneas leaves Carthage for Rome, thus leaving Dido, whom he loved, behind. The same basic journey is in view in the *Confessions*. Augustine is about to leave Carthage for Rome. Second, it's the gods who ensure that Aeneas doesn't stay in Carthage. When Jupiter (the Latin Zeus) finds out that Aeneas and Dido have fallen in love, he sends Neptune (god of the sea) to remind Aeneas that his destiny lies in Italy, not in Carthage. Similarly, in the *Confessions*, we get the sense that God is behind all the actions which are taking place. Third, since Aeneas can't bear to tell Dido that he has to leave, he tries to set sail without saying goodbye. Yet, suspecting Aeneas is up to something, Dido confronts Aeneas before he can leave. Aeneas responds that he is sailing for Italy "not of my own free will."[15] This causes Dido to kill herself by falling on Aeneas' sword. Just as Aeneas left Dido, causing her to be heartbroken, so Augustine leaves his mother, breaking her heart in much the same way (thankfully, without the suicide of Monica).

The most important part of this allusion, however, is the role of the gods. In an epic poem like the *Aeneid*, it becomes apparent that while fate is really in control, the gods work hard to manipulate the situation. In the *Aeneid*, the gods are fickle and fallible. This is not the case in the *Confessions* as God is not capricious, but worthy of praise.

The central point for the *Confessions* is that it was the true God who facilitated Augustine's leaving. As Augustine puts it, "You applied the goads (*stimulos*) at Carthage which moved me to wrench myself away from there, and you displayed before me the allurements of Rome to attract me there" (5.8.14). It was ultimately God who used Augustine's ambition to draw him ever closer to himself. For Augustine, the Christian God, not fate, is in control of reality. Thus, Augustine is employing similar imagery as the *Aeneid* in telling his story, but he re-interprets the key part of the story.

The Imagery of the Sea

Another important item we shouldn't miss is the connection of the waters of the sea to baptism. Augustine makes this connection explicit in Focus Text 5C. When Augustine sets sail on the water, this is a significant event. It is loaded with meaningful symbolism. We should realize that Augustine's readers would have understood the waters of the sea to represent death.[16]

In ancient literature, the sea is often depicted as being treacherous. For example, Odysseus, the main character in Homer's *Odyssey,* loses all of his sea-faring companions on his way back to Ithaca. Aeneas encounters similar troubles in his various sea voyages. The "wine-dark sea" was not a particularly friendly place. It was mysterious, foreboding and deadly.

In Chapter Thirteen of the *Confessions,* when Augustine is giving an allegorical interpretation to the creation account in Genesis One, he also sees the sea is foreboding terms. There, Augustine interprets the sea as the gathering of sinful humanity in contrast to the redeemed which have been separated onto the dry land (13.17.20).

Augustine is transforming the pagan image of the sea by offering a solution to sin. He does this by connecting the sea to Christian baptism. This makes perfect sense because Christians see baptism as a kind of death before one is raised to life. This image comes directly from the Apostle Paul's writings in the Bible:

> *We were buried therefore with him by baptism into death, so that as Christ was raised from the dead by the glory of the father, we too might walk in newness of life. For, if we have been united with him in a death like his, we shall certainly be united with him in a resurrection like his (Romans 6.4-5).*

Augustine understands the connection in Roman mythology between the sea and death in distinctively Christian terms when he transforms the image to invoke Christian Baptism. This is so because Christian baptism is a death – a death to being held by the realm of sin – and an anticipation of the resurrection which is to come. Augustine does not understand this association as he moves to Rome. But, looking back on it, he cannot help but marvel at the work of God – both literally and figuratively – in transforming his life.

Questions for Reflection

1. What was your experience with your parents as you gained your independence? Was this a difficult or a smooth process for you?
2. Are there any ways in which your desires might be conflicting with God's plan for yourself or your children?
3. Is it troublesome for you that Augustine is so influenced by pagan literature? Is it possible to Christianize non-Christian influences?
4. Augustine is trying to get us to "read" the signs of God's creation well. Does the symbolic reading of the waters of the sea provide a clue for how we're supposed to interpret life?

CHAPTER SIX

AUGUSTINE TURNS

Introduction

As we transition to Chapter Six, Augustine is thirty-years old and in Milan. We have seen him become disillusioned with much of his life. Augustine may love his girlfriend, his career and his Manichaean contacts, but real happiness has eluded him. The search for wisdom, which he began eleven years prior after reading Cicero, had not yielded much fruit. With his embrace of academic skepticism at the end of the last Chapter, Augustine has found himself wondering if truth even exists. Perhaps the search for wisdom through philosophy was just a youthful burst of enthusiasm on his part.

Reversal of Misplaced Loves

In Chapter Six, Augustine questions each of the misplaced loves he has previously embraced. Interestingly, he presents his questioning in reverse order to how he initially introduced them in Chapters Two through Four. For example, Augustine questions his career ambition when he realizes a drunken beggar that he encounters is probably happier than he is. He may have effectively left the Manichees, but he questions his on-going commitment to materialism when he considers the Epicurean philosophical system. He questions his commitment to *curiositas* through events in his friend's Alypius' ("*A-lip-ee-us*") life. Then, the Chapter culminates when Augustine questions his on-going sexual lust when he sends away his girlfriend and the mother of his son, Adeodatus ("*Ah-deo-datus*").

Augustine's decision to send away his girlfriend is less poignant than tragic. Modern observers are often deeply troubled by it. As we'll see, Augustine sends his girlfriend away so he can become engaged to a ten-year-old girl who has money and political connections. If it seems absurd that a girl this young would be engaged, we should realize that this was standard practice in the Middle Ages. As late as the thirteenth century, for example, Dante became engaged to his wife when she was eleven.[1] When puberty came, this meant it was time for marriage.

As a result, many have rushed to defend Augustine, arguing that the dismissal of a concubine was standard practice in the Roman Empire for an up-and-coming official. We'll have to figure out whether or not this dismissal is warranted. As usual, the answer is more complicated than we might expect. I think Augustine cares deeply for his girlfriend, but there is no denying this is one episode from his life that is difficult for many to fathom.

Alypius and Friendship

One of the most important elements in Chapter Six occurs when we are introduced to Alypius, Augustine's best friend. Since both Augustine and Alypius are from Thagaste, it is almost certain their paths crossed many times before Augustine introduces him here. Augustine tells us that Alypius was his student in Carthage, that he came to Rome to study law and that they wound up together in Milan. Alypius has been in the background of our story for some time. I'll need to explain why it is that someone so important suddenly makes an entrance. After all, it is Alypius who is with Augustine in the garden scene of Chapter Eight and is baptized with him in Chapter Nine. Why wait until now to talk about him?

We should realize the focus in Chapter Six is not so much on Augustine, but on his friends, particularly Alypius.[2] The theme of friendship, so prominent in Chapter Four, re-emerges, albeit with a very different twist. This is not a coincidence. In contrast to Augustine's inability to be useful to his dying friend in Chapter Four, we observe a much more outwardly-focused Augustine here. We observe Augustine actively attempting to curb Alypius' poor moral choices which were leading him astray. Said another way, he's acting like a true friend.

I think a key reason why Augustine gives so much space to Alypius is for the benefit of Paulinus of Nola.[3] In the Introduction to this Guide, I discussed how Augustine came to write the *Confessions* at the behest of Paulinus who wanted to know more about his life and his struggles with the Manichees. For example, Paulinus writes the following in a letter to Augustine (if it seems flowery, this was simply the typical letter-writing style of the day):

> *Dearest brother, so in accord and admirable in Christ the Lord, no-*
> *tice with what intimate friendship I acknowledge you, with what*
> *surpassing wonder I admire you, with what great love I hug you.*
> *Every day I converse with your books and feed on the breath of your*
> *mouth...With your five books against the Manichees, you have pre-*
> *pared sufficient armor for me. If you have prepared any other de-*
> *fenses of the Catholic faith against her enemies, I ask you to provide*
> *me with the weapons of justice from your arsenal and to not refuse to*
> *provide them to me (4.2).*

It could very well be that the *Confessions* is Augustine's attempt to help Paulinus understand his struggle with the Manichees and, in turn, to describe Alypius' struggle with his own issues. After all, Paulinus probably wanted to know something about Alypius as well. If so, Augustine is responding to Paulinus for his friend because, out of modesty, Alypius didn't think he could write about himself.[4] Of course, I'm speculating that this is the case, but it's an educated guess based on the literature we have.

Other Key Structural Markers

Speaking of literature, another interesting feature of Chapter Six is the lack of literary references. Up until now, Augustine has made literary allusions everywhere. In fact, Augustine's whole journey seems to take place with Virgil's *Aeneid* in the background. Yet, all of a sudden, the literary allusions cease. Augustine may just be doing this to move the story along, but he may be subtly making a more important statement by breaking with the literature which had dominated his life for so long. Just as he sends away his long-time girlfriend in Chapter Six, he also starts seeing life not in terms of made-up myths, but in terms of Scripture.

Finally, we become aware that Augustine has a more complicated relationship with Ambrose than he let on previously. In Chapter Five, we only hear words of praise for the man whom Augustine considers to be his "spiritual father." But the reality is somewhat different in Chapter Six when we discover that Augustine and Ambrose really weren't so close. Ambrose, being a busy Bishop, simply doesn't have time for Augustine. While Ambrose's spiritual interpretation of the Old Testament is critical to the story, they don't have a particularly warm relationship. This has implications for how we interpret Augustine's story.

Summary

Chapter Six divides neatly into four sections. First, Augustine's mother, Monica, re-appears into our story. Now that Augustine has a big job, she moves to Milan (probably along with Augustine's brother and sister) to be near him. Augustine's career is taking off and Monica wants to be there to observe it. We also see how Monica and Ambrose interact in this section which sets up some interesting issues. Both Monica and Ambrose seem to be happy, but Augustine decidedly is not.

Next, we get an update on Augustine's career. His job is to deliver "panegyrics" on behalf of the Emperor. This means Augustine gives beautiful speeches designed to promote the Emperor Valentinian II's policies, whatever they might be. It is in the aftermath of one of his speeches that Augustine encounters a drunken beggar and wonders why the drunkard is the happy one.

By far, the longest section of the Chapter is dedicated to Alypius and his various troubles. Here, the lust of the eyes is in the forefront. Just as Augustine's *curiositas* didn't make him happy, it doesn't do much for Alypius either. Interestingly, Alypius' besetting sins are different than Augustine's, but the deleterious effect they have on happiness is similar.

The Chapter concludes with Augustine's sending away his girlfriend and his subsequent engagement to a ten-year-old. At the very end, Augustine tenuously embraces Epicurean philosophy, which is essentially materialistic in its orientation. The lust of the flesh is certainly not crushed, but Augustine starts taking actions which will eventually lead in that direction.

Ambrose and Monica

Augustine begins Chapter Six by noting that his mother came to Milan to be with him. She endured a difficult sea crossing. While doing this, she was a rock of stability to the worried passengers, as "she assured them a safe arrival" because of a vision (*visum*) she had received from God (6.1.1). By contrast, Augustine, securely in Milan, was depressed (*desperatione*) and despaired of ever "finding truth." Nevertheless, upon her arrival, Monica was overjoyed to learn that Augustine was no longer a Manichee. This news caused Monica to declare with certainty that she would see her son a baptized Catholic Christian before her death, yet another prophecy which would come to pass as Monica had anticipated.

We also learn that Monica was popular with Ambrose, the Bishop of Milan. However, she was surprised to learn that the practice of taking cakes, bread and wine to the "relics of the saints" (*memorias sanctorum*) was prohibited by Ambrose (6.2.2). This was something she had done with regularity in Thagaste, but the norms were different in Milan. Augustine is astounded when Monica simply submitted to Ambrose's authority. Likely in response to rumors that Monica was an alcoholic, Augustine specifically mentions that Monica's practices were for devotion, not pleasure. Not surprisingly, whenever Ambrose ran into Augustine, he would praise his mother for her piety.

Augustine next notes that Ambrose was "a successful man as the world judges such things" (6.3.3). This is an interesting comment. In many ways, Ambrose was the model for what Augustine wanted to be. He was happy, respected, a good speaker and even had confidence that he knew what was true. Moreover, he was celibate, which seemed "painful" to Augustine.

Yet, we get the sense that there was distance between Augustine and the great Bishop (6.3.4). For example, Ambrose did not know about Augustine's emotional agitation (*aestus*). Augustine found it difficult to gain an audience with Ambrose since he was so busy with other matters. Augustine tried to go see Ambrose, but found him reading silently, a practice that was rare in those days, since most were taught to read out loud. Augustine did not want to bother Ambrose, and was likely looking for a closer relationship.

The longer Augustine listened to Ambrose's sermons the more he realized his prior criticisms of the Church came from misunderstandings. For example, Augustine thought when the Scriptures discussed humankind being made in the "image and likeness of God" (Gen 1.26) this meant God had to be corporeal. Listening to Ambrose, he figured out this was not the case. Augustine realized he had been falsely accusing the Church, a fact which left him "confused and turned upside down" (6.4.5).

He discovered that if he followed Ambrose and read the Scriptures spiritually and not with wooden literalism, he could make sense of the Old Testament. Because Augustine did not yet have a strong grounding in the Scriptures, he was not quite sure if Ambrose was right, but he started reconsidering his assumptions (6.4.6). In fact, from this time on, Augustine started to prefer "Catholic teaching" (*doctrinam catholicam*) (6.5.7). We should not underestimate how important this turn is. Augustine has not yet fully embraced the teachings of the Church (in particular, the Incarnation); but, he has taken a major step forward in at least being willing to admit that its teachings are not ridiculous.

I should point out that Augustine's tentative embrace of the authority of the Church has brought us full circle. In Chapter One, when Augustine remembered his childhood, he noted that in the absence of first-hand knowledge, he had to rely on authorities to tell him what the truth was. Augustine realized he could not have known anything about where he came from unless an authority – his parents – had told him.

Although some things the Church taught "could not be demonstrated," Augustine increasingly found the Church's teaching believable, especially compared to the Manichees (6.5.7). After long deliberation, Augustine started to trust the Christian Scriptures which he surmises must have a divine source (6.5.8).

Suspicion About Ambition

Augustine, however, was still weighed down by his worldly cares. He was consumed by "public office, avarice and marriage," none of which were eternal (6.6.9). Augustine may have had a terrific job, delivering flowery speeches about the Emperor and his policies, but he had no joy.

After delivering one of his speeches on behalf of the Emperor, Augustine realized that he had less happiness than a destitute beggar whom he observed on the street. The beggar was "making merry and rejoicing" while Augustine was in anguish because of his ambition. Something must be wrong, he thought. The beggar, having acquired wine by offering good wishes to passer-byes, had even done more good than Augustine who sought success by "lying" (6.6.10). At the apex of his success, Augustine saw his life as a sad state of affairs.

Alypius

Augustine next introduces his best friend, Alypius. Alypius was from Augustine's hometown of Thagaste, where his parents were "leading citizens" (6.7.11). Although he was originally Augustine's student in Carthage, Augustine was drawn to Alypius as a friend for his great virtue. Despite this, we learn that Alypius is also a sinner.

Augustine presents us with four vignettes from Alypius' life to demonstrate that even in this virtuous lad there was a sinful streak. God uses the sins in each of the four vignettes for his own purposes, again demonstrating that while God may not be the author of sin, he uses our actions – both good and bad – for good. Since Alypius would eventually become a Bishop in Thagaste, Augustine sees these vignettes as preparation for spiritual leadership.

The Circus Games

Alypius was drawn to the Circus games, a reference to competitive charioteer races, in Carthage (6.7.11). One day, Augustine unwittingly dissuaded Alypius from attending these races during a sarcastic aside which Augustine used in a lecture. Employing great self-control, Alypius simply gave up going to them (6.7.12). Augustine sees this as ample evidence of God's providence at work. Augustine had not intended to confront Alypius; yet, an unplanned remark because the impetus for moral improvement. We see here a good example of Augustine's belief that nothing good happens from a moral perspective apart from God's grace.

Unfortunately, Augustine's influence also drew Alypius into an association with the Manichees. In particular, Alypius was drawn to their asceticism. Since most of Augustine's friends were Manichees, we should not be surprised that Alypius found the Manichees convincing, at least for a time.

Gladiatorial Games

Augustine was clearly impressed that Alypius, through sheer self-discipline, had been able to rid himself of a vice. But we see Alypius relapse when he got to Rome. Alypius had come to Rome to go to law school (6.8.13). One day, his fellow students wanted to go to see the gladiators fight to the death, perhaps in the Roman Forum. As he describes Alypius' actions, Augustine makes it a point to note what happened with his eyes.

During the spectacle, Alypius "closed the gates of his eyes," figuring he had enough self-control to not drink in the violence. But after one of the gladiators fell in combat, causing the crowd to roar in approval, Alypius was overcome by curiosity (*curiositate*). The result was that Alypius was "struck with an ever deeper wound in his soul than the gladiator he longed to see suffered in his body." The notion that wounds we incur spiritually are more important than those incurred physically is an important theme in Chapter Six and one we will explore further in the Focus Text Section.

What was the result? Alypius "looked, he shouted, he broke out in flames." This is Alypius' fall. Alypius' own *curiositas* has taken him down. Augustine is again emphasizing that this was all occurring according to God's providential plan.

False Accusations

Augustine next recounts how Alypius was falsely accused of a crime in Carthage. A thief came to a silver shop and, employing a hidden hatchet, hacked away at the covering to the shop (6.9.14). The silversmiths heard this and sent someone to check out what was happening. When the thief heard the silversmith coming, he dropped his hatchet and ran away. Alypius, who was walking along, saw the hatchet on the ground, picked it up and was trying to figure out what had happened. When the silversmith arrived, he found Alypius holding the hatchet and immediately accused him of attempting to break into the shop.

The authorities arrested Alypius, since he appeared to be guilty, and was led away to the city magistrates. A mob formed, insisting that Alypius be punished. On the way, Alypius ran into a city official who recognized him and, when he explained the situation, helped figure out who the real culprit was (6.9.15). When evidence was found which corroborated his testimony, Alypius was exonerated to the seeming disappointment of the boisterous crowd. Augustine finds this event to be providential since Alypius would one day have to decide difficult disputes as a Bishop of the Church. As Augustine puts it, Alypius, who was "destined to become a such a great man, began to learn already that in judging, one must not condemn (*deambulabat*) anyone out of reckless credulity" (6.9.14). God was at work in Alypius' life.

Perks of Power

The last vignette Augustine recounts is a later one while he Alypius was in Rome. Alypius was a kind of law clerk in the courts, an assessor. Unlike most in his position, Alypius could not be bribed (6.10.16). This caused a problem when a powerful Senator, who was used to getting his way, ran into Alypius. Alypius not only refused the Senator's bribe, but also refused to budge even when threatened. Alypius' character impressed everyone (except perhaps the Senator).

We even observe Alypius' character in little things. Alypius loved books and could have made use of the court's stenographers to copy them for personal use. No doubt this was standard practice. However, Alypius refused to do so. Augustine could barely contain his admiration for his friend, as his character was terrific.

We should note that someone of Alypius' sterling character would not likely have associated himself so closely with Augustine if Augustine had been the scoundrel many perceive him to be. From a human perspective, both Alypius and Augustine were honorable Roman gentlemen. This is why Nebridius, who we last met in Chapter Four, is so eager to come join Alypius and Augustine in their search for "the happy life" (*beatae vitae*) (6.10.17). Upon moving to Milan, Nebridius, Alypius and Augustine form a close bond of friendship.

Ambrose and Augustine

Having recounted how Alypius and he became good friends, Augustine contrasts their close friendship with the distant relationship he has with Bishop Ambrose. As I noted previously, Ambrose plays a seminal role in Augustine's life, but their relationship is more complicated than it appears on the surface. This is the case because "Ambrose had no time" for Augustine (6.11.18). Ambrose had made a major impact on Augustine since through the spiritual interpretation of the Scriptures. Augustine had come to see that the Old Testament was not the absurdity the Manichees said it was. Yet in Ambrose, Augustine encountered someone he could not manipulate, impress or control. This must have been a relatively new experience for him. He wanted to ask Ambrose probing questions, but he couldn't get access. This clearly causes Augustine some grief.

Had Ambrose made more time for Augustine, he would have told him to abandon his pursuits of false wisdom and become a Christian by being baptized in the Church. Augustine knows this, but has difficulty doing so. Augustine concedes secular victories are "pleasant," but are also "superficial."

Augustine's Women

Augustine cannot quite get himself to give up his misplaced loves. No doubt, he is making progress in that direction. But, he realizes that to continue advancing in his career, he needs to marry someone "with some money" (6.11.19). In other words, Augustine needs cash to buy an office if he is going to continue to advance. Moreover, he admits that he would be miserable if "deprived of female embraces" (6.11.20). This marks the transition to a discussion of the lust of the flesh.

Alypius thought it was silly to a take a wife since she would inevitably get in the way of the "untroubled leisure" (*securo otio*) needed for philosophy (6.12.21). Alypius found it easier to lead a celibate life, having had a bad sexual experience as a younger man.

For his part, Alypius couldn't understand why Augustine found it so difficult to give up sexual pleasure (6.12.22). But, he also wondered what he was missing. Alypius was curious enough even to consider marriage for a brief time, but he never really pursued it.

Augustine's Engagement

By contrast, Monica was putting pressure on Augustine to have a "real" marriage so he could advance in his career. Under pressure and through the focused efforts of Monica, Augustine became engaged to a young girl (6.13.23). It appears Monica was using the proposed engagement as a manipulative way of ensuring Augustine would be baptized in the Church. Since presumably the girl was Catholic, she would have required any would-be husband to marry her in the Church. Augustine wryly notes that "the girl who was asked for was almost two years under the legal age," meaning she was likely about ten years old.

An ominous sign developed when Augustine's philosophical society fell apart because the spouses refused to live in such a community. The strict rules proposed for the community – including a prohibition on private property – were too unyielding for the spouses. Consideration of the wives was an afterthought, causing the entire project to collapse (6.14.24).

Augustine's Girlfriend(s)

One implication of Augustine's engagement was that it forced him to send away his long-time girlfriend, an act which clearly was difficult for him. As Augustine describes it, "My heart, which cleaved to her, was chopped up and wounded, dragging a trail of blood" (6.15.25). For her part, the unnamed girlfriend returned to North Africa, "vowing to know no other man." She left Adeodatus, their son, with Augustine. This is an odd result since Roman law would normally have given custody rights to the woman.[5] We do not know the circumstances of her return to Africa, but it could very well be that Augustine's girlfriend allowed him to keep Adeodatus so he might receive the advanced education Milan could provide. Unfortunately, Augustine tells us little about what we want to know.

The action of sending away his girlfriend created a dilemma. What was Augustine supposed to do about his continuing sexual needs? As lustful as ever, Augustine simply found another girlfriend. As Augustine puts it, "I was impatient because of the two-year delay to obtain the girl I had proposed to...so I procured another woman."

Could it be that God was at work even in these actions? Augustine notes that the only thing that kept him from greater sexual license was the "fear of death and God's future judgment" (6.16.26). The lust of the flesh was still consuming Augustine, but, he was at least aware that the caldrons of lust which enveloped him were making him ever unhappier.

The Epicureans

Augustine closes out Chapter Six by noting that he had a brief flirtation with the Epicureans. This continues the pattern of ending each Chapter with a descent into a different thought system. Epicurus denied that there was any eternal punishment since there was no afterlife. If there is no future judgment, then why not live to maximize the present? Wouldn't this bring more happiness? Augustine chides himself in the strongest terms for his puerile thinking.

Augustine was still a long way from happiness and peace. But, he was making progress. He has taken the first definitive steps to deal with the lust of the flesh, even if it has resulted in greater misery, both for himself and others. He quickly recognized that the Epicureans, while sounding good, are not going to make him happy either. He is surrounded by friends, yet lonely; he is surrounded by success, yet dissatisfied. The unravelling process has begun in earnest.

Focus Texts

Chapter Six is a rich resource for potential texts to study. In fact, one commentator on the *Confessions* even claims that the entire story of the *Confessions* could be summarized by the various vignettes and stories of Chapter Six.[6] I think this is a bit of an overstatement, but nevertheless it hints that Chapter Six breaks the mold of some of the other Chapters we have read to this point. There is something unique going on here.

In this Section, we will be exploring Augustine's relationship with Ambrose, Alypius' fall, and Augustine's decision to send his girlfriend back to North Africa. These three areas of focus are intended to provide a sense for the unravelling of the three misplaced loves which occur in Chapter Six. Of particular importance is the focus which the "lust of the flesh" receives as Augustine sends away one girlfriend, gets engages to another and retains yet another woman to satisfy his lust, both for sex and for position.

Augustine and Ambrose

In Chapter Five, I noted I was going to wait until now to discuss Ambrose. The reason for this is hopefully becoming clearer. Augustine presents Ambrose in Chapter Five as a dear mentor, one who had an enormous impact on his life. Yet, when we get to Chapter Six, we observe that Ambrose and Augustine are not really close. After cordially welcoming Augustine to Milan, Ambrose doesn't give Augustine the time of day. Reading between the lines, we might get the sense Augustine was a bit put off by this relatively cool reception. He wanted another close friend, but Ambrose was not going to be that for him. Just how influential was Ambrose for Augustine? This is not an easy question to answer. Consider the following text:

Focus Text 6A

Ambrose I considered a successful man according to how the world judges things, as the powerful greatly respected him. Only his commitment to celibacy appeared painful to me. But I was not yet acquainted nor had I experienced what hopes he bore and what struggles he encountered against the temptations of his own excellence, what source of comfort he found in such struggles, what impeccable joy was in his heart and hidden in his mouth when he chewed on your word (*pane*). He did not know my agitation or the dangerous pit menacing me (Matt 15.14). I had no opportunity to ask questions of him as I wished since crowds of busy people, whose infirmities he served, made demands on his time...That agitation in me needed to find him at a moment of leisure so that it might be poured out. But such an opportunity I never found. Yet, I heard him 'rightly dividing the word of truth' (2 Tim 2.15) to the people every Lord's day. I became ever more convinced that all those knotty and wily pretenses of those who betray the divine books could be resolved. I discovered that your spiritual sons (whom you regenerated by grace through their mother, the Catholic Church (*matre catholica*), did not understand the truth that man was created by you in your image (Gen 1.26) as meaning they believed and confessed you were defined by the form of a human body (6.3.3-4).

I get the sense Augustine isn't very happy that Ambrose won't get close to him. We need to remember that before Ambrose became a Bishop, he was a very good politician, serving as governor of two small Italian provinces.[7] Ambrose had come from a political family, as his father was head of the government in Gaul (modern-day France and Germany). Ambrose had known people like Augustine his whole life – smart, educated, ambitious and pagan. Perhaps for the first time, Augustine had run into someone who was not terribly impressed with him. Yes, Augustine was impressive on the surface, but Ambrose, as a Christian Bishop, saw right through him and realized that there was little in the way of substance from a spiritual perspective. Ambrose was interested in building Christ's Church, and Augustine, at the time, did not seem like a particularly good candidate for that.

The second thing to notice in the text – and I admit it looks like a superfluous comment – is that Augustine couldn't figure out Ambrose's celibacy. It was increasingly the case by the fourth Century that those in higher ecclesiastical positions were embracing celibacy. In fact, for those who served the Church in Milan under Ambrose, celibacy was not optional. While plenty of priests were married, they were expected to abstain from sex after being ordained in Milan.[8] This stands in marked contrast to other places that were not so rigorous.

For Ambrose, celibacy was critical because it was something which promoted the special status of those who were ordained. Although all who were baptized into the Church were equal before God, Ambrose expected the clergy to reflect holiness on earth. So potent was this demand for clerical celibacy that by the sixth century, it was the *laity* which demanded that priests be celibate, thus setting in motion the later practice of uniform clerical celibacy in the Roman Catholic Church.[9] Although clerical celibacy would not become the official practice of the Catholic Church until the twelfth century (at the first Lateran Council of 1123), Milan in the late fourth century was a place which anticipated this position.

As we've already seen, the issue of sex is not a minor one. It is going to play a key role in Augustine's understanding of what it means for him to come into the Church and be baptized. When he encounters Ambrose, Ambrose does not treat Augustine like an up-and-coming successful man. He treats Augustine as an unbaptized pagan, having sex out of wedlock. In other words, Ambrose is not very impressed with Augustine.

Augustine clearly sensed this and was stung by it. Could it be when Augustine describes Ambrose as one who "received me like a father" this is not meant to be taken literally? Augustine is likely speaking here about Ambrose as his spiritual father, the one who would eventually baptize him and welcome him into the Church. Despite the occasional language to the contrary, Augustine and Ambrose were not particularly close.

How can we explain Augustine's seemingly heart-felt conviction that Ambrose made a major impact in his life? I think the impact is real; it's just not relational. The impact is in two key areas – the Scriptures and in Neoplatonism (which we'll get to in the next Chapter). When Augustine first listened to Ambrose preach, it was primarily to assess his style. Ambrose was a good preacher whose rhetorical skill was impressive.

As Augustine listened longer, however, he started to realize that the Manichaean claims about what Christians believed were simply not credible. This is also something we have observed previously. What's new in Chapter Six is that even as Augustine starts to buy the idea that the Old Testament isn't ridiculous, he still struggles with the idea of an immaterial God.[10] This is why Augustine tells us in Chapter Six he wasn't completely sure whether Ambrose's teaching was true (6.6). The Old Testament might be understandable if interpreted non-literally, but the notion of who God was still puzzled Augustine. How could material humans be created in the image of an immaterial God? He still had not worked this out by the end of the Chapter.

This also leads to the discussion of authority in Chapter Six. I noted in the Summary Section that there is a connection between Augustine's childhood experience of recognizing he needed an authority to tell him true things with his struggles to understand God and the beliefs of the Catholic Church. In the absence of direct knowledge, we are forced to rely on authorities to fill in the gaps (something we do all the time). When we consider things that cannot be known through sensory experience like God or the soul, the Church steps in to fill that gap.

But this encompasses only one sense of authority. In our day, we usually picture authority as something coercive, such as a government's mandating certain behaviors or actions. As usual, there is a deeper sense at work in this passage. What Augustine also means by authority is "coherence."[11] I am grateful to Michael Cameron for the insight that Augustine understands authority the way a rhetorician would – that symmetry and beauty are what provide moral consistency.[12] To Augustine, authority is what brings symmetry to seemingly incoherent events such as the immaterial God taking on flesh in the Incarnation.

Said differently, Ambrose is important for Augustine because he is supplying the coherence for his formerly disjointed understanding of life.

Augustine knows he is not happy. He observes that Ambrose is. What's the difference? Ambrose is a celibate follower of Christ who has dedicated his life to the Church, while Augustine is a sexually active, ambitious intellectual who has given up on ever finding truth. The contrast is significant.

It is absolutely true that Augustine learns how to read the Bible differently after hearing Ambrose preach. It is also true that Augustine realizes the Manichean claims about the Christian faith are misstated. But what is most important in Chapter Six is that Ambrose provides the link to authority – the coherence – that will ultimately answer his questions. He can't quite understand how people are created in the image of an invisible God. He can't quite understand how the Incarnation works. But he is starting to change his direction. To get there, he'll need the help of Neo-Platonist philosophy, which we will observe in Chapter Seven.

Questions for Reflection

1. What images do the word "authority" conjure up for you? When we discuss the authority of the Church as an aid to understanding, does this give you pause?
2. Ambrose thinks celibacy is essential for ministry and believes that it is the preferred state for all people. What do you think about that? Have you ever considered adopting the practice of celibacy?
3. Have you ever tried to get close to someone influential, only to be rebuffed? Describe a relationship where you wanted greater closeness than you received.
4. If Ambrose met you, how would he size up your spiritual life?

Alypius and the Fall

We observed Augustine's fall in Chapter Two when he stole some pears and got his girlfriend pregnant. We are going to see something similar occur with Alypius here in Chapter Six. Augustine and Alypius are tempted by different things. While Augustine is constantly beset by sexual lust, this hardly affects Alypius at all. In fact, Alypius' flirtation with marriage is more out of curiosity about what he's missing than genuine interest. In the end, he concludes that he's not missing very much and prefers the quiet life of the scholar to the busy life of a husband.

What proves damaging to Alypius is something different. It is the "lust of the eyes," which we have been describing as *curiositas* which really gets to Alypius in this Chapter, leading to his fall. Here, we will observe a connection between what we allow into our eyes and our wills. Let's consider the following text:

Focus Text 6B

In Rome, Alypius was extraordinarily blown away, by an unbelievable passion for gladiatorial shows. He was utterly against such shows, but when some friends and fellow students met him by chance on their return from lunch, and although vehemently refusing and resisting, they employed friendly intimidation and lead him to the stadium at the time of the savage and deadly games...when he was brought there and they sat down where they could, the most terrible of all the pleasures seethed throughout the place. But, Alypius, closing the gates of his eyes, prohibited his mind from advancing to any such evil. And if only he had shut up his ears! During the battle, a mighty cry of the whole crowd vigorously beat on him. Overcome by curiosity (*curiositate*), and believing himself to be equipped to disregard and overcome whatever he saw, he opened his eyes. He was struck with an even deeper wound in his soul than the gladiator he longed to see suffered in his body. He fell more pitiably than the one whose fall had brought the roar of the crowd in the first place. By invading his ears and unfastening his eyes, it made way for the striking down and routing of the strength of his soul....what can I add? He looked; he shouted; he broke out in flames. He carried away with him an insanity that caused him to return not only with those who first dragged him off, but even without them, dragging others along (6.8.13).

Let's first consider the similarities between this scene and Augustine's theft of the pears in Chapter Two. Both involve the sight of something that is not particularly desirable. You may remember how Augustine puts himself into the Biblical story of the fall of mankind in Chapter Two, yet notes that the fruit he was stealing wasn't even attractive to the eyes. With Alypius, he considers himself strong enough to withstand the temptation to drink in the murderous sights of the gladiatorial games. Yet we quickly find out that he is not. When Alypius opens his eyes, he sees the gore of the games, and is transfixed by what he observes. Both Augustine and Alypius see things which are not attractive, but which nevertheless transfix them.

Secondly, we should notice that Alypius' trip to the games never would have happened had he not had the encouragement of a group. Alypius did not want to go to this event and had no particular desire to see people fight to the death. Yet, under pressure, he goes along for the ride and suffers real damage to his soul. The power of a group (or a society) to perpetuate sin is a real concern. Of course, the same holds true for Augustine since he freely admits that he would never have stolen the pears had he not been in a company of friends who encouraged him to do so. Friendships, which can be so valuable in life, can also drive us towards sin.

In the way he tells both stories, Augustine is really teaching that we are bound together with Adam.[13] The story of the fall in Genesis 3 is not just something which happened to one man a long time ago. It is the story of everyone. As a human race, we share in Adam's fallen nature and reap its fruits. This is a central theme which Augustine describes in the *Confessions*. We cannot choose not to sin.

Thirdly, we observe in this passage that there is a connection between the eyes and curiosity. I noted previously in this Guide, when discussing *curiositas*, that there is a sense the word carries of being "wasted by cares."[14] For both Augustine and Alypius, the fleeting pleasure of sin leaves behind a legacy of disintegration. This is because satisfying the inquisitiveness of the eyes can have lasting effects on the soul. The lasting effect of sin on the soul is significant.

Why is this? Augustine is adamant that the damage from the gladiatorial games is ultimately spiritual, not physical. He believes that the wound Alypius incurs from observing this event is more significant than the lost life of the gladiator. He even tells us that Alypius is not the same person after he drinks in the blood and violence. There is real damage done in this event.

To Augustine, damage done spiritually is far more important than that which is done physically. This is the case because spiritual damage can have eternal effects. Allowing base physical things into our sight weighs the soul down and inhibits it from ascending and enjoying the ever-present reality of Christ.

For Augustine, our central problem is our corrupted will, driven, in turn, by misplaced loves.[15] We end up taking ourselves far away from God when we focus on temporal pleasures at the expense of our eternal desire to be with God. Augustine is less interested in laying down stark rules to follow; he is simply trying to assert that the fleeting pleasures of the world will never bring the satisfaction and the wholeness we crave. Both Augustine and Alypius want to be happy, but their behavior and their choices have led them to things which cannot make them happy. The damage done to the soul by the "lust of the eyes" is significant because it reorients the soul towards temporal physical things and away from eternal spiritual things.

What's missing in this discussion is the realization that we, as fallen humans, cannot unite with Christ on our own. We might aspire to ascend, but the weight of sin always pulls us down. This is why Augustine eventually comes to realize that participation with Christ happens only by the grace of God. It is the gift of God who gives himself to us that enables our souls to ascend to him.

This is what Augustine is preparing us to observe. Alypius does damage to his soul by going to the gladiatorial games. His eyes drink in the carnage of death as entertainment. Such a spectacle does damage because it ends up affecting his will. It takes him further away from God. The good news is that this damage can be undone through God's grace which is freely offered to everyone. However, since our wills are free, we can also resist the grace offered to us.

While we are in our mortal bodies, our wills affect the life of the soul. We are free to fill our minds with images that do not edify. We are free to take ourselves away from God. We can even refuse God's love and the means of his grace (especially the sacraments). Etienne Gilson says it well:

> *Thus, every movement of the soul is directed either towards a good to be acquired or retained or away from an evil to be avoided or removed; but the soul's free movement to acquire or to retain a thing is the will itself. Every movement of the soul, therefore, depends on the will.*[16]

If we desire to rise up and see Christ with the eyes of the mind, the misplaced loves of 1 John 2.16 – the lust of the flesh, lust of the eyes and the pride of life — have to be curbed. We were created for something ultimate and unchanging. To spend our lives in the pursuit of temporal things is illogical. Augustine implores us to strive for something greater, and, with the help of the grace of God, to make progress in the spiritual life which enables the soul to ascend.

As we will observe when we get to the next Chapter, this progress in the spiritual life takes the form of a ladder of ascent. We start with the need for authority, but this is the lowest rung of the ladder. We ultimately make progress in the spiritual life by focusing on God who is eternal and unchanging rather than on temporal things which are always subject to change and deterioration. Unwholesome images weigh down our souls and prevent us from rising up and joining with Christ. Augustine is not trying to kill off fun; he's simply trying to direct us toward things that will edify and away from things that will not and cannot.

Questions for Reflection
1. Do you have friendships which have driven you either toward or away from God?
2. Alypius' soul was damaged because he drunk in violence in the gladiatorial games? What impact are images from TV or the movies having on you?
3. What do you do which detracts from your spiritual life? What brings you happiness?
4. How do you deal with the constant bombardment of sexual images in our society? Are you even aware of its effects?

The End of the Affair
Augustine has been with his girlfriend since he was sixteen and in Thagaste. They have been together for sixteen years and had a son, Adeodatus, together. In one of the most troubling scenes in the *Confessions*, Augustine sends his girlfriend back to North Africa at the end of the Chapter so he can get engaged to a ten-year-old girl with appropriate societal status.

Viewed from the standards of our day, these actions on Augustine's part are just impossible to understand. It never even crosses his mind that he could put his career on hold and marry the woman who had loyally served him for almost two decades. Augustine tells us that this decision grieved him deeply, but this fact engenders little sympathy among most modern readers. What are we supposed to make of this series of events? Let's start with the text:

Focus Text 6C

Meanwhile, my sins were being multiplied. The woman with whom I regularly slept was ripped from my side since she was an impediment to my marriage. My heart, which cleaved to her, was chopped up and wounded, dragging a trail of blood. So she returned to Africa, vowing to you to know no other man, and leaving my natural-born son with me. But I was too unhappy to imitate the example of a woman. I was impatient because of the two-year delay to obtain the girl I had proposed to, and being no lover of marriage, I was a slave to lust. So, I procured another woman, though in no way a wife, that my soul's sickness might endure and be brought through by this protection until I came to the kingdom of marriage. Of course, my wound, made by the former departure, was not cured, but after inflammation and sharp pain, it putrefied. The pain made me cold, but it hurt with hopelessness (6.15.25).

The first thing to consider is that Augustine's actions of keeping a girlfriend to satisfy his sexual needs are not at all out of line in late fourth century Italy. In fact, because they had a child together, Roman law might have even recognized their relationship as a legal marriage, even though no official ceremony had taken place.[17] Roman law understood that upper-class men, especially those who were on the rise, could keep a concubine until they found a suitable wife.

It was understood, by both the man and the concubine, the relationship would never end in a "legitimate" marriage. Marriages were usually about the acquisition of property, position and power, not about love. Augustine's girlfriend would have known the day of her dismissal would come at some point. This might not let Augustine off the hook; but, it was the reality in the society at the time.

To complicate matters, the Church even agreed with this Roman practice for a time. In the year four-hundred, Bishops at the First Council of Toledo issued the following judgment:

If a man has no wife, but a concubine instead of a wife, let him not be refused communion; only let him be content to be united with one woman, whether wife or concubine.[18]

This seems like a clear statement from the Bishops of the Church in support of what Augustine was doing. However, the *Apostolic Tradition*, a church manual written by Hippolytus used in the early third century, has a different perspective:

The man who has a concubine must cease and take a wife according to the law. If he will not, he shall be rejected [from being a catechumen].[19]

Keep in mind that Hippolytus was outlining a rigorist position against his arch-rival Callistus whom he reviled because of his permissive attitude toward the sexual practices of upper-crust congregants. The point here is that there is conflicting evidence about the Church's acceptance of those who had concubines. Yet the evidence closest to Augustine's time suggests that it was an acceptable practice.

We should remember that the relatively permissive attitude of the Church only applied to the laity since it was not acceptable for the clergy to engage in such practices. The point I'm making is that as long as the relationship was monogamous, it was treated like a common-law marriage by the Church of the late fourth century. It was a concession given to those high-up in Roman society, but, as we'll see, one that did not last.

There is some justification from the Old Testament for such an arrangement. After all, Abraham (Gen 22.24), Saul (2 Sam 3.7), David (2 Sam 5.13), Caleb (1 Chronicles 2.26) and Manasseh (1 Chronicles 7.14) all had concubines. Remarkably, Rehoboam had sixty concubines (2 Chronicles 11.21). Not to be outdone, Solomon had three-hundred concubines along with seven-hundred wives (1 King 11.3). Clearly, having a concubine was standard practice during the time of the Old Testament patriarchs and prophets.

The New Testament was not so amenable to the idea. The Apostle Paul clearly envisions sex occurring between one man and one woman within the bounds of marriage. Yet, for the apostle Paul, celibacy is the preferred state and marriage is a concession:

But because of the temptation to immorality, each man should have his own wife and each woman her own husband...I say this by way of concession, not of command. Yet I wish that all were as I myself am. But each has his own special gift from God, one of one kind and one of another (1 Cor 7.2, 6-7).

Paul recognizes that different people are called to different ways of living. Not everyone — in fact, only a distinct minority – are called to keep vows of celibacy. This is why leaders in the Church like Ambrose thought of celibacy as a higher order of things. The decision to pursue celibacy is a vocation. In fact, in his work *On Virginity*, Ambrose says the following:

I do not then discourage marriage, but recapitulate the advantages of holy virginity. This is the gift of a few only, that is, of all...I am comparing good things with good things, that it may be clear which is the more excellent.[20]

Ambrose is following Paul's instructions when he suggests that chastity is a matter of calling:

Only, let everyone lead the life which the Lord has assigned to him, and in which God has called him. This is my rule in all the churches (1 Cor 7.17).[21]

Marriage is a good thing, but celibacy is better. Since Augustine continued to have a hard time even envisioning what life would be like without sex, he opts for marriage and gets engaged. His engagement is done primarily for the utilitarian purposes of wealth and career advancement. We know this because after dismissing his girlfriend, he finds another woman to satisfy his sexual needs.

The other thing to consider is the role of Monica. Monica was probably never particularly happy about Augustine's girlfriend, and we can surmise that it's no coincidence the girlfriend is dismissed shortly after Monica arrives in Milan. I pointed out before that Monica wanted to arrange a proper marriage for Augustine to manipulate her son into being baptized. Monica clearly plays a role and is perhaps *the* significant cause behind the girlfriend's dismissal.

The most damning evidence against Augustine, however, is his later decision, when he is a Bishop, to completely disavow the practice of concubines. He may have had one, but when he is in a position of authority, he comes to see that this practice is inappropriate. In a post-modern world, which is ever-sensitive to power relationships and sexuality, Augustine's actions appear hypocritical. Consider what Augustine says in his later work *On the Good of Marriage:*

> *If fact, if a man should make use of a woman for a time until he should find another worthy of his station or financial means to be his partner, then that state of mind is adultery, not with the one he desires to find, but with the one he is sleeping with without being a partner in marriage with her (5.5).*

At best, Augustine is inconsistent in his later condemnation of the practice. More optimistically, we might surmise that Augustine learned something from his prior life. Looking back, even if his actions were within the bounds of acceptable behavior for the time, what he did seems wrong. With the benefit of hindsight, he knows it. Sin begets sin. This much Augustine sees clearly.

Questions for Reflection

1. Many accuse Augustine of being a misogynist because of how he treats his girlfriend. How do you assess his actions?
2. Have you done anything in a past relationship which you regret?
3. How do you evaluate fourth-century attitudes toward celibacy? What (if any) are the spiritual advantages to the celibate life?
4. How do we teach young people about Christian views of sexuality? Would it be easier to do this if we had less of a rule-based ethic and taught celibacy as a calling?
5. How could ancient views on celibacy inform modern discussions of homosexuality and gay marriage?

CHAPTER SEVEN

AUGUSTINE ASCENDS

Introduction

We face a difficult task in Chapter Seven. We have to answer one of the central questions Augustine has been wrestling with – how can we see God if God is incorporeal? Throughout this Guide, I have been suggesting that Augustine is leading us to a mystical vision through the story of his life. I have also been suggesting that the apex of the spiritual life is having an interior vision of Christ with the eyes of the mind, enabling participation in Christ. Up until now, I have not fully explained what I have meant by that.

What is a mystical experience? There is a great diversity of views on this subject. As a result, let me be as clear as I can about what I mean. I take my understanding of what a mystical experience is mainly from St. Teresa of Avila, one of the great mystics of the Western Church. St. Teresa said that she sometimes experienced "a consciousness of the presence of God of such a kind that I could not possibly doubt that he was within me or that I was wholly engulfed in him."[1] Bernard McGinn, a Professor at the University of Chicago and an expert on the history of Christian mysticism, employs Teresa's understanding to explain that a mystical experience is simply the conscious awareness of the divine presence.[2] I am relying on McGinn's understanding in this Chapter. A mystical experience is a conscious and heightened awareness of the presence of God, not some strange trance or ecstatic experience.

What Augustine is going to demonstrate to us in Chapter Seven is that it's entirely possible to experience the presence of God in this life. This is a very brief experience for Augustine, but it's also powerfully real. What Augustine will help us see is that we can't engineer mystical visions because they're an act of grace. God has to enable our participation in divine realities.

Augustine and Mysticism

Chapter Seven represents an important milestone in the *Confessions*. In the Chapter, Augustine has a mystical experience in which he has a vision of the divine nature. He describes this experience across two sections of the Chapter. This experience is incomplete, but it represents an essential step on his journey. It also provides strong evidence that the ultimate goal of Augustine's journey is not a once-and-done conversion experience, but an ever-closer relationship with Christ, which Augustine finds through the mind. To me, Augustine's experience of mystical union is a remarkable event.

I should admit that during my first several times through the *Confessions*, I completely missed this aspect of it. Chapter Seven seemed like a lot of dry, boring theology and philosophy, which appeared to detract, not enhance, Augustine's story. I couldn't have been more wrong.

But I should admit that seeing Augustine as the fountainhead of Western mysticism is controversial. Some will find all this talk of mystical visions uncomfortable. This probably happens because some readers of Augustine have put so much emphasis on his so-called conversion that the experiences he has beforehand tend to be ignored as superfluous.

You can probably tell by now that I think seeing Augustine's turn as a point-in-time conversion experience to be a rather significant misreading of the *Confessions*. All through the book, we've seen Augustine expressing his story as a gradual journey, not a sudden "decision for Christ." In fact, Augustine would say it was the grace of God which was doing the essential work all throughout his journey. One by one, his objections to Christianity have melted away. By the end of Chapter Seven, we'll see almost all his intellectual objections have been met.

Plotinus and Neoplatonism

One thing that I am intending to help you observe is that there are allusions to Plotinus ("*Ploh-tine-us*") all over the Chapter. To understand Augustine's experience in Chapter Seven, we're going to have to see it like Augustine does – through the lens of Neoplatonism.

Plotinus is a philosopher who interprets and extends Plato's philosophical system. I write "system" euphemistically since Plato probably never intended for his dialogues to be turned into a grand system of thought. What Plato wrote was so influential his later followers tried to systematize it. This is mainly what Plotinus is doing.

Plotinus provides a conception of God which is, on the one hand, pagan and, on the other, not too far away from Christian belief. This is one reason why Church leaders in the late fourth century like Augustine and Ambrose like him so much. They were amazed that he got so close to Christian belief just through reason. Augustine's embrace of the Platonic tradition is one of the chief reasons why Plato would exercise such an outsized influence on the Church, even though most of his writings were lost.

Augustine says some remarkable things in Chapter Seven. He actually thinks that his reading of the "books of the Platonists" is more or less saying the same thing as the prologue to John's Gospel. He even quotes Romans 1.20 – "Ever since the creation of the world, his invisible nature, namely, his eternal power and deity, have been clearly perceived *in the things that have been made* so they are without excuse" – four times in the Chapter. Augustine believes that some things are knowable just because of the effects of the creation. God has left his fingerprints everywhere. This ushers in a discussion about the interaction of faith and reason, thus introducing a centuries-long debate about it. The central question is whether we can know anything about God without revelation to guide us.

It's important not to take this point too far. Towards the end of his life, Augustine criticizes himself for his writings prior to the *Confessions* because he accepted a bit too uncritically what the Platonic tradition was claiming. For example, in his *Retractions* (1.4), Augustine writes the following:

> *I have been especially displeased with myself for offering up effusive praise to the Platonists, Plato and the Academic philosophers beyond what was proper for such impious men, especially those great errors against which Christian teaching must be defended.*

Plotinus was enormously influential, but ought not to be a source above the Scriptures for uncovering truth. Augustine's more balanced view of the Platonic Tradition would be a later development in his intellectual journey. In Chapter Seven, we'll find that the "books of the Platonists" provide the basic framework for understanding God's interactions with humankind.

Summary

As a whole, Chapter Seven forms the center for the *Confessions* (as measured by Chapters or Sections). When Augustine composed the work, it came in thirteen Chapters, so we're right in the middle of it. In saying this, I should mention there is not uniform agreement among scholars that Chapter Seven is the center of the book, since different methodologies can produce different results. [3]

The typical approach to the *Confessions* is to just read the first nine Chapters, which (more or less) form the autobiographical portion of the book. This is the approach we're taking in this Guide. However, we should not forget that the last four Chapters, while not strictly autobiographical, were intended to be part of the complete work. They provide a more advanced example of what it is to read the Bible and to pray.

It is no coincidence that Augustine encounters Christ right at the center of the book. In fact, Augustine's reading of the "books of the Platonists," occurs right at the center of the Chapter (section thirteen), which, in turn, represents the literal center of the book. Augustine's reading of Plotinus is the key to Augustine's mystical encounters with Christ and is the precise center of the story.[4]

In Chapter Seven, we are also continuing our unravelling of the misplaced loves of 1 John 2.16. This time, the lust of the eyes is in focus. When Augustine sent away his girlfriend, we observed that this process of unravelling was by no means complete. After all, Augustine got engaged and then took on another concubine to satisfy his sexual needs. We'll have a similar experience in Chapter Seven. Augustine's intellectual problems may be largely answered, but his journey is not complete since he has not yet come into the Church. In fact, the largest difficulty of all – how to explain the Incarnation – still remains unresolved for him.

Yet Augustine's new-found ability to envision God in incorporeal terms helps him solve the problem of the lust of the eyes. This is one reason why the Platonists are so essential to Augustine's journey. This incorporeal conception of God also proves enormously helpful in providing an answer to the problem of why evil exists. As a result, his break from the Manichees becomes complete in Chapter Seven. This results in a full intellectual conversion to Christianity.

The Final Rejection of the Manichees

Augustine begins by noting that he had transitioned from a youth to being an adult (7.1.1). Despite this, he was still mired in beliefs that were not true. He knew God to be "incorruptible, imperishable and unchangeable," but could not figure out how to imagine him as an incorporeal substance. At this stage, Augustine was conceiving of God as something invisible like light or wind, not something truly incorporeal. If God is omnipresent, how could such an incorporeal substance take up space, he wondered? He saw God as taking up "infinite space" (*infinita spatia*) and "penetrating the whole mass of the world" (7.1.2). But this had to be wrong since a larger part of the world would then get more of God.

Augustine had figured out enough by this point to know that what the Manichees believed wasn't true. In part, he had his friend Nebridius to thank for this (7.2.3). The Manichees believed that there was a force of darkness which existed which was fighting against the light. Nebridius simply asked what would have happened if God had decided not to fight back against the darkness. Since, as a perfect being, nothing evil could injure God, this would mean that the dark substance would have no power. The Manichees had no way to reconcile this problem.

Moreover, how was Augustine supposed to answer why evil existed? After all, this was a chief reason why he had been attracted to the Manichees. Once Augustine turned to the question of the source of evil, he became convinced that Manichaean ideas were false (7.3.4). Augustine observed that it was our fallen wills that were the source of evil, an insight which forms the basis of Christian teaching on the problem of evil to this day (7.3.5). Augustine knew he existed because he could will things. He also surmised his will was the cause of sin. He couldn't blame evil on the Devil, since he had acted freely.

Augustine believes that God is incorruptible. After all, if God were corruptible, then it would be possible to attain something better than God, which Augustine knows to be nonsense. If God is incorruptible, this means, that "there is no way corruption can impair our God" (7.4.6). It follows that God can't be compelled to do something against his will. So if God made everything good, this means God could not be the source of evil, which results in the utter collapse of the Manichaean system.

Augustine has come to see that the Manichaean answer for the problem of evil didn't hold up. But this wasn't the only difficulty he found. He also turned his attention to astrology since this was a favorite practice of the Manichees (7.5.7). Remember, back in Chapter Four while Augustine was in Carthage and Thagaste, both Vindicianus and Nebridius had tried to get him to give up the practice of astrology, arguing that it was simply by chance that their predictions had come true. He had basically ignored their counsel.

But in Chapter Seven, another friend comes along, Firminus ("*Firm-in-us*"), who once and for all provided proof that the practice of astrology had nothing to offer. Firminus told a memorable story about his father who had the opportunity to observe the births of two children at exactly the same time. One child came from a slave girl, the other was Firminus himself (7.6.8). By the logic of the astrologists, since they were born at the same place and time, their destinies should have been the same. Yet the exact opposite occurred. Firminus saw his wealth increase as a nobleman while the salve girl remained in servitude and poverty her whole life. Thus the prediction of the horoscope was purely by chance (7.6.9).

Armed with this story, Augustine realized that he could have proved the error of astrology from the Bible. Jacob and Esau were twins, after all. They should have had the same destiny. Yet, by divine providence, the blessing of Isaac went to Jacob, not Esau (Gen 27), meaning that the younger son became a great patriarch while the oldest did not. Through this, Augustine observed it was God who has passed "just judgment" (*iusti iudicii*) on everything (7.6.10).

This leads Augustine to some core convictions. He believes God exists. Further, he believes God, who is judge, cares for humanity. Moreover, he believes Christ offers a way of salvation for humanity which ends in eternal life (7.7.11). These three items form the basis of his worldview – God exists; He cares; He redeems. His intellectual conversion was largely complete.

The Books of the Platonists

Augustine next turns to Neo-Platonist philosophy. Up to this point, Augustine had dealt with the problem of evil, coming to see it as a privation. To Augustine, evil is the absence of a thing, not a thing itself. I'm grateful to Philip Cary for pointing out that this is kind of like a hole in a shirt.[5] It exists and affects everything that was made. But the one who created the shirt did not make the hole; rather, it's a deprivation of what was made. The hole exists, but is not a thing in itself; it's the absence of something.

Augustine's first step is to purify his soul by ceasing to fix attention on external things. To Augustine, "images of corporeal things opposed his soul's return" (7.7.11). Said another way, if evil is in our hearts, it is blocking us from the contemplation of God. This unsettled state terribly troubled Augustine (7.8.12).

An unnamed person (likely Victorinus) translated the books of the Platonists from Greek into Latin which enabled Augustine to read them (7.9.13). What Augustine found is remarkable. He claims that by reading Plotinus and other Neoplatonic philosophers, he found the same thing as he would read in the prologue to John's Gospel – "In the beginning was the Word and the Word was with God and the Word was God" (John 1.1). The only thing – and it's a big thing – he didn't find was a reference to Christ. As we're going to observe throughout this Chapter, Augustine is saying that Plotinus revealed many things, but left out the most important thing, Christ. As I pointed out above, this act of reading the "books of the Platonists" is at the literal center of the *Confessions.*

Augustine also discovered part of the message of Philippians Two in the books of the Platonists as well (7.9.14). He discovered that Christ "took the form of a servant and emptied himself" (Phil 2.6-7). This is a key New Testament reference to the humility of Jesus' coming in his Incarnation. Augustine claims to find this message expressed in different words in Plotinus. Yet Plotinus missed any reference to Jesus' being God, meaning that he missed the entire story of redemption that Jesus brought. As such, the understanding of the Platonists is incomplete.

Moreover, the books of the Platonists hinted at Christ's participation in divine wisdom, but missed that he came to die for the ungodly (Rom 5.6). In fact, they missed the whole notion of the atonement which claims that God sent his son "for us all" (Rom 8.32). The facts of the Incarnation and the atonement of Christ are things which God has hidden from the wise, but has given to the humble (Matt 11.26-29). Thus the key thing Augustine has to learn is humility, something which had been sorely lacking in his years as a Manichee and as a rhetorician.

Augustine also discovered the message of Christ's pre-existence in the books of the Platonists. From before all time, Christ has eternally abided with the Father, which Augustine sees as a reference to the reception of "his fullness" in John 1.16. But, once again, the Platonists miss the most important part concerning redemption, that Christ "died for the impious (Rom 5.6) and that [the Father] did not spare his own son, but gave him up for us all" (Rom 8.32). Augustine summarizes his assertion that the Platonists understood part, but not all, of the Gospel by referencing Rom 1.21-23, charging the Platonists as being "fools."

Augustine also compares the incomplete assertions of the Platonists to the selling of Esau's birthright in Gen 25 for some "Egyptian food" (7.9.15).

The result was the inscrutable wisdom of God which fundamentally altered the order of things to make the older son (Esau) serve the younger (Jacob). Once again, the Platonists pointed in the right direction, but their conclusions were incomplete since they missed the point of the revelation.

The Mystical Vision

Augustine next realizes that the books of the Platonists are incomplete, but they have proved helpful because they pointed Augustine in the right direction. Augustine continues this theme by describing the first of his mystical experiences.

Plotinus had admonished Augustine to "return" into himself (7.10.16). We should not miss how influential this short statement is. Augustine understands the path to God as an interior journey through the soul which is enabled by God's grace. A mystical experience is a more vivid realization of our participation in the divine presence.

This interior journey, enabled by God, passes through several stages. Augustine turns inward and finds with the "eyes of the soul" an "immutable light" above his mind. This light was different than anything else. The light transcended Augustine's mind and was only known by love. God raised up Augustine to discover eternal truth and love. As Augustine puts it, what he saw was "being" (*esse*) itself. In other words, Augustine has been shown a real vision of the divine essence. He held this vision only briefly before the vision faded. At the moment of the vision, however, "there was no room for doubt" because he had seen God, pure being, with his mind's eye. Through this experience, Augustine became aware that his very existence was contingent because he was dependent on God for his creation (7.11.17). The issue for Augustine is the vision's fleeting character.

The Problem of Evil and Conversion

After this vision, Augustine suddenly becomes convinced about the problem of evil (7.12.18). He realizes that all things which God has created are good. Just because they were created good doesn't mean that they'll stay that way. In fact, if a created thing has no potential for corruption, it would no longer be a created thing – it would be God. Thus all things were created good, but if they are "deprived of good," they are deprived of parts of their being, just like the hole in the shirt. Hence

God, who created all things, could not be the author of evil. Evil is not a thing. It is literally "nothing."

For God, "there is no evil at all" (7.13.19). This means the Manichaean teaching that there were two cosmic forces at war with each other had to be wrong. There was no dark substance opposed to God. At this point, Augustine breaks into a confession of praise when he realizes that God could not be the author of evil. When Augustine "awakes" from his vision, he has discovered an infinite God who was good, an insight which he realizes could only have come from God himself (7.14.20).

To spend time attached to temporal, changing things is to focus on what is "finite" (*finita*), not what is infinite (7.15.21), another indication that something profound has occurred in this first vision. Coming back into himself he finds wickedness again, not just externally, but internally. However, Augustine's understanding has profoundly changed. Augustine discovers his perverse will is what has brought him down (7.16.22). Hence, sin is not some external force such as the Devil acting on a helpless agent. Rather, sin is a corrupted and misdirected will, which causes him to focus on misplaced loves which simply cannot satisfy him.

What was the result? Augustine discovered that he loved God and wanted to be in relationship with him. The sad part was that this desire wasn't stable because he was still weighed down by sin. As Augustine puts it, "I was snatched up to you by your beauty and then torn away from you by my own weight...by the weight of my sexual activity" (7.17.23).

He again encounters the remarkable assertion of Romans 1.20 – that although he is dragged down by temporal things, it is those same created things which testify to God's existence. Yet Augustine's interpretation of the situation has changed as he finds the "immutable and eternally real truth rose up over [his] mutable mind." The frustration is that Augustine now knows with some certainty what he is supposed to do (attach to that which is eternal), but finds himself unable to do it because of his flesh.

The Mystical Vision, Part II

Augustine then experiences the grace of a mystical experience a second time. This time, he is even clearer about what the steps of the experience were. He starts as he did before, turning inward and thus ascending from the body to the sensible soul where humans process external sensory information. He then ascended to the rational soul where the higher reason functions are accomplished. From there, he transcended reason by ascending to the "intellectual soul" where he again discovered light. This light enabled him to declare that the "unchangeable is in command of the changeable" (7.17.23). Lastly, the soul ascended to pure being. As Augustine describes it, "in the flash of a trembling glance, I came to 'that which is'" (*id quod est*). Augustine saw God's "invisible nature understood through the things which are made," the fourth reference in the Chapter to Rom 1.20. Through God's grace, Augustine has ascended to capture a vision of God with the eyes of the mind.

As before, however, Augustine does not possess the purity of heart and the strength to sustain the vision (7.18.24). Augustine quickly realizes he cannot attain this on his own, but is dependent on Christ. The problem is that Augustine is still not able to describe Christ well since he has not yet discovered an orthodox Christology. In essence, what Augustine needs is the humility to accept the Church's teaching on who Jesus is.

Christ the Mediator

So who is Jesus? At this point, Augustine admits that he did not yet understand the Incarnation and did not yet possess an orthodox conception of Christ. He thought of Jesus as someone having "excellent wisdom," an idea Augustine could have found in the philosophers of the day (7.19.25). Augustine moves past these philosophers to accept Jesus' virgin birth, but was still stuck on how the unchangeable, eternal Word took on human flesh. At this point, Augustine seems to be holding the heretical Christology of Photinus, who denied that Christ eternally existed and thus was "adopted" into the Godhead at some point.[6]

Augustine also brings Alypius back into the story to tell us that he held an expressly Apollinarian Christology wherein the flesh and the Godhead were pushed together into one person.[7] Said more simply, Apollinarians thought Christ had one nature, not two, meaning he wasn't really human. According to Augustine, Alypius' progress was even slower than his. The point is they both struggled to conceive of how Jesus could be both fully human and fully divine.

Augustine now sums up what he knows. He's convinced that God is infinite, that he exists and that he doesn't change (7.20.26). He's further convinced that all things came into existence through Christ. Because he doesn't yet hold to an orthodox conception of Christ, Augustine still needs to grow. Yet Augustine believes that all his struggles have occurred according to divine providence. Augustine had taken some giant steps forward, but still had some progress to make.

Augustine and Paul

Augustine's progress would proceed much more rapidly once he started reading the Bible and, in particular, the Apostle Paul closely. Remarkably, whereas Augustine used to think Paul contradicted himself and the rest of the Old Testament, his intellectual objections had vanished. This is yet another significant step which Augustine takes in Chapter Seven.

Augustine discovers that the things he had learned from Plotinus could be found in the Bible, albeit with a greater emphasis on God's grace (7.21.27). What Paul taught was true. His writings had led Augustine to a much fuller understanding of the truths which the Platonists espoused.

Of course, Augustine discovered that the books of the Platonists missed many things. There was no devotion, confession, redemption, salvation, repentance or humility. The Platonists pointed toward the true God, but in an opaque way. Augustine again concludes that God has hidden the fullness of the truth from the wise and disclosed it to the humble. In short, the Platonists were a means to an end, not an end in itself.

Focus Texts

There are three main areas which we will explore in this Section. The first is Augustine's reading of the books of the Platonists. The second is the description of Augustine's mystical vision which came after he read the books of the Platonists. Finally, we will explore Augustine's advance when he rejects the Manichees by discovering their solution to the problem of evil makes little sense.

Plotinus and His Influence

Thus far, we have seen Augustine encounter several thought systems. He spent almost ten years as a Manichaean proselyte. He also investigated Academic Skepticism, Epicureanism and Aristotelianism. None of these thought systems were able to help Augustine find the rest he was seeking. This changes when he reads the books of the Platonists. Why? Consider the following passage:

Focus Text 7A

> You first wanted to show me that God 'resists the proud, but gives grace to the humble' (1 Pet 5.5) and with what mercy you show the way of humility to men since 'your word became flesh and dwelt among men' (John 1.14). Through a certain man massively swollen with pride, you procured for me some books of the Platonists in Latin translation from the Greek language. Therein I read, of course not in the same words, but suggested by many of the very same multi-layered arguments, that 'in the beginning was the Word and the Word was with God and the Word was God. He was in the beginning with God. All things were made through him and without him nothing was made. In him was life and the life was the light of men; and the light shines in the darkness and the darkness could not comprehend it' (John 1.1-5). Furthermore, the human soul, even though it bears witness to the light, yet it is not that light, but God, the Word, is 'the true light' because 'he illuminates all men coming into this world.' Moreover, 'he was in this world and the world was made through him and the world did not recognize him.' However, that 'he came to his own and his own did not receive him, but as many as received him, to them he gave the power to become sons of God to those who believe in his name,' that I did not read there (John 1.7-12). Furthermore, I read there that God, the Word, 'was born not of flesh, nor of blood, nor of the will of men, nor of the will of the flesh, but of God' (John 1.13). But, that 'the word became flesh and dwelt among us,' that I did not read there (John 1.14). I detected in those books, expressed in various sayings and in multiple ways, that the Son, being 'in the form of the Father, did not consider it theft to be equal with God' since, by nature, he is just that. But that 'he emptied himself and took on the form of a servant and was made in the likeness of men, being found in human form' and that 'he humbled himself, becoming obedient unto death, even the death of a cross' (Phil 2.6-11)... these books did not contain such things (7.9.13-14).

Augustine does something remarkable in this passage. He reads the books of the Platonists and finds the truths of the Scriptures embedded therein. This might seem like a fantastic claim, which is why it is going to take some unpacking. Before we get there, what books did Augustine read? This is a favorite question of scholars and frankly one that no one has been able to answer with any reasonable degree of precision. The most probable answer is Augustine was not reading Plato himself, but was likely reading the Neo-Platonist philosopher Plotinus along with Plotinus' student and popularizer, Porphyry, in Latin translation.

Plotinus seems to be especially influential on Augustine, even if he spends most of his time pointing out the incompleteness of his ideas. To Plotinus, humans were never fully part of the material world – they kept one foot in it but had an eternal spiritual part which stood outside the world.[8] The soul, which, to the Neoplatonists, was eternal and uncreated, was designed to ascend to a higher realm of consciousness. This takes no external help on anybody's part to do, even if it is rarely accomplished. Rather, by purifying the soul through contemplation, the soul rises up and participates in the transcendent realm. So the soul is stuck in the physical body in this life, but its real home is elsewhere. Thus contemplation of "that which is eternal" is what enables the soul to ascend. Plotinus describes his own experience this way:

> *Oftentimes, I have been raised up out of the body, having ventured outside of all things, penetrating into myself, and inspecting closely such an unspeakable beauty. Being assured, above all, that I was of the better part, pursuing the noblest life, and having come to identify with the Divine, I was established in it and have come to that supreme energy above all else in the sphere of the intellect (4.8.1).*

We'll talk more about Augustine's own mystical vision below, but the important part here is that the Platonists had figured out many things. This might seem strange. Without divine revelation, how were they able to intuit anything true about God? Doesn't this go against the need for divine illumination which we discussed in Chapter Four?

What Augustine is telling us is that the Platonists knew quite a bit about God, even if they hadn't figured out that the *Logos* (the Word) was an eternal person. Think about that for a minute – Augustine is claiming that some Greek Philosophers *reasoned* their way to knowing something true about God. Some might find that absurd, but I believe it is something that Augustine and other early Christians believed. It tells us that reason can be a very powerful instrument for discovering what is true. The problem is that it's also an imperfect instrument and a thus it's a rare thing to reason this well.

This is why Thomas Aquinas, in the very first part of the *Summa Theologiae*, discusses the interaction of Scripture and reason. He asks if reason is fully treated in philosophy, why do we need revelation? After all, both Plato and Plotinus seemed to get pretty far just using reason. His answer is as follows:

> *In order that the salvation of men might be brought about more fitly and more surely, it was necessary that [humans] should be taught divine truths by divine revelation.*[9]

Said differently, what the Platonists did with reason was remarkable, but was not something that could be expected of most people. We need reason to understand the revelation God has given us in Scripture. The Platonists may not have known Christ (which, as we'll see, is a huge problem), but they discovered the *Logos* (or the Word) of John 1. The *Logos*, which Christians took to be Christ but could also mean "reason," was special because it was uncreated and eternal, quite unlike a spoken word which quickly fades away. In fact, to the Greek philosophers the *Logos* was the same as eternal forms.

What do I mean by that? What are eternal forms? Put simply, the forms are divine ideas which act as archetypes for things or ideas in the world. These eternal ideas account for the unity which exists between incorporeal and material things. For example, an idea like justice on earth is always imperfect. According to Plato, earthly justice participates in a perfect form of justice which is elsewhere. If all this sounds a little strange, it is because the modern world has done everything possible to rid itself of this way of thinking. We much prefer to reduce things so we can see, categorize and manipulate them. Plato is inviting us to something greater, something otherworldly, something mystical.

Note that Augustine had no problem suggesting that our immaterial souls must participate in a greater, invisible reality. All Plato's theory of the forms is trying to do is to explain how unchangeable, perfect realities in heaven can interact with changeable, imperfect realities on earth. Put simply, the forms are perfect, timeless, unchanging ideas in the mind of God. For Augustine, there is such a thing as objective truth because of the existence of these archetypes.

Notice how Augustine begins Focus Text 7A. He begins it by noting that "God resists the proud, but gives grace to the humble" (1 Pet 5.5). It takes some humility to believe that your sensory experience is not all there is! Isn't this, at its root, what it is to be a Christian? Don't Christians believe in realities they can't see?

This is how reading the books of the Platonists gave Augustine humility and brought him into the Christian fold. As we've seen, a central problem for Augustine is that he's puffed up with pride. He was a great student who became a great rhetorician. Yet what Augustine was realizing – and what we all need to realize – is that learning is impossible without humility. Unless we recognize our own ignorance, it becomes very difficult to learn anything.

But let's admit that the books of the Platonists would seem an odd place to find humility. Augustine himself tells us that Plato (or perhaps his later followers) was suffering from monstrous pride. After all, the Platonists were simply speculating on the soul and why it longs for something greater than itself. Isn't this where Augustine began the *Confessions*? Right at the beginning of the book, Augustine asked this key question:

> *But who calls upon you who does not know you? For the one who does not know you might call upon another instead of you (1.1.1).*

Augustine was trying to find God. But he knew so little about God and was so completely lost in his pride, he found it impossible to find rest in God.

This is where the Platonists made their contribution. They provided Augustine with a framework for a transcendent reality. They taught him that the innate desire he felt for something eternal was perfectly natural. His soul kept trying to ascend, but his unhealthy fixation with the temporal things of the world prevented him from rising up and finding rest.

As we've seen, Augustine has been unhappy throughout the *Confessions*, but now he knows why. Tethered to earthly things, he cannot find rest. Augustine realizes that by untethering himself from earthly things, his soul can find rest by returning to God.

Augustine takes this idea much farther than the Platonists do when he comes to realize that Christ is the *Logos*, the source of the divine ideas, and the very same reason contained in the books of the Platonists. Remarkably, Augustine and the Platonists have been talking about the same things using different language! Augustine can finally find happiness because he has figured out where truth resides. Etienne Gilson puts it well:

The knowledge of truth may be essential to happiness, but in Augustine truth is pursued only because truth alone can make him happy, and it is pursued only to the extent that it can make him so.[10]

The Platonists have only gotten Augustine so far. They do not know Christ and this omission is ultimately fatal for their understanding. All that was left for Augustine to do was to connect the dots between what he had heard from Ambrose and what the Neo-Platonist books had taught him about spiritual ascent. That connection resulted in his coming to realize the wisdom of the philosophers was the *Logos* of John 1. Wisdom was Christ, who was Truth personified. Augustine had taken a leap forward in his struggle to find rest.

Help has come, by means of the grace of God. God sent the books of the Platonists to Augustine so that he might become humble enough to understand the Scriptures. The central point is Augustine was unable to ascend alone – he needed divine assistance. He received it in abundance through the preaching of Ambrose and the books of the Platonists.

Questions for Reflection

1. The project of modernity is inherently reductionist. We categorize and control our world. Talk about ways that our perception of control is an illusion.
2. Does it disturb you that truth might reside in philosophy? What does this say about how the Holy Spirit works?
3. What do you think about other religions? Is the Holy Spirit at work in Islam, Judaism and Hinduism? Why or Why not?
4. Augustine finds truth in non-Christian fields and sources. Has that been true for you?
5. Why is the Incarnation important for Augustine? Is it for you?

Augustine's Mystical Visions

Now we come to what I believe is one of the real high points of the *Confessions*. I have been trying to suggest throughout this Guide that Augustine is involved in a long process of conversion. This process will not be completed until he is resurrected from the dead. Even when Augustine gets to heaven, he will still be in a process of development, albeit one very different than what he has been experiencing on earth.

Augustine's search for God takes a step forward once he encounters "that which is" directly. It's a fleeting experience since he is still weighed down by sin. Nevertheless, Augustine directly experiences the presence of God. The result is that his intellectual objections to Christianity and to the Scriptures melt away. Augustine may not understand everything about Christian orthodoxy – particularly with regard to the Incarnation – but his turn toward Christ becomes much more concrete.

Let me admit that not everyone reads the text this way. Some have been uncomfortable with the idea that Augustine could turn without a dramatic point-in-time conversion experience and without the Church. These are reasonable objections, especially since Christians in Augustine's day believed the laying on of hands at baptism actually brought the Spirit into one's life.[11] The problem with this reading, in my opinion, is that it tries to pinpoint conversion to a particular point in time. I don't think this is Augustine's understanding in the *Confessions*.

Readers who try to figure out just when Augustine was converted are asking the wrong question, in my opinion. As I mentioned, there's evidence that Augustine may have started his conversion way back in the first Chapter when he was first made a catechumen in the Church and requested baptism. It's not about *when* Augustine decides to drop his objections to the Christian faith; it's about *how* he encounters the very presence of God by grace. Ultimately, Augustine turns towards God and away from sin which is what the on-going process of conversion entails. I like how Jose Reta describes this process:

> *Pagan philosophers place conversion's goal in the return of oneself, as the path to reaching transformation in the "One"; Christian conversion is the return to God, the Supreme Good, from which the soul has distanced itself through sin. However, this 'return to self' is also a return to God, from whom disobedience and sin have caused such distance.[12]*

Hence Augustine still has more conversions to undergo. Make no mistake Augustine takes a big step toward Christ and the Church here. But the mystical visions of Chapter Seven represent *one* of his many conversions. Its implications are so profound that it will change Augustine's life forever. Let's look at how Augustine describes what he encountered:

Focus Text 7B

So I was amazed that I was already loving you, not as a phantasm in your stead, and not steadfast in the enjoyment of my God. But I was snatched up to you by your beauty and then torn away from you by my own weight, sinking down with a sigh into lower things by the weight of my sexual activity. But staying with me was the memory of you. I harbored no doubt that you were the one I was to be bound to, while not yet being bound since 'a corrupted body oppresses the soul and the earthly tent weighs down upon many things' (Wis 9.15). My greatest certainty was that 'from the creation of the world, your invisible nature is clearly seen, being understood by the things that are made, even your everlasting power and divinity' (Rom 1.20). I was searching for why I so admired the beauty of bodies, whether heavenly or earthly, and what it was that enabled me to judge soundly about mutable things so I could say, 'this ought be so and that not so.' I made an enquiry into this, trying to find out how I judged, and seeing that I did so judge, I discovered that immutable and eternally real truth rose over my mutable mind. And thus little by little did I ascend, from the realm of bodies to the soul which uses the bodily senses for perceiving and which conveys sensations exterior to the body. Such are the limits of the capabilities of beasts. From there, I came to the reasoning faculty by which the senses of the body are judged. I discovered that this was also mutable within me, raising itself up to its own understanding and directing my thoughts away from the power of habit. It withdrew itself from the tumult of phantasms so that it might come upon the light with which it was splattered (making known in no uncertain terms that the unchangeable is in command of the changeable). Then, in a thrust (*ictu*) of trembling contemplation, I came to 'That Which Is' (*id quod est*). Right then, I saw 'your invisible nature understood by the things that are made' (Rom 1.20), but I did not have sufficient strength to fix my glance. Because of my weakness, I was made to go back and I returned to my normal state. Within me was only a dear memory and a desire to consume what I only got a whiff of (7.17.23).

Augustine begins by noting, to his surprise, that he already loved God. Apparently, he didn't rationally wake up one day and "decide" to love God; his ability to do so was a gift. The problem was that his love was unstable, weighed down by his "sexual activity" (*conseutudo carnalis*). I'm not going to comment on it here, but the need for Augustine to rid himself of his constant need for sexual gratification is going to be a major theme in the next Chapter. For his soul to live in communion with God, Augustine is going to have to purify himself of lust, the sin which has been hindering him the most.

What Augustine does next is to describe the steps of ascent which his soul made to come into the presence of God. These steps are not something which Augustine invented. Rather, he borrows them from Plotinus. However – and this is very important – Augustine evidences a Christianized take on Plotinus. Whereas the Platonists believed that one's soul could rise up and unite with "the One" unaided, Augustine thinks this is impossible. Moreover, Plotinus would never have seen a vision of God as fleeting and impeded by sin.[13] By contrast, Augustine understands that a vision of God is a gift. We cannot ascend to God apart from his grace.

Yet Augustine and Plotinus share much in common. The most important thing that Augustine takes from Plotinus is the idea that the ascent to God is an intellectual one. What do I mean by that? An intellectual vision "sees" that which cannot be seen. If we desire to see God, this is obviously impossible to do with human eyes since God is invisible right now. Rather, the ascent to God happens internally when the eyes of the mind transcend the soul and are enabled, through an act of grace, to catch a vision of God. To both Plotinus and Augustine the soul desires to participate fully in a mystical vision, a real sense of the presence of God. This is what Augustine has been talking about when he says the soul seeks its rest in God.

The soul which has ascended finds that its true home is with God, not in the material realm. This does not mean that the material realm is bad; it simply means that abiding in God and participating in the divine nature are far better. This is why I have been claiming throughout this Guide that the climax of the earthly spiritual life is a spiritual vision of God.

I also want to emphasize that Augustine's Christian interpretation of Plotinus is not just retrospective.[14] Augustine is not looking back on this event and imposing a later understanding on it. Instead, I think this is how he really read Plotinus at this point in his life. This detail is crucial for my conclusion that Augustine is acting and reasoning as a Christian in Chapter Seven. In other words, Augustine was thinking Christianly before he came into the Church, before he was baptized and before the famous garden scene of Chapter Eight.[15] I can only conclude that the reason for this is he is an incomplete Christian. Augustine is weighed down by lust, and does not understand the Incarnation. He is awaiting baptism, Christian instruction in the sacramental mysteries and entry into the Church. Said another way, there's still a lot of progress for him to make.

What was his mystical encounter like? Augustine starts by ascending from the body to the soul. He moves from that which is material and visible to that which is incorporeal and invisible. Said another way, he starts this experience by turning inward in a state of contemplation. To Augustine, the only way the soul can ascend to God is for it to turn away from earthly things. This is why Augustine has become disillusioned with his fixation on things in the world. These corporeal things have impeded his spiritual ascent.

Augustine describes next that he ascended to the "reasoning faculty." This represents the rational part of the soul which is the part which separates humans from animals. Unlike lower life forms, humans can engage in higher reasoning, a fact which has proved essential for Augustine's use of the books of the Platonists thus far. This reasoning faculty is shared by all humans, but still represents a very changeable reality. Augustine is after something greater – he wants to participate in that which is unchangeable.

Augustine next ascends to the realm of intelligence. This is what I have been describing as the "mind's eye," but is technically called the intelligible soul. The intelligible soul can see visible things invisibly. For example, we employ memory to "see" places we have been in the past even if we're not presently there. Such places are not things that we see with our physical eyes, but we catch an intellectual vision of something we have physically seen before.

The problem is Augustine's soul is still seeking the God who can't be seen. This is the next step on Augustine's ladder of ascent. This last step is seeing "that which is" (*id quod est*) or pure being. Unlike humans, God's being has nothing contingent – it depends on nothing else for its existence. By contrast, all created entities depend on something else – God – for their existence. God only depends on himself and thus stands separate from created things.[16] The technical term for God's lack of contingency is "aseity." This literally means that God is "from himself." As an uncreated being, he depends on nothing external to himself for his existence.

We shouldn't miss the allusion to the Exodus story here. After Moses encounters God in the burning bush and God calls Moses to a mission for him, Moses asks God how he should answer when the Israelites inevitably ask what the name of God is. God famously responds to Moses, "I Am who I Am." God reveals himself to Moses as pure being. Thus when Augustine says that he saw "I Am," this means he encountered the "ground of being" itself. Just as Moses was sent on a mission to call the Israelites out of darkness, God will also call Augustine to do something analogous as a Bishop in the Church.

Note how this dovetails with Augustine's discussion of John One from Focus Text 7A. When Augustine encounters the *logos* in the books of the Platonists, he believes they are talking about the uncreated word. The uncreated word – the *logos* – is being itself. Augustine has caught an intellectual vision of Christ who was revealed in the Bible as the Word.

This is also why Augustine's repetition of Romans 1.20 is so important to this vision. Paul writes that God's "invisible nature" is able to be seen by the things which are made. In context, Paul is proclaiming that God's creation testifies to the creator. Augustine has simply taken this a step further and asserted that as a created being, he has been enabled to see God.

At this point, you might wonder how it is than anyone can see God? Did not God say to Moses later in the book of Exodus, "You cannot see my face, for man shall not see me and live" (Ex 33.20)? Augustine addresses this difficulty in a letter he wrote about fifteen years later in response to Paulina who asked whether it was possible to see God with bodily eyes. Augustine's basic answer is that it is possible, but it's the eyes of the mind which can see God, not the eyes of the flesh. Here's how Augustine puts it:

> *Now, however, you pressed me for an explanation about something difficult to explain. Recalling what was said, pay careful attention to see whether I have explained it. So, if you ask, 'is it possible for God to be seen?' I respond: 'It is possible.' If you ask how I know this, I respond, 'since it is found in the Scriptures, which speak the truth, 'blessed are the pure in heart, for they shall see God' (Matt 5.8) and other similar passages. If you ask, how was he invisible if he can be seen, I respond, he is invisible by nature, but is seen with his will and as his will. In fact, he was seen by most not as he is, but in the kind of form he was pleased to take on…So, 'the Lord is Spirit' (John 4.24), and thus 'the one who clings to the Lord is one spirit [with him]' (1 Cor 6.17). As a result, if one can see God invisibly, then one can cleave to God incorporeally (147.15).*

This quote represents Augustine's mature thinking, but I think we can already find hints of it in the *Confessions*. The point is that seeing God is possible for those who are pure in heart. Can we make the claim that anyone is pure in heart? For most, such a claim is difficult to sustain. This is why Augustine's mystical vision of God has to be a gift. It's also why the vision does not sustain. Yet by withdrawing from the world into the soul and by ascending to "that which is," Augustine has glimpsed the divine nature. He was utterly transformed by the experience and his life would never be the same.

Questions for Reflection

1. Contemplation on the words of Scripture has been a Spiritual Discipline for centuries. Is this something you practice?
2. Have you experienced God's presence in an especially real way?
3. Augustine understands his mystical vision happened by grace. What does this mean?
4. If conversion is a process that is completed at our resurrection, how does that affect your life?
5. Many claim to have had experiences with God. How can we tell if such experiences are distinctively Christian?

Christ, The Problem of Evil and The Gospel

One of the major strides forward which Augustine makes in Chapter Seven is his final rejection of the Manichees. For several Chapters, Augustine has become less and less convinced about their truth claims. Chapter Seven represents the final nail in the coffin. He becomes a convinced anti-Manichaean after this point.

Although the discussion of this in the *Confessions* comes before the prior two Focus Texts, I have waited until now to discuss it because I want to show how it ties to Augustine's discovery of the real presence of God. We saw in Focus Text 7B, Augustine has an encounter with "that which is." This is a reference to the divine name, "I Am." Just like Moses, Augustine had a direct encounter with God before being sent on a mission.

What I did not discuss in the preceding section was how this discovery of "that which is" makes the Manichaean beliefs impossible. Remember, the Manichees believed that there were two opposing forces at work in the universe – the kingdom of light was allied against the kingdom of darkness. According to the Manichees, there exists an evil substance which is fighting as hard as it can against the good. This dualistic explanation of why evil exists in the world sounded pretty convincing until Augustine encounters a God who is infinite, but also simple in substance. In other words, there were not two gods at war with each other. Rather, everything was contingent on God. Since God had created everything good, evil could not be a substance opposed to God.

Augustine became convinced that God was not the author of evil, but man's twisted will was. It's his discovery that evil is not a substance, but the absence of good, that precipitates his mystical experience. Consider the following:

Focus Text 7C

> Now, then, you had released me from those fetters, and I was trying to find out where evil came from but found no solution. But you did not permit any flux of thought to snatch me away from the faith which I accepted as true, that you exist and are an unchangeable substance and that you care for men and judge us. Further, in Christ, your Son, our Lord, and also in the Holy Scriptures entrusted to the authority of your Catholic Church, you have set the way of man's salvation for that life which is to come after death. These things were safely and immovably settled in my mind, as I was ardently trying to answer where evil came from. Such were the tormented birth pangs of my heart, and O what grief, my God! Your ears where right there, though I was unaware of it (7.7.11).

Augustine starts to gain some certainty on the problem of evil, a relatively new event in the *Confessions*. It seems like every Chapter has Augustine trying out a different thought system or approach to life. Once he throws off the chains of the Manichees once and for all, however, things start to become clearer.

What did he discover? First, Augustine doesn't doubt God exists. This was hardly novel for his day. As in our lifetimes, most believe that God exists. But Augustine goes further and describes God as an "unchangeable substance." If God really exists and doesn't change, this lays the groundwork for the idea that God isn't made up of two opposing substances. If he were, this would mean that God would be constantly in flux, since the opposing substances would be working against each other.

Secondly, Augustine notes that God "cared" for humanity. This belief in God's providence makes the Manichaean conception of God impossible.

After all, if God is made, in part, of an evil substance which is wreaking havoc upon the world, Augustine could not have observed God's care for the world.

Notice how all this is coming full circle. Right on the first page of the *Confessions*, we learned that without God, Augustine himself would lack something essential to his being. If evil is the absence of good, then to lack God's indwelling presence is to be mired in a state of privation. Those lacking God's presence might exist bodily. They might also have souls. They just lack completeness since they lack God.

God cares for all of humanity through his providential grace. As Jesus puts it in the Sermon on the Mount, the Father "makes his sun rise on the evil and on the good" (Matt 5.45). God cares for all of humanity providentially. Yet he cares in different ways for those he indwells. When Augustine repeats that "God resists the proud, but gives grace to the humble," (1 Pet 5.5) this is, in part, what he is indicating. Ultimately, God is present as the judge of humanity. God's resistance of the proud is manifested in his judgment.

What Augustine is telling us is that he has discovered the Gospel. He has discovered that Christ is the way to salvation which ends in eternal life. Augustine has been humbled when he realizes his only hope for salvation is Christ. The books of the Platonists may have taught him how to ascend through contemplation, but only Christ can provide him with the rest he has been seeking.

In short, Augustine's intellectual objections are over. Augustine may not fully be able to articulate an orthodox conception of Christ, but he has met Him. Augustine, in rejecting the Manichees, has embraced the Gospel and taken a big step toward his ultimate homecoming.

Questions for Reflection
1. If someone asked you to articulate the Gospel, how would you explain it?
2. What is humility? Describe someone you know who you consider to be genuinely humble. What is he/she like?
3. Paul says in Romans 1 that he "is not ashamed of the Gospel of Jesus Christ." Are you? What prevents you from being more active in Evangelism?
4. Christians believe that evil is an absence of a thing rather than a thing in itself. Does this help explain why bad things happen to good people?

CHAPTER EIGHT

AUGUSTINE TAKES UP AND READS

Introduction

If Chapter Seven represents a significant intellectual high point in Augustine's story, Chapter Eight represents the emotional high point of the book. Once again, it's a sight to behold. When people think about the *Confessions,* they often think about Augustine's conversion in a garden, which many think happens here.

Of course, by now, you're probably aware that the popular view that Augustine converts to Christianity suddenly after reading a passage from the book of Romans is a difficult position to sustain. As we've seen, Augustine has many conversions throughout the *Confessions.* He's been trying to show that conversion is a process of intellectual, moral and spiritual reformation that continues throughout one's life, culminating in one's resurrection.

A very real turn takes place in Chapter Eight – it's just not what most people think. What I will try to show is that Augustine's turn in Chapter Eight – his "conversion"– is to celibacy. After encountering several different conversion stories, he makes a decision to never have sex again, a state which I'll refer to throughout this Chapter as "continence."

Not have sex again? I know this might sound strange, but it's the obvious conclusion we'll have to draw if we read the text closely. You'll see that Augustine deliberately brings continence to life. He ends his engagement and commits to live a celibate life.

But why would he do such a thing? By this point, it shouldn't be too surprising. As we saw in Chapter Seven, Augustine encountered "that which is," but the vision did not sustain very long because he was weighed down by his attachment to fleshly lusts. Augustine, after experiencing God, wanted more. He realized that lust was the thing holding him back from experiencing a more perfect union with God.

In fact, we should probably see Chapter Eight as the logical response to the brevity of the mystical experience of Chapter Seven. Augustine told us in Chapter Seven that he was not able to sustain the vision since his sin kept his soul from ascending. He caught a brief glimpse of God, but it did not last very long. So it's natural that Augustine would want to remove the thing that was impeding his soul's ascent.

As such, Chapter Eight is really about the work of moral reformation Augustine undergoes between the mystical visions of Chapters Seven and Nine. This moral reformation represents a turn in his will, done in cooperation with the power of grace. In other words, the central point of Chapter Eight isn't his conversion to Christianity; it's about experiencing God, who is immanent in his creation.

Augustine was hardly alone in making the decision to be celibate. In late fourth century Italy, virginity was thought to represent a significantly elevated spiritual state. This is why Ambrose demanded that all his clergy in Milan remain celibate, even if they were married. Married couples who were not ordained were also frequently pledging to live in a state of continence. We'll see this in several of the examples Augustine provides in the lead up to the famous garden scene. Why this occurs is a question I'll try and answer over the course of the Chapter.

Hence Chapter Eight is ultimately about Augustine's turn from sexual sin and his embrace of a life of continence. In his continuing use of Scripture, we'll notice the return of the story of the Prodigal Son and the reversal of the fall described in Genesis Three. We find Augustine (1) confessing his sins, (2) confessing praise to God through prayer and (3) making a confession of faith. The only thing missing is his formal coming into the Church through baptism, which will happen in the next Chapter.

One thing to notice is Augustine begins Chapter Eight telling us that he had no more intellectual doubts. He no longer feared about eternal life. He knew Christianity was true. How did he know that? He knew it because he had encountered God directly, much as Paul did on the road to Damascus. Augustine had already turned intellectually. In response to the vision of Chapter Seven, Augustine takes several positive steps to purify his soul because he knows that, according to Jesus, only the "pure in heart" could see God. This is why Chapter Eight centers on the turn in Augustine's will.

In Chapter Eight, we also observe the final unravelling of Augustine's misplaced loves. In Chapter Six, Augustine started to reverse the "lust of the flesh" by sending away his girlfriend. In the last Chapter, Augustine reversed the "lust of the eyes" by finally rejecting the Manichees and by realizing it was his mind's eye which would see God. In this Chapter, he reverses the "pride of life," when he starts to devote himself full-time to the pursuit of Christ, wisdom and celibacy. We should see Chapter Eight as the final reversal of Augustine's unruly will from Chapter Two when he stole the pears along with his ruffian friends.[1]

Summary

Chapter Eight divides neatly into three main sections. The first two sections describe various vignettes in which the protagonists turn to Christianity, often by taking a pledge of celibacy. We'll see this first with Victorinus ("*Victor-eye-nus*"), one of the most famous intellectuals of his day. In a different way, we'll encounter this through a brief reference to the Apostle Paul and his famous conversion in Acts 13. Paul encounters Christ on the Damascus road, leads a celibate life, ceases to persecute the Church, and becomes one of its greatest evangelists. We'll also see this in Pontichianus' ("*Pon-tick-ee-ahn-us*") description of Antony, the first famous monk, who gave away everything he owned, moved to the desert and conducted spiritual warfare through prayer, fasting and celibacy. Finally, we will see this through Pontichianus' friends who, upon reading about the life of Antony decide to give up their careers, and, together with their fiancées, dedicate themselves to a life of celibacy. Given these examples, we can see the clear thrust of the Chapter is about the humility that comes from celibacy. Just as Antony humbled himself, gave up his wealth, committed to celibacy and did great things, Augustine would seek to emulate his example.

The third section of the Chapter, however, is the most famous. After being deeply moved by the story of Antony, Augustine is in a garden adjacent his house with his friend Alypius. Augustine's descriptions of his inner turmoil are dramatic. After hearing a child continuously chant "*tolle lege*" (which he understands to mean "take up and read"), Augustine opens to Romans 13, reads a passage and decides to convert to celibacy, just as Pontichianus' friends, Antony and Paul had done. This so-called garden scene is one of the most famous passages in all Christian literature.

Simplicianus and Victorinus

Augustine begins by quoting verses from four different Psalms in praise to God. He then claims "Concerning your eternal life I was certain (*certus*)... all doubt had removed from me that there was an imperishable substance from which every other substance derives its nature" (8.1.1). Having encountered Christ, Augustine desired to become "more stable" in Him. The problem was Augustine found himself reluctant to give up everything and follow Christ.

Augustine admits that he was disgusted with his worldliness (*saeculo*) and that his old zeal for financial gain and public adulation had vanished (8.1.2). Yet Augustine's central problem was he still "steadfastly enthralled by a woman" (*ex femina*). Said differently, his fleshly lusts were still weighing him down. This seemed tragic because he had met the incarnate Christ of John 1 in the last Chapter, but his sexual lust kept his soul from ascending. In Biblical terms, Augustine had discovered the pearl of great price (Matt 13.46); but, he was hesitant to give up everything, particularly his sexual habit.

Augustine went to visit Simplicianus ("*Sim-plick-ee-ahn-us*"), who was Ambrose's teacher, baptizer and counselor (8.2.3). Augustine describes Simplicianus as "a deeply learned old man" with knowledge of "all the liberal arts." Augustine was seeking advice about what to do about his unsettled state. Augustine mentioned he had "read some books of the Platonists" which had been translated into Latin by Victorinus ("*Victor-eye-nus*"). Augustine's reading delighted Simplicianus (8.2.3).

Simplicanus then went on to describe Victorinus' conversion. Victorinus, born about fifty years before Augustine, was a famous Neoplatonist philosopher.[2] He was so famous that he was the recipient of a statue in the Roman forum.[3] Like most Romans, Victorinus had been an ardent worshipper of the gods of the Roman pantheon and had vigorously defended the pagan practice (8.2.4). Almost out of the blue, Victorinus embraced Christianity and was baptized. Victorinus did this after making a careful investigation of the Christian Scriptures, concluding that Neoplatonist philosophy and the Bible were talking about the same God.

One day, when they were together, Victorinus admitted to Simplicanus that he had become a Christian. Simplicanus challenged this assertion since Victorinus had not presented himself for baptism in the Church. Victorinus deflected this challenge by asking "Then do walls make Christians?" At the root of his deflection was his concern that a public confession of faith, which baptism usually entailed, would embarrass his philosopher friends. As he continued to read the Bible, Victorinus became concerned that "he would be "refused" by Christ "in the presence of the holy angels" (Luke 12.9). His concern led him to seek a proper Christian baptism.

He said to Simplicianus, "Let's go to Church; I wish to be made (*volo fieri*) a Christian," a statement which filled Simplicianus with joy. So Victorinus, one of the best minds in the Roman Empire, went to the Church to be catechized and, in time, baptized.

It was standard practice to allow one who was embarrassed or had public stature to confess the Apostles Creed and be baptized privately.[4] The details of why this option was standard practice are somewhat unclear from the available literature, but we can surmise this was a practice the Church developed during its years of periodic persecution when making a public profession of faith could have imperiled one's life. It was also perhaps an expression of mercy to those who were too shy to address a large, boisterous audience. Nevertheless, Victorinus waved off this option and, from an elevated platform, made a public confession.

Augustine makes it a point to tell us that "there was no salvation in the rhetoric which he was teaching" (8.2.5). When the gathered congregation saw the famous Victorinus ascending the platform to make his confession, a great murmuring came over the crowd. They started chanting "Victorinus, Victorinus!" in unison, so overjoyed were they that one who had publicly opposed Christianity had embraced it. Victorinus then proceeded to "announce his truth faith with splendid boldness."

Augustine next recounts two parables to make the point that what had just happened with Victorinus was exactly what the Scriptures had predicted. The first was from the parable of the lost sheep (Luke 15.6) when Jesus says that there is more rejoicing "over one who repents than over ninety-nine just persons who need no repentance" (8.3.6). The second was a reference in the same Chapter of Luke to the Prodigal Son "who was dead and is alive again, was lost and has been found" (Luke 15.32). The homecoming of both brings rejoicing and humility.

Augustine then ponders why it is that the soul takes more pleasure in something found anew than it does in something which it has always possessed (8.3.7). He proceeds to provide six examples of how this is the case, everything from (i) an emperor's victory in war, (ii) to surviving a storm at sea, (iii) to becoming well after a lengthy illness, (iv) to the pleasure of eating when one is hungry, (v) to the habits of drunkards and finally (vi) to an engagement period which delays the consummation of a wedding, thus heightening its pleasure. All of these increase the exhilaration of what comes afterwards.

Augustine especially observes this phenomenon in the one who "was dead and is alive again, was lost and has been found" (8.3.8), an obvious allusion to the Prodigal Son. This is also what Victorinus had done in submitting himself for baptism. He had found the humility to come into the Church. Augustine repeats the reference to remind us that, ultimately, he is the Prodigal Son who needs to humble himself and come home. Augustine tells us about Victorinus' integrity by recounting that Victorinus left his post as a famous rhetorician when the Emperor Julian later passed an edict no longer allowing Christians to teach. In short, his confession was genuine.

Augustine also briefly mentions the Apostle Paul as another example of the humility involved in embracing Christianity. Augustine noted God has chosen the "ignoble" and "contemptible" things of the world, a reference to 1 Cor 1.27 (8.4.9). Paul, one of the greatest persecutors of the Church, was humbled on the Damascus road and became a great missionary. By citing Paul's conversion, Augustine was claiming a link to his story.

What was Augustine's reaction to all this? He ardently wanted to follow Victorinus. But he was still held back by the "irons" which kept him prisoner (8.5.10). This is a reference to his corrupted will and, ultimately, his sexual habit. Augustine describes it this way, "So my two wills, the one old, the other new, the one carnal, the other spiritual, were in conflict within me and in their discord, they undid my soul." Since Augustine had accepted the truth of Christ, he could no longer fall back on his excuse of being uncertain. He was simply afraid of what a life of continence might entail (8.5.11). Augustine knows that the love of Christ is better than his lust, but was having trouble taking the next step forward (8.5.12). It was lust which was holding him back.

Augustine recounts that God eventually delivered him from the "bond of sexual pleasure" (8.6.13). The rest of the Chapter is largely a depiction of how this occurred. Augustine mentions he went to Church a lot, but also surrounded himself with like-minded friends who lived in a community with him. Chief among these friends was Alypius ("A-lip-ee-us"), employed at this point as a lawyer, Nebridius ("Neb-rid-ee-us"), who we met in Chapter Four, and Verecundus ("Ver-eh-kun-dus"), a literature professor in Milan. All of them, but especially Nebridius, were seeking to devote themselves to "reading or listening to wisdom," a statement which indicates they were giving themselves to philosophy.

Ponticianus and Antony

One day, Augustine received a surprise visit from Ponticianus. Ponticianus was a fellow African, who held an important position in the Imperial Court. During the ensuing conversation, Ponticianus noticed a book lying open on an adjacent gaming table. Expecting to find a book on literature, Ponticianus was surprised to find that it was the Bible. Since Ponticianus was a baptized Christian, this both amazed him and brought him joy.

Augustine tell us that Ponticianus "often prostrated (*prosternebatur*) himself before God at Church in repeated and continuous prayer" (8.6.14), an obvious sign of his humility before God. Ponticianus proceeded to tell Alypius and Augustine about Antony, a famous Egyptian monk. Despite his fame in Christian circles, neither Alypius nor Augustine had heard of him before Ponticianus told the story.

Ponticianus recounted the story of Antony to Alypius and Augustine. They were both moved by what they heard. Ponticianus went on to describe the development of the monastic movement. Again, both Augustine and Alypius were unaware of these developments. In fact, Ambrose had even founded a monastery outside Milan, which was news to both Augustine and Alypius.

Ponticianus himself had become familiar with Antony through some colleagues of his while he was in an administrative position in Trier (in modern-day Germany and the place where Ambrose spent his early childhood). Ponticianus' friends wandered off on a walk one day and came upon a house where they were discovered *The Life of Antony*, a book written by Athanasius. The book recounted Antony's pursuit of a monastic vocation in Egypt. One of the friends read parts of it and "was in awe and enflamed." During his reading, he began to think of leaving his civil service job and following Antony's example. (8.6.15). He thought about his goals in life and realized the path Antony had pursued was a higher calling than service to the Emperor. Right then, he "shifted inwardly," and "his mind was stripped of the things of the world." The word "stripped" (*exuebatur*) here carries the idea of being undressed, an image of reversing the sexual tension which was dominating his life.

Both of Ponticianus' friends thus came to leave their governmental jobs and turned to serve God. Remarkably (and tellingly for the times), since the friends were both engaged to be married, their fiancées also decided to dedicate to their lives and their virginity to God. Ponticianus notes that he wept since he was not ready to take this step of renunciation.

What was Augustine's reaction? He starts alluding to the Psalms (Ps 50.21). But, then he launches into a review of his own life, which appalled him (8.7.16). Augustine's language is very strong, describing himself as "crooked and defiled, disreputable and ulcerous." As disgusted with himself as Augustine was, he simply put it out of his mind and deflected his emotions again.

Truth be told, Augustine had trouble with the deflection. He really admired these men who had surrendered their posts and their pursuit of pleasure in order to serve God. As he looked back on his life, it had been about fifteen years since his original conversion to philosophy after reading Cicero's *Hortensius* (Chapter Three). What did Augustine have to show for it? His answer is one of the most famous sentences of the whole *Confessions* which sums up his life: "grant me chastity and continence, but not yet." (8.7.17). Once again, Augustine knows that his penchant for lust isn't making him happy, but he's having trouble taking the next step to rid himself of it.

Augustine was uncertain what to do. Once again, His language is very strong: he was "confounded with horrible shame that gnawed away" at him." He had no excuses to offer. "All the arguments had been swallowed up (*consumpta*) and refuted (*convicta*)" (8.7.18). Having finished his story, Ponticianus left the house.

The Garden Scene

After the departure of Ponticianus, Augustine was alone with Alypius. Describing himself as having "a violent quarrel" within his "interior house" (8.8.19), he turned to Alypius, and asked:

> *What is wrong with us? ...the unlearned rise up and take heaven by force and we, with our heartless teaching, wallow in flesh and blood. Are we ashamed to follow because they have surpassed us? Should we not be ashamed not to follow?*

Augustine retired to the garden to work this out, noting that God "knew but I did not, what was to take place." Augustine's turmoil was all part of the process of bringing him to a place of decision regarding celibacy. As

Augustine recounts, "But as far as I knew, I was going nuts yet dying to live, aware of what an evil thing I was, but unaware of the good thing I was about to become."

When Augustine went into the garden, Alypius followed him. Even though he was with his best friend, he felt like he was alone. The only thing that stood between Augustine and a closer walk with God was his will. He had the power to turn his will toward the health of his soul and not toward the satisfaction of the flesh (8.8.20).

Although the mind might command the body with ease, turning the soul required grace (8.9.21). In fact, drawing on Romans Seven, Augustine wonders if he has two wills. Yet Augustine concluded a dualistic view of the will was closer to Manichean belief than the truth. He was in conflict with himself, not a foreign evil substance "unconnected" (*alienae*) to himself (8.10.22).

Thus an old excuse starts to melt away. He was going to have to solve the conflict with his will by affirmatively deciding to serve God, which meant giving up sex. Augustine admits "And so it was not I that brought this about 'but sin which dwelt in me'" (Rom 7.17-20), a reference to original sin. He continues, "sin was the punishment of a different freely-committed sin, since I was a son of Adam." Manichaean dualism had provided a handy, but lazy, excuse for why Augustine hadn't turned toward God, but it was no longer a tenable one. Put simply, "eternity delights, but the pleasure of temporal goods holds us down" (8.10.24).

As Augustine looks back on it, he sees that this turmoil was implanted in him by God to bring him to a decision about what kind of life he was going to lead. As Augustine recounts, "I was wavering between dying to death (*mori morti*) and living to life (*vitae vivere*)" (8.11.25). In fact, Augustine brings his temptations to life as he describes them "nipping at him stealthily," attempting to make him "look back" (8.11.26), a likely allusion to Lot's wife who looked back and turn to salt (Gen 19.26). In the end, the decision was simple. Could Augustine turn toward Continence or not? Having brought sin to life, he now does the same with his goal – celibacy:

> *from that region toward which I had set my face and to which I feared to cross over, there appeared the chaste, dignified Continence, serene yet not dissolute, cheerfully and honorably coaxing me to come without further deliberation. Receiving and embracing me, she stretched*

forth her godly hands, filled with crowds of good examples to follow (8.11.27).

Chastity personified was calling to Augustine. Augustine's own words are telling: "Cast yourself without care. He will receive you and heal you." The path to healing in his soul was through celibacy.

Augustine started to weep at all of his emotional turmoil. He left Alypius' side and sat underneath a fig tree. He then wept more profusely, prompting more references to the Psalms. Augustine then "offered up these dramatic words: 'How long? How long? Tomorrow! Tomorrow!' Why not now? Why not an end to my indecency this very hour" (8.12.28)?

Just then, he heard a child chanting from a nearby house. The child sang again and again, "Take up and read, take up and read" (*tolle lege, tolle lege*) (8.12.29). At this, Augustine reports his facial expression changed. His words are important here: "I interpreted it as none other than a command from God to open the book and read the first passage I might come across." The great monk Antony was his model. Antony had heard the story of the Rich Young Ruler read by another, he gave up all his worldly goods so that he might turn and serve God.

Having opened the book, Augustine's eyes came immediately to Rom 13.13-14: "not in rioting and drunkenness, not in promiscuity or in sexual impurity, not in strife or envy, but put on the Lord Jesus Christ and make no provision for the flesh to obey its lusts" (Rom 13.13-14). He recalls, "I neither wanted nor needed to read further. Right then, at the end of this sentence, as if freedom from cares were infused into my heart, all the darkness of doubt dispersed."

Augustine next recounts what happened to Alypius, who opened the book to the same place. Coming upon the next verse (Rom 14.1), he read "Receive the one who is weak in faith" (8.12.30). Augustine writes that Alypius, "without any disturbed hesitation," made the same vow as Augustine. Alypius thus joined Augustine in his pledge to live a celibate life.

Augustine then went inside and told his mother what had happened, causing her to rejoice. Her prayers were answered. Her son's fight with God was over. Augustine concludes that he would neither "seek a wife nor any hope in this world (*spem saeculi*)." He decided to live by the "Rule of Faith" which God had revealed to Monica in a vision years ago. Augustine's conversion to the celibate life was complete.

Focus Texts

Given how important the garden scene of Chapter Eight is to the story, I would highly recommend reading all of Chapter Eight of the *Confessions*. You won't be disappointed. I recommend reading it directly, not only because it's dramatic and famous, but also because you'll get more out of the Focus Text section if you do. All the Focus Texts will come from the garden scene because it's one of the most famous and beloved parts of the *Confessions*.

As I hinted above, we're going to see familiar themes emerging here, but with greater maturity. As usual, Scripture is at the center of Augustine's experience. Even if the key element in all of this is the turning of Augustine's will, I want to continue emphasizing that it all occurs within the context of God's grace.

The Garden Scene

Let's first set the scene through Augustine's description of where Alypius and he were. The location in a garden is critical for the continuing development of the story.

Focus Text 8A

> Our place of lodging had a little garden (*hortulus*). We enjoyed the use of it as well as the whole house since our host, the master of the house, was not living there. The commotion in my heart snatched me away to the garden where no one would impede the fiery quarrel which had engaged me until it was discharged. You knew, but I did not, what was to take place. But as far as I knew, I was going nuts yet dying to live, aware of what an evil thing I was, yet unaware of the good thing I was about to become (8.8.19).

This scene takes place in a garden. This is a significant detail. We should remember back to Chapter Two as we're doing this. Where did the scene with the theft of the pears take place? It was in a vineyard with a single pear tree in view. In Chapter Two, I noted this represented the Garden of Eden. Hence the garden scene of Chapter Eight is the recapitulation of Augustine's "great fall" from Chapter Two. Augustine's commitment to celibacy is the final reversal of the lust of the flesh from Chapter Two when he got his girlfriend pregnant.

Chapter Two came with lots of imagery of the fall of Adam and Eve. As I pointed out in the discussion to that Chapter, Augustine put himself in the Biblical story and depicted himself as Adam. His soul was sharing in the fall of mankind.

What is Augustine saying? He, along with many of his late fourth-century peers, believed that they could imperfectly re-create the pre-fall conditions of Eden if they could just crucify the lusts of their flesh. In a Neoplatonic mindset, it's the bodily passions that are weighing the soul down from its natural desire to ascend and to be with God. If that's the case, the natural thing to do is to rid oneself (as much as possible) of the things that are hindering this ascent. So, for Augustine, the garden scene represents the reversal of the fall.

But that's not all. Where was Jesus just before he was crucified? He was in a garden (the Garden of Gethsemane). What happened in that garden? Jesus experienced emotional turmoil as the reality of his impending crucifixion weighed on him. Jesus then separated himself from his disciples to pray. In the meantime, Jesus was filled with anxiety, asking his Father to take "this cup" away from him. Importantly, Jesus finished by saying, "Yet not my will, but yours be done" (Luke 22.42). If Chapter Eight is about a turn in Augustine's will, the Garden of Gethsemane is a rather obvious parallel. Moreover, the garden scene is about Augustine's decision to purify his flesh, providing an interesting parallel to the physical crucifixion Jesus would undergo.

Further, did you notice how many trees were in the garden scene? There's one tree. This is not an insignificant detail since there was a single tree in view in Chapter Two.

What kind of tree was it? It was a fig tree. As you might suspect, there's all kinds of pertinent imagery this fits. In Homer's *Odyssey*, for example, two sea monsters, Scylla ("*Sil-lah*") and Charybdis ("*Car-ib-dis*"), play an important role. These monsters almost killed Odysseus, the hero of the *Odyssey*, but for a fig tree which Odysseus hung unto which saved his life. Hence it is not a coincidence that Homer makes his way back into our story. The fig tree in the *Odyssey* and the fig tree of Chapter Eight function as symbols of salvation.

What about the Bible? Here, too, the fig tree proves significant. In John's Gospel, Jesus revealed himself to the Apostle Nathanael by saying that he saw him while he was sitting under a fig tree. Note the following verse from

John: Nathanael said to him, "'How do you know me?' Jesus answered him, 'before Philip called you, when you were under the fig tree, I saw you'" (John 1.48).

Thus, both in Biblical and extra-Biblical literature, the fig tree shows up in important ways as characters are about to make significant turning points in their lives. Both Odysseus and Nathaniel needed to be rescued. Augustine again puts himself into key Biblical stories to make his point.

But the fig tree also serves as an important symbol for the Old Testament prophets as well. In several sections of the Old Testament, the biblical text associates the fig tree with rest for the prophets, kings and people of Israel.[5] This is true for Solomon (1 Kings 4.25, Song of Songs 2.13), Rabshakeh (2 Kings 18.28, Isa 36.13), Jeremiah (8.13) and Micah (Micah 4.4). The promise, particularly in the Minor Prophets, is that a time would come when the people of Israel would find rest under a fig tree. Consider what Zechariah says:

> *I will remove the iniquity of this land in a single day. In that day, says the Lord of hosts, every one of you will invite his neighbor under his vine and under his fig tree (Zech 3.9-10).*

What Augustine wants us to notice is that the association of rest and the fig tree is well established in the Old Testament.

Perhaps most importantly, however, we should think back to the fall and the Garden of Eden. Once again, a garden is in view. In Genesis, the Biblical text doesn't tell us what kind of tree is in the Garden, just that it was "the tree in the middle of the garden" (Gen 3.3) and that the tree "was good for food and that it was a delight to the eyes and that the tree was desirable to make one wise" (Gen 3.6). But we should keep reading. In the very next verse, after Adam and Eve had eaten the forbidden fruit, what did they use to cover their nakedness? They used fig leaves (Gen 3.7). They cover their shame with the leaves from this same tree.

Do you see how the fig tree in Chapter Eight of the *Confessions* serves as a symbol of the reversal of the fall and the fulfillment of the hopes provided by the Old Testament prophets? After pledging his life to celibacy, Augustine will no longer be ashamed. As he comes into the Church and has his sins wiped away by baptism (Acts 22.16), his guilt and shame will be no more. The fig tree of Chapter Eight depicts the reversal of the curse of Chapter Two.

Not only that, but did you notice how Augustine describes this reversal in Focus Text 8A? Augustine says that he was "dying to live." Was Augustine ill? Well, yes, at several points in the *Confessions*, he has described himself as being physically ill. In fact, his excuse for why he quits his job as a rhetorician will be chest pains.

But, as usual, there's more to the story. It seems pretty straight forward that Augustine is talking about spiritual health here. What he's suggesting is that the disintegration of his soul, the problem he identified at the beginning of the book, is starting to be healed. He has to die to his fleshly lusts in order to live.

In this Guide, we have talked a lot about conversion as a process, but I have waited until now to provide a fuller sense of what I think Augustine means by this. For Augustine, conversion is about becoming whole again. It's about finding integration for his soul where before there was only disintegration. I really like the way Paul Henry, a particularly insightful commentator on Augustine from the 1930s, describes conversion:

> *As apostasy is the dissolution of the constitutive elements of religion, so conversion is the integration of previously dissociated elements. Well before his conversion, Augustine possessed a philosophy and was familiar with Christ. The Hortensius had shown him that happiness could be found in the pursuit of truth. His mother, then Ambrose, had taught him that Christianity is a source of light for the intellect and peace for the heart. Still, he did not become a convert. The elements remained isolated: Manichaean materialism declared itself incompatible with Christian beliefs. However, should another philosophy with a spiritual foundation reveal itself through an elaboration of the ideas implied in the Hortensius and, above all, parallel the doctrine of St. John and St. Paul, and should this synthesis become possible, then conversion will not be far off. Augustine saw this possibility in a flash and at once began to search for a way to bring it about.*[6]

Said another way, Augustine is in a life-long process of conversion which climaxes in several stages. In Chapter Seven, he experienced "that which is" and became intellectually convinced. He no longer doubted that an immaterial God existed and that the Church's teachings were true. This is his intellectual conversion.

Here, in Chapter Eight, Augustine converts to celibacy. This moral reformation provides the essential transition between the intellectual vision in Chapter Seven and his baptism and final vision in Chapter Nine. As Augustine comes into the Church, is baptized and ascends to God, his mind, body and spirit are all involved. Thus Augustine experiences many conversions over the course of the *Confessions*. What he ultimately finds is the integration of all these diverse elements where only disintegration was characteristic before. Ultimately, what he finds is Christ.

By asserting that Chapter Eight is about a moral conversion, I am suggesting that Augustine experiences nothing less than the reformation of his disjointed will. This is ultimately what grace does – its power restores the will, enabling us to make better choices. In particular, grace enables Augustine's turn towards God and away from sin. In a well-known passage from his later masterwork *On the Trinity*, Augustine describes this process of reformation as follows:

> *For God to be contemplated, who by nature we are not, we had to be spiritually cleansed by him. God became what we are by nature and what we are not because of sin. So by nature we are not God. By nature, we are human beings and because of sin, we are not just. Yet God became a just man in order to intercede before God on behalf of sinful man. For there is no congruency between the sinner and the just, but there is congruency between men (homini) and the man (homo). Therefore, by joining to us the likeness of his humanity he has taken away the unlikeness of our iniquity. Having participated in our mortality, he made us a participant in his divinity (4.2.4).*

The ultimate goal of redemption is participation in God which, in turn, could only come about because of Jesus' Incarnation. His mystical vision in Chapter Seven provided Augustine with a small foretaste of what an encounter with God entails. But, as we saw, the experience was fleeing, since Augustine's will was still weighed down by sin. Augustine turns from lust towards celibacy so that he might experience God more fully. Augustine's moral reformation, crucifying the lust which has been ever-present in his life from childhood, is an essential part of his Christian journey. Let's see how he describes this turn toward celibacy:

Focus Text 8B

> But now such doubts spoke weakly. For, from that region toward which I had set my face and to which I feared to cross over, there appeared the chaste, dignified Lady Continence (*continentiae*), serene yet not dissolute, cheerfully and honorably coaxing me to come without further deliberation. Receiving and embracing me, she stretched forth her godly hands, filled with multitudes of good examples to follow. There were so many boys and girls, a throng of youth of every age, also burdened widows and older virgins. And Continence herself was in them all, not barren, but 'the fruitful (*fecunda*) mother of children' (Ps 113.9), the joys which come from you, Lord, her husband. Then she smiled at me with encouraging mockery, as if to say, 'Can you really not do what these men and women have done?' 'Do you actually think they did this on their own and not by the Lord, their God?' Their Lord God gave me to them. Why stand on your own strength, so as to not stand at all. Cast yourself upon him! Do not be afraid. He will not remove himself, so that you fall. Cast yourself without care! He will receive you and heal you. (8.11.27).

It should be perfectly obvious to us that no one named "Continence" came down floating out of the sky. Augustine is personifying his turn to celibacy. He is describing Continence as the exact opposite of the inner turmoil which he had found within himself. Whereas he was filled with anxiety and indecision, continence was fruitful, confident, godly, joyful, smiling and encouraging. She was offering to bring healing to Augustine's disordered soul. These are all characteristic traits which Augustine very badly wants to experience in his life.

Continence then describes many examples of people who have managed to be celibate. Some – boys and girls, in particular – may not have the same sexual temptation that Augustine does. But, virgins and widows do. The point is that people across all ages and backgrounds have managed to be continent, controlling their fleshly lusts in order to reach a higher spiritual plane. Continence is suggesting Augustine can do the same.

Yet it might seem bizarre to us to deny something so natural. To Augustine, this is what was so appealing about celibacy. It wasn't natural. It was beyond someone's natural abilities. Celibacy was the ultimate outward statement that a Christian was dedicating himself to eternal spiritual things and not to temporal things.

It was also a strong statement that the effects of the fall could be mitigated in this life. After all, Adam and Eve had walked around the Garden of Eden naked and without shame before the fall. As soon as they eat of the forbidden fruit, the first thing they do is to cover their bodies out of shame. Augustine takes this shame to mean that something dramatic has taken place which brought shame and disordered desire where none existed before.

The most important thing to notice here is the need for grace. Continence, after suggesting that Augustine should be celibate, says that none of the examples cited above were able to do it on their own. They could only be continent by the aid of God through his grace. In fact, Augustine's own will had proved unreliable. Aided by grace, however, his will could be shaped to the point where it would able to fulfill his vocation.

As we first saw in Chapter Four, we observe that grace is a power to Augustine. It is not some spiritual non-entity out there in the ether somewhere. The natural and the supernatural are not radically separate, but co-inhere with one another, meaning that grace is the very power of God imminently at work in us. Grace is necessary, but not irresistible, since we retain our free will. [7] Augustine could decide that celibacy is too hard and he'd rather get rich and famous as a public speaker. But Continence is telling him is that he can embrace celibacy with God's help.

God is calling Augustine to a life of celibacy and to his Church. God is calling Augustine to give up that which would never satisfy him for the only thing that will. God is calling Augustine into a deep, abiding relationship with himself. To get there, Augustine will have to admit that his will is not strong enough on its own. He needs the strengthening hand of God to enable his vocation.

In fact, it is only after we understand that God's call is a gracious gift, not a call to an endless struggle, that we can understand the garden scene fully. God's grace is not just external help and does not obliterate our nature.[8] It works to perfect us so that we might live in closer fellowship with God. In what is arguably the most famous extended passage from the *Confessions,* Augustine describes his dramatic moral turn this way:

Focus Text 8C

I offered up these pitiful words: 'How long? How long? Tomorrow! Tomorrow!' Why not now? Why not an end to my indecency this very hour? I was saying these things and weeping in the bitterest despondency of my heart. Just then, I heard a voice (whether it was from a boy or girl, I do not know) from a nearby house, repeating over and over while singing, 'Take up and read! Take up and read!' (*tolle lege, tolle lege*). Immediately, my expression changed and I thought intently about whether there was any kind of children's game which used this kind of song. No such children's tune came to mind. Repressing a torrent of tears, I arose and interpreted it as none other than a command from God to open the book and read the first passage I might come across. Now, I had heard of Antony, who just happened to enter [Church] at the reading of the Gospel and understood it as a warning addressed directly to him when he heard read: 'go, sell everything you have and give it to the poor and you will have treasure in heaven. Then come and follow me' (Matt 18.21). By such an inspired saying (*oraculo*) he was turned (*conversum*) toward you. Moving quickly, I returned to the place where Alypius was sitting, since I had left the volume of the Apostle there when I arose. I snatched it up, opened it and read in silence that passage on which my eyes first fell: 'not in rioting and drunkenness, not in promiscuity (*cubilibus*) or in sexual impurity (*impudicitiis*), not in strife or envy, but put on the Lord Jesus Christ and make no provision for the flesh to obey its lusts' (Rom 13.13-14). I neither wanted nor needed to read further. Right then, at the end of this sentence, as if freedom from cares were infused into my heart, all the darkness of doubt dispersed. (8.12.29).

First, I want to point out two allusions which are easy to miss because they are more thematic than textual. After hearing the child, Augustine tells us that his facial "expression changed" (*mutato vultu*). This little detail may seem insignificant, but I think it should remind us of what happened in Chapter Four (Focus Text 4B) when Augustine told us that his soul was "cast down" (*conturbaret*). I noted at the time that this was likely pointing us to the story of Cain and Able in Genesis 4 since Cain's countenance was cast down after he murdered his brother.

What Augustine is showing us when his facial expression changes is that the garden scene is also the reversal his earlier identification with Cain. You may remember from our discussion in Chapter Four that Augustine uses Cain and Abel to represent two cities – one the City of God and the other the City of man. Cain is a murderer and in strife, while Abel is a martyr and at peace. We should observe how Augustine's turn toward continence and away from his addiction to lust is a turn toward wholeness and healing. Said differently, Augustine identifies with Cain and the City of man earlier in the story, but now he is moving toward the City of God.

The second allusion which is also easy to miss, occurs when Augustine tells us that he "read in silence" (*legi in silentio*). This should remind us of what happened in Chapter Six when Augustine tried to go in and see Ambrose, but didn't want to disturb him in the midst of his concentrated study. When he encountered Ambrose, Augustine was amazed that he was reading silently, which was against the custom of the day. Yet I think this seemingly insignificant detail is important. By picking up the Scriptures, Augustine is no longer identifying with his pagan friends who read aloud, but has come to imbibe the Scriptures as Ambrose did. Augustine's turn away from his addiction to lust and his embrace of the pure life which Ambrose had modeled suggests that a real turn occurs in this Chapter. Augustine's embrace of Continence is an embrace of Ambrose's way of life.

Yet what is truly central to Focus Text 8C is the story of Antony. Before Ponticianus told this story to him, Augustine had never heard of Antony and was unaware of the monastic movement. Given its importance to our story, let me explain who Antony was.

The Life of Antony was written by Athanasius during the middle of the fourth century during one of his many periods of being exiled under persecution for being an orthodox Bishop. Athanasius claims to have interviewed people who served Antony directly, including the person charged with bringing him water, which lends an air of credibility to the story.

Antony was an Egyptian Christian living in Alexandria. His parents died when he was relatively young, but he used his industriousness to manage the family's agriculture holdings and carve out a comfortable life for his sister and himself. One day, while Antony was on his way to Church, he was thinking about how the members of the Early Church held their goods in common. The result was that no one was in want in the community. Upon entering the Church, he heard the New Testament passage being read, which was from the parable of the Rich Young Ruler. In it, Jesus exhorts the protagonist of the parable to sell everything and give it to the poor.

Antony decided that this exhortation was directed at him. So he went and sold everything he had and gave it to the poor. He created a small endowment for the care of his sister and divided up his fields among his neighbors so no one would feel slighted.

Antony then moved to the edge of town to learn from those who were living in seclusion as hermits. Similar to those pursuing celibacy, he believed that he could re-create the conditions of Eden by denying his flesh the things that it craved. He fasted frequently, prayed without ceasing and did simple jobs to support himself.

Having apprenticed with those living an ascetic life, he then proceeded to do something which no one had done before. He moved deep into the desert and lived alone apart from the support structure of a town. The story of the *Life of Antony* is really the story of how one man sold everything and moved to the desert to pray. There, he became the chief antagonist against the devil and his angels. When Antony was "discovered" twenty years later after living as a recluse in the desert, people were amazed that it appeared he hadn't aged. Athanasius describes this memorable scene this way:

> *So, for close to twenty years, he continued in spiritual training by himself, never venturing out and rarely being seen by anyone. Now, after this time, many were anxious and zealous to imitate his training and others who knew of him came. As they were tearing down and shattering his door, Antony emerged from a kind of inner sanctum having been initiated into the mysteries* (mystagoge) *and indwelt by the Spirit of God* (theophoria). *Then, for the first time, he was seen by those who came to him outside his hut. Those standing there, when they saw him, were astounded that his body was in the same shape as before, having not grown fat, though unexercised, nor gaunt from fasting and battling it out with demons. But he looked just the same as before he had withdrawn from them. Now again his whole self* (psuche) *was pure in its outward bearing, for it was neither weighed down with distress nor buffeted by pleasure or laughter nor downcast with grief. In fact, when he observed the crowd, he was not troubled nor stirred up by the appearance of so many. But he was completely measured as one governed by reason and set in his nature. Through*

him, the Lord healed the bodily sufferings of many of those present and he made others clean from demons (14.1-5).

In Chapter Seven, Augustine genuinely wanted to sustain an experience of the presence of God. But, Antony, an illiterate man, who gave away all earthly goods, managed to sustain it over more than twenty years through the practices of asceticism. In so doing, he greatly facilitated the development of the monastic movement in which devout Christians realized that there was great power and worth in dedicating a life to prayer and experiencing the presence of God. What Athanasius described was what Augustine had been seeking for some time.

There is evidence that Antony's asceticism accomplished remarkable things. Towards the end of Antony's life, for example, Constantine, the Roman Emperor wrote to him looking for some counsel. Antony wasn't going to bother to respond because he was not impressed by politicians. Yet, when someone pointed out that this might be a bit disrespectful, he responded with remarkable wisdom. One particularly memorable passage is the following:

> *Now Antony was also exceedingly wise and the marvelous thing was that, though unlettered, he was a clever and intelligent man. One day, two Greek philosophers came to him, believing they could use their powers on Antony. Now he was at the outer mountain. Realizing who the men were from their outward appearance, he went out to them and said (via a translator), 'O philosophers, why have you expended so much effort on an ignorant man'?' But they replied, 'you are not ignorant, but full of practical wisdom' (phronesis). Antony said, 'if you came to a fool, your effort is in vain, but if you consider me wise, then 'become as I am' (Gal 4.12), for it is necessary to 'emulate what is good' (3 John 1.11). Now, if I had come to you, I would have imitated you. But if you come to me, 'become as I am,' for I am a Christian. Then they went away amazed, for they observed that even the demons feared Antony (72.1-5).*

Augustine and Alypius both marvel that an uneducated man could have the kind of impact he did by simply having the courage to follow the commands of Christ. After a lifetime of experiencing Christ's presence in the desert and waging a spiritual battle against demons, Antony dramatically influenced the world.

Hence the garden scene must be in observed in light of Antony's story as well as the other vignettes which precede it. When Antony pursues asceticism and goes to the desert to pray, he has a real impact. He takes territory in the desert which was considered Satan's domain. Despite Augustine's prodigious learning, he had accomplished little thus far in comparison to Antony.

The idea that an uneducated man from Egypt could change the world obviously impresses Augustine greatly. Thus when he hears the famous words "*Tolle Lege*" (take up and read), he's being driven back into the very Scriptures that Antony obeyed, the catalyst that caused Antony to sell everything and move to the desert.

Yet here is where the story gets even more interesting. I am intrigued with what Alexander Sizoo, writing in the 1950s, discovered. Sizoo suggests that Augustine misunderstood what the child was singing. Augustine writes that the child is singing a song that says, "Take up and read."[9] But it's probable Augustine actually hears a Roman harvest song which instead says: "lift up and sort."[10]

Why mention this seemingly insignificant detail? I mention it because there was a concerted effort in the twentieth century to claim that this famous scene is fictional, just a stylized literary account which Augustine invents. One of the best pieces of evidence that the garden scene is not fictional is the misunderstanding of the song. If Augustine actually misunderstood the song the child was singing, this is good evidence for its authenticity. After all, why tell the story this way if there's a significant mistake in it?

Here's why this is important. Augustine has been teaching us all along how he wants us to read the Scriptures. To Augustine, it simply will not do to spend all our time in the literal sense of the text. This is where a reader should start, but there are deeper layers of meaning to peel back. In fact, this was Ambrose's great gift to Augustine – to teach him that a mature reader of the Bible should expect to finds layers of meaning hidden in the text.

I think Augustine is still trying to teach us this in Chapter Eight. There are some parts of the story which are figurative (like personified Continence), but we should be searching for the deeper meaning in everything we come across when we read Augustine. Similarly, when we read the Old Testament, we have not read it properly unless we interpret it in light of Christ (Luk 24.27).

To say that Augustine just made up the garden scene is to miss one of the central goals of the *Confessions* – namely, to teach Christians how to read the Bible. Augustine wants us to assume that he's a trustworthy witness and that the literal sense of the text is true, but is pointing to something deeper and more profound.

What this means is that Augustine is teaching us a sacramental reading of the Bible. There's an outward and visible sign, the literal sense, which is pointing to something deeper, the spiritual sense. This is analogous to how the Eucharist takes simple elements like bread and wine, but after their consecration, insists they point to, and indeed participate in, a divine reality. In a sacrament, both the literal and the figurative co-inhere. Thus the text does not just contain symbols, but evokes an actual participation with the referent of the symbol.

In a similar way, Augustine brings a sacramental understanding to the garden scene. There was literally a garden; there was literally a fig tree; and there was literally a child singing. But the deeper point is the change of the will that comes about in Augustine by the end of the Chapter. The tree, the song, the inner-turmoil, the references to Romans and the climactic exhortation to rid the flesh of its lusts are all very real, but they're markers for the most important thing, which is the changed interior reality that Augustine experiences by grace. Augustine's will has changed – he'll pursue celibacy, which is a step toward the ultimate healing and integration he'll experience by coming into the Church.

Augustine is not saying everyone needs to be celibate. Rather, he's calling everyone to a sacramental relationship with Christ and to a sacramental reading of the Scriptures. To pursue his particular calling, Augustine makes a commitment to not have sex again. As we know, the impact that Augustine had on Christendom and the world is profound. The reason why this impact was possible was because Augustine surrendered, in humility, to Christ. Augustine and the world would never be the same. His moral conversion was complete.

Questions for Reflection
1. What habits hold you back from a deeper Christian life?
2. What is grace? How is it possible to have free will if God acts on us through his grace?

3. How does the commitment to celibacy that almost everyone in this Chapter exhibits strike you? Do you find it repressive? Liberating? Misguided?
4. What would it mean to be completely consecrated to God within your own vocation? What would you have to change to get there?
5. Augustine does not experience his turn alone. What is the role of others in discerning what God wants for us?

Appendix - Asceticism

Given the emphasis Augustine places on celibacy, we might want to explore why he feels so compelled to "convert" to asceticism. What would make him, and many others in the fourth and fifth centuries, attach such a high premium to the celibate life? Given our culture which puts sexuality on display almost everywhere, Augustine's assumptions might seem more than a little foreign.

Augustine and Asceticism

There is one obvious thing we should realize. Augustine does not live in a post-Freudian world where it's assumed that human sexuality is at the center of all we really are. We should realize by now that Augustine thinks the soul plays a primary role in our consciousness, our spiritual existence and in our decision making. As we saw in Chapter Seven, it's the intellective part of the soul that desires to ascend and see "that which is."

In fact, it's that last part – our decision making – that causes the problem in Chapter Eight. We come into this world with damaged wills and we're not able to choose a different kind of existence. This is the legacy that has been handed down to humanity as a result of the fall, something that we've explored at length in other Chapters.

In fact, the whole disjointed character of the post-fall world came about because of disobedience. When Adam and Eve chose to set their wills in opposition to God's, the result was a disintegration of the harmony which had previously been present.[11] Prior to the fall, body, soul and spirit were an integrated whole, living in harmony with nature and with God. After the fall, the reality is different.

When we talk about a post-fall conversion to asceticism, we have to answer the question of how this helps our damaged wills. Make no mistake: Augustine believes that in order for him to be baptized and to live as a genuine believer faithful to his vocation, he has to be celibate. If he is going to lead a life consecrated to God, he cannot go on sinning like he has. The only answer for him is to stop having sex. This is how Augustine describes his decision to be celibate in his work called the *Soliloquies*, composed shortly after the events described in this Chapter:

> *Above all, I have resolved to flee sexual relations. I am of the opinion that nothing brings a man's mind down from its stronghold more than womanly charms and bodily contact without which a wife cannot be*

had. So, if it is the wise man's obligation to give care to children (such
I do not know yet for certain), anyone who has sexual relations only
for this, I will admire, but, in truth, I have no wish to imitate him. In
fact, the attempt is more dangerous than the happiness to come. So, for
the sake of righteousness and the freedom of my mind, I have resolved
not to long for, wish for or seek a wife (1.10.17).

But this is where we often become uncomfortable. Does that mean sex within marriage is sin? We might get this impression by reading some later medieval literature, which equated the seminal transmission of our corrupted nature with sin. In fact, Augustine's linkage of the sexual transmission of the soul and our fallen nature contributes significantly to the development of that point of view. Most medieval theologians who link sin and sex believe that they're faithfully interpreting Augustine.

I think this linkage is understandable, but nevertheless unfortunate. There is no doubt that Augustine leads the tradition in that direction and is open to criticism for doing so. I should emphasize that Augustine is not against marriage and is not against sex within marriage. The problem he has is with lust, which he has a hard time separating from the sex act itself.[12]

Augustine is, of course, critical of his own sexual behavior before he came into the Church. But he thinks that marriage is a good thing, even if the state of virginity and continence is better. Augustine believes that marriage is good since the Scriptures ascribe a high degree of value to the institution.[13] After all, did Jesus not perform his first miracle at a wedding and forbid divorce? The problem is not with marriage; the problem is with our disjointed wills.

The proof that our corrupted wills have had a dramatic impact on our world is the reality of death. Everyone dies. But, this did not have to be the case. To Augustine, had Adam and Eve not sinned, the reality of death would not have come to plague humanity.

It is interesting to consider what would have happened if the fall hadn't occurred. Augustine thinks Adam would still have had offspring.[14] This must be the case because of God's command to "increase, multiply and fill the earth" (Gen 1.28). Augustine describes it this way in his book *On the Good of Marriage*:

Therefore, through sexual intercourse, generations of bodies might be
able to exist, which would have a fixed mode of development and yet

would not incline toward old age or even into old age, nor unto death until the earth is filled up with that blessed increase. For if the clothes of the wandering Israelites, which God furnished for forty years, did not suffer any deterioration, how much more would he apply this to bodies which had faithfully obeyed his precepts through a certain fixed moderation of condition until they should be changed for the better. This would not occur by the death of a man, whereby the body is separated from the soul, but by a blessed translation from mortality to immortality, from animal nature to spiritual nature (2.2).

What Augustine is trying to tell us is that Adam and Eve had sexual relations in the garden. It's part of their nature and the means of carrying out God's command to multiply and fill the whole earth. But something had gone terribly wrong after the fall since this stability of body and soul became disintegrated. In short, they managed to have sex without lust getting in the way before the fall. All Augustine is doing is saying that this disintegration has had a profound effect on human sexuality, first for Adam but also for us. There is now a compulsive need for sex. Before the fall, no such compulsion existed. There is now disintegration where formerly integration was the norm.

In his *Literal Commentary on Genesis*, Augustine describes Adam and Eve's post-fall condition this way:

Of course, by this deed they lost that marvelous state which was to be provided to them by the mysterious power of the tree of life... This led to the loss of the state of their body, that reality of disease and death, which is even now in the flesh of animals. Consequently, this same motion [of the genitals] which causes in animals the appetite for sex thus enables those born to succeed those who die. But, even in light of that, the rational soul provided a sign of its excellence in this very penalty by causing embarrassment at the bestial motion in its carnal members and instilling it with shame. This occurred not only because it perceived something there it had never experienced before, but also because the shame which came from that motion occurred as a result of the transgression of the commandment. So, in that member previously clothed with grace it perceived something [new] there even when its nakedness had suffered nothing unseemly (11.42).

In other words, before the fall, Adam and Even were not ashamed by sex. Their desire for each other was ordered and there to fulfill the commands which God had given them. But, after the fall, the nature of sex had changed. It was now disordered and uncontrollable. Thus in their pre-fall state, sexual desire existed, but the desire was perfectly congruent with the will.[15] Now, the will was forced to fight against the desire to keep it under control. Augustine knew this fight well, since he had succumbed to his sexual desires time and again.

This is another reason why marriage is a good thing. It provides a proper (and dare I say, ordered) place for those desires to be fulfilled. This is precisely what the apostle Paul has said – if one finds himself burning with lust, it's better for that person to marry than to burn (1 Cor 7.9).

Why is virginity an even better state than marriage? One reason is the example provided by the Virgin Mary. Peter Brown describes this well:

> *For Augustine, Mary's conception of Christ stood rather for an act of undivided obedience. It recaptured the ancient harmony of body and soul, in which the will was not the maimed thing that it so soon became.*[16]

Unlike Augustine, Mary was faithful. She was not wracked with the lust. Rather, she was chaste and pure. Put more simply, she managed to retain the harmony that humankind had lost in the fall. By grace, she was able to become the bearer of God ("*Theotokos*").

For Christians in the fourth and fifth centuries, virginity and celibacy allowed a person to recapture a little bit of Eden. We might find it odd to consider the celibate life paradise, but Augustine was trying to get there by crushing his sexual appetites, which were keeping his soul from ascending. He understands his life will be more fulfilled if he lives in harmony with God, rather than living in a disjoined existence. But, as hard as he tries, he cannot make this change on his own. It requires divine assistance.

Why does God not simply take away the sexual impulse? If sin is so bad and God is omnipotent, why does he leave us here on earth in such a disjointed state? Augustine's answer is that it requires us to look to God for help. Our disintegrated condition is a constant reminder that we cannot live the Christian life without grace.

This is a helpful answer, but one the tradition after Augustine finds less than satisfactory. Towards the end of Augustine's life, parts of the Church, particularly in the East, would find Augustine's notion of original sin difficult to swallow. Everyone agrees that something damaging had occurred because of the fall and that grace is necessary to live the Christian life. But the question becomes the degree to which the fall has damaged us and how that condition was transmitted. Augustine says that the implications are catastrophic – that we cannot choose not to sin. But the broader Catholic tradition (at least until the Reformation) did not agree that our wills are so damaged we cannot make right choices.

The reason for the disagreement is that it's hard to ascribe moral culpability if we can't really make free moral choices. Said differently, how can God be just in judging us if, by our very natures, we cannot choose good things? The Medieval Church and the broader Catholic tradition tends to side with the critics rather than with Augustine here whereas the Protestant tradition kept Augustine's notion of total depravity, sometimes without the sacramental remedy.

Augustine, however, recognizes this problem regarding free will. He writes the following in the *City of God*:

> *In fact, just because God foreknew that man would sin does not make a man sin. On the contrary, it is not to be doubted that man sins on his own, since God, whose foreknowledge cannot be fallible, foresees not by fate nor by chance nor by anything else, but he has foreseen that man by his own accord would sin. Of course, a man does not sin unless he should will to do so. But if he had refused to sin, then God would have foreseen that act (5.10).*

The problem is that Augustine says different things at different times. Free will is something Augustine will defend, particularly in his earlier writings, but in some of his later battles with the Pelagians, Augustine makes statements which seem to contradict it.

The chief spokesman for the critics is a monk named John Cassian, who was instrumental in bringing eastern monastic practices to the West. Although a celibate monk, Cassian believed sexual desire was not a perversion, but was put there by God. Cassian believed God gave us sexual desire to help us. The sexual urge reminds us that even if our outward behavior is chaste, our inner conscience might not be.

> *So, we also read in the apostle that this battle has been sown in our members for our advantage... and this fight, which in a certain way is*

helpful, has been introduced to us by the administration of the Creator, challenging and driving us to a better situation. Now if it were removed, there is little doubt that an inverted and pernicious harmony would follow (4.7).

After Augustine, the Church has been characterized by diversity of thought on this issue. What really matters is grace. Augustine decides he has to live a celibate life in order to fulfill his vocation. The only way he can do this is through grace. It's inconceivable that one can live the Christian life without it. We might find some of Augustine's teachings on human sexuality foreign, but his insistence on the importance of grace is his most lasting legacy.

CHAPTER NINE

AUGUSTINE ASCENDS...AGAIN

As we come to the end of the narrative portion of the *Confessions*, and consequently this Guide, the year is AD 387 and Augustine is thirty-three years old. The amount of change he has undergone in his life during the past three years is simply stunning. Having progressed from being a convinced Manichaean to a believer in Jesus Christ, having moved from North Africa to Milan and having abandoned his addiction to carnal lust for a life of asceticism, Augustine is not the same man he was just a few years prior.

Yet his journey is by no means complete. As I have been emphasizing throughout this Guide, Augustine sees his life as a lengthy spiritual journey, one that will only be complete after his resurrection. He believes his deeds, feelings and thoughts in this life really matter. He also has become convinced he has progressed in the spiritual life solely because of God's grace.

In a sense, Chapter Nine recapitulates many of the struggles Augustine has narrated along the way. For example, Augustine exhibits a depth of joy in his encounter with the Psalms of David, which represents a reversal of his rejection of the Bible during his youth. We also encounter five deaths in Chapter Nine, yet Augustine reacts to each death wholly differently than when he bewailed the loss of his friend in Chapter Four. These deaths are narrated together with Augustine's own enactment of spiritual death and resurrection which is his baptism.

After his baptism, Augustine has another mystical experience. He doesn't have experience it alone this time, but is with his mother when he "sees" God. In fact, the mystical experience occurs while looking down at a garden, a reversal of his fall in Chapter Two and a reminder of his turn to celibacy in Chapter Eight. Thus this Chapter has a focus on spiritual rebirth, thus completing the story of physical birth with which began the *Confessions*.[1] Moreover, Augustine considerably advances his teaching in the Chapter. From the beginning of this Guide, my claim has been that one of Augustine's main purposes in writing the *Confessions* has been to teach us to read the Bible and to pray. Right in the middle of the Chapter, we find a more advanced investigation of Psalm Four. Augustine interprets Psalm Four in light of his own story, demonstrating that "repose" is found only in God. This references his prayer from the start of the *Confessions* that "our heart is restless until it finds rest in you." While not complete, Augustine has found a degree of rest which is unimaginable from where he started.

Augustine then experiences a miraculous answer to prayer, as a toothache which had been obstructing his work suddenly went away after his community prayed for him. If the *Confessions* is one long prayer, Augustine is careful to show us that prayer works powerfully.

Overview

Given the framework we have been using to track our way through the *Confessions*, we discover that the misplaced loves of 1 John 2.16 have been resolved. Augustine's gaze is no longer drawn to fleshly lusts, but eternal things, exemplified most beautifully in the mystical experience at the end of the Chapter. This reverses the lust of the flesh. His gaze is no longer drawn to *curiositas*, or knowledge of things that are not beneficial. Now, Augustine formally comes into the Church and accepts its teachings. Finally, the pride of life is reversed when he formally vacates his position as a teacher of rhetoric to devote himself full-time to the pursuit of Christian wisdom. Even his way of resigning his position represents a remarkable advancement over the younger Augustine. Augustine is now putting others before himself and has reversed the pride of life which so dominated his earlier descriptions of his existence.

We can break down Chapter Nine into two main sections. The first deals with Augustine and the philosophical community of friends which forms around him. Here, we meet Verecundus ("*Ver-eh-kund-us*"), who lends his country estate to Augustine and his friends; we become re-acquainted briefly with Nebridius and we see him interact with Adeodatus, his son, as well as Alypius, his best friend. The first section shows how important community has become.

The second part of the Chapter has Monica in focus. We've seen that Augustine and Monica have had a tempestuous relationship at points in the

Confessions, but here Monica is presented as the Saint she will become. She is the patient, dutiful mother who lives on as a model for all mothers.

Fellowship with Friends

As usual, Augustine begins with a confession. He admits his soul was in "the darkness of death" and his heart was an "abyss of corruption." Augustine squarely sees his disjointed will as the center of the problem. He knows he needs to reform and embrace God, but only Christ who is his "helper and redeemer" could enable him do that. Yet Augustine had turned from his fleshly desires, in particular, his desire for gain, his penchant for lust and his obsession for status. He was seeking to replace temporal things with the Lord who was his "brightness, riches and salvation" (9.1.1).

One of the key pieces of evidence of Augustine's turnaround was his decision to resign from his position as a "marketer of words" (9.2.2), a reference to his career as a rhetorician. But he did not resign in haste, wanting to leave his post in an honorable way. In a telling change, Augustine sought the counsel of his friends for how to do it. Augustine decided to leave quietly at the end of the term and blame a sickness – lung and chest pains – for his inability to continue. He was very careful not to cause scandal or gossip (9.2.3). Augustine admits that he was looking forward to the leisure which would allow him the space to contemplate God full time with his friends (9.2.4). He also confesses that his "enthusiasm for greed had receded."

Verecundus

Augustine next describes his friend Verecundus, a non-Christian whose wife was a believer. Augustine describes his friend as being "held back from the road on which we had advanced" because of his "remaining shackles," a reference to his marriage vows (9.3.5). To Augustine's thinking, Verecundus could not really give himself to Christianity in the same vigorous way unless it came with abstinence from sex. Yet he would also insist that Verecundus should live out his faith "with fidelity to his position, that is, to a life of marriage" (9.3.6). Augustine may have thought that celibacy was a higher form of devotion, but he did not believe it was the only way.

Verecundus offered Augustine and his friends the use of his vacation house at Cassiciacum without charge. This is probably the modern-day Italian town of Cassiago di Brianza where an inscription bearing Verecundus' name has been found.[2] At Cassiciacum, Augustine and his friends were able to "rest" in Christ "away from the raging passion (*aestu*) of the world." Within a year, in 387, Verecundus would be dead after an illness, but "he departed this life as a faithful Christian," likely meaning that he was baptized at roughly the same time as Augustine and Alypius. Verecundus represents the first death in Chapter Nine.

Nebridius

Augustine next re-introduces one of his best friends, Nebridius, someone we met originally in Chapter Four. Similar to Verecundus, Nebridius was also not a Christian and, likely under Augustine's influence, "had fallen into that pit of destructive error [Manichaeism] which would have him believe that the flesh of [Jesus] was just a phantasm" (9.3.6).

Augustine describes Nebridius as a "most ardent investigator of truth." After Augustine came into the Church, Nebridius also become a baptized believer. Characteristically, Augustine says, "not long after our conversion and regeneration by baptism, he also became a devoted Catholic (*fidelem catholicum*), serving God "with perfect chastity and continence among his own people in Africa." To Augustine, Christian conversion was connected with leading a celibate life if done at the highest level.

Nebridius died soon after his baptism while he was in Africa, thus representing the second death in the Chapter. After his death, Augustine harbors no doubt about the fate of his soul, saying that he was "in the bosom of Abraham" (Luke 16.22). We shouldn't miss how different Augustine's reaction to Nebridius' death is in Chapter Nine compared to his reaction to the death of his unnamed friend in Thagaste in Chapter Four. There is no more angst, evidence that his soul was in a much greater state of rest.

Cassiciacum, The Psalms and Prayer

Augustine next describes what was probably the happiest period in his life, his time at Cassiciacum doing philosophy with his friends and family (9.4.7). As I described in the Introduction to this Guide, Augustine composed several philosophical dialogues during this period which represent his earliest extant writings.

Augustine describes the great joy he experienced as he prayed and studied the Psalms of David. Together with Alypius and two catechumens preparing for baptism, Augustine discovered the richness of the Old Testament, a dramatic reversal from his former rejection of the same during his Manichaean years.

Augustine provides a window on his handling of Scripture by writing extensively about his interpretation of Psalm Four (9.4.8). As he has been teaching us to do, Augustine places himself in the Psalm and interprets it in light of his own life. He pictures what it would be like to recite the fourth Psalm while his former Manichaean colleagues were watching. What would he tell them?

He would tell his listeners that the true God had heard his prayers and had "opened wide" for him (Ps 4.2). Augustine stands in awe at the mercy of God especially in light of his former life when he "delighted in vanity and strove for falsehood" (Ps. 4.3, 9.4.9), a key verse which he repeats six times. Despite Augustine's earlier life, God had "enlarged" him (Ps 4.4). Here, Augustine both looks back and looks forward, intimating that in his baptism (which is still to come) God would raise him from the dead (Eph 1.20) and send his Spirit (John 14.16). Augustine sees his own story in light of the story of Christ in the Scriptures, but ultimately in light of Christ's resurrection, which his baptism will re-enact.

Christ had called Augustine out of his earlier life, which is intoned by the key question of the Psalm: "why do you delight in vanity and strive for falsehood" (Ps 4.3-4)? Augustine sees this admonition squarely directed at him. What is Augustine to do about it? The Psalmist says: "be angry and do not sin" (Ps 4.5, 9.4.10). Augustine felt righteous anger at the Manichees for leading him astray from the truth that God was incorporeal and that the Old Testament was the Word of God.

In their pride, the Manichees never asked "who will reveal good to us" (Ps 4.6)? The Manichees misunderstood light. It was not trapped, held under wraps by an evil substance, but was freely given by Christ. As the Psalmist confesses, "the light of your countenance is stamped upon us, O Lord" (Ps 4.7). Augustine admits that his recollection of the Manichees made him angry. But he also admits, "nor did I want earthly goods to be multiplied, nor to absorb time or to be absorbed by time." Good had come out of his former life lived apart from God. In the context of eternity, Augustine was looking forward to another kind of "grain, wine and oil" (Ps 4.9).

By the time Augustine got to the end of Psalm Four, he describes himself as being "enflamed" (9.4.11). Augustine believes he can "fall asleep and grasp his repose" (Ps 4.9) because he has found his rest in Christ. The Lord had formed him "in a singular hope" (Ps 4.10). He was finally at peace, even if he was still angry with the Manichees for leading him away from the straight path.

Augustine concludes his recollection of his time at Cassiciacum by recounting a remarkable answer to prayer he received. At some point, he was in terrible pain because of a toothache which was agonizing enough to render him mute. He begged his friends to pray for him. As soon as "we had gotten down on our knees with humble devotion, the pain fled" (9.3.12). Augustine admits that he had never experienced such a direct and dramatic answer to prayer before this incident.

The Baptism

After formally notifying officials in Milan that he would not be returning to his post the next semester, Augustine wrote Bishop Ambrose to inform him of his contrition for his past life and his desire to be baptized (9.5.13). He asked Ambrose for suggestions on what he might read in preparation. In response, Ambrose suggested he read the book of Isaiah, which Augustine admits he did not understand. His application for baptism accepted, Augustine and Alypius moved to Milan so that they could be catechized in the mysteries of the faith.

Adeodatus, Augustine's son, now appears, as he is to be baptized with his father. Augustine mentions that Adeodatus was between his fifteenth and sixteenth years during this time, a fact which we employed in Chapter Two to suggest that Augustine had gotten his girlfriend pregnant when he was sixteen in Thagaste. We shouldn't miss the irony that while Augustine was busy sinning during his sixteenth year, his son, by contrast, was presenting himself for baptism and engaging in philosophical debates. Augustine couldn't have been more proud.

Next, Augustine was baptized. Augustine wept during the baptism, noting that the "anxiety from our past life fled away from us" (9.6.14). He had finally come home. The Prodigal Son was no longer a vagabond. Augustine's baptism represents a key marker on his on-going spiritual journey.

Augustine then recounts a political battle Ambrose fought against Justina, the mother of the boy emperor Valentinian (9.7.15). We met Justina in Chapter Five during Ambrose's resistance to the attempted takeover of a church by an Arian congregation. Ambrose's stand against her reinforces Augustine's respect for Ambrose.

Augustine also describes the discovery of the relics from the martyrs Protasius and Gervasius, which, upon being dug out and transferred to the basilica in Milan miraculously healed several people (9.7.16), a relatively common occurrence in the literature from the time. Augustine's initiation into the mysteries of the Church had become very real.

Monica and The Vision at Ostia

The second half of Chapter Nine is taken up with a discussion of Augustine's mother, Monica. This discussion takes place while Augustine and she are at Ostia, at the mouth of the Tiber River, which is the place where she would pass away. On the whole, this section, presents a flattering, but also realistic, portrait of his mother.

Augustine notes that Monica grew up in a "household of faith" which was quite severe in discipline (9.8.17). Despite (or, perhaps, because of) this severity, Augustine recounts Monica's wine addiction which she developed as a young person. One of her chores was getting wine for the table from a cask. What started with a few sips grew to a full-fledged addiction to wine (9.8.18). One day, her wine habit drew a sharp rebuke from one of the servant girls during a dispute. After calling her an "alchie" (*meribib-ulam*), Monica "considered her shame, at once condemned it (*damnavit*) and stopped it." Augustine sees this as God's providence at work at helping Monica in her addiction, as her ability to kick the habit did not happen by her own will power, but was assisted by God's grace.

Augustine next recounts what happened when Monica married Patricius. Although she tried to win him to the Christian faith, this did not happen until he was much older. Monica had to put up with Patricius' frequent "cheating" and "hot temper" (9.9.19). As we discussed in the Introduction to this Guide, this does not mean Patricius was abusive to Monica or Augustine, but it does mean that he exercised little self-control.

Yet Monica was forced to adopt strategies for dealing with her husband's temper. Although other women "bore the marks of blows and suffered disfigurement to their faces" because of their violent husbands, Augustine recounts that "it has been never reported nor is there any indication that [Patricius] had beaten his wife or that there had been any domestic strife between them even for a single day." In short, Patricius was no saint, but his temper was mollified by Monica's humble spirit.

Monica also managed to win over her mother-in-law, which appears to have been no small feat. Just as she had calmed down her angry husband, she also used her "steadfast perseverance and meekness" to win her initially-skeptical mother-in-law to her side (9.9.20). The result was that the servant girls who plagued Monica with their insolent tongues and gossip were subjected to punishment. This eventually led to greater peace and gentleness in the house.

Monica also became known for her work as a peacemaker. She had great discretion in sharing information. Augustine finds this ability especially remarkable given how prevalent gossip was in the community.

Monica's patience ultimately paid off when Patricius became a Christian at the end of his life, won over as he was by her gentle demeanor (and, likely, his impending death). After his baptism, Monica no longer had "reason to complain," (9.9.22), more evidence of Augustine's belief in the efficacy of the sacraments.

Right before her death, Monica has a mystical experience together with Augustine. It occurred at Ostia while Monica and Augustine were "gazing out a certain window which looked out onto the garden" (*hortus*) (9.10.23). The experience occurred as they were speculating about "what sort of eternal life is in store for the saints," a question which led them to the contemplation of God.

Their conclusion from this contemplation was that "the carnal senses, however pleasurable and however illuminating for this material world are not worthy of comparison, not even of mention, to the sweetness of that life" which is to come (9.10.24). Together, Augustine and Monica ascended and experienced "Wisdom" for a time "by a total thrust of the heart." I'll have much more to say about their experience of "eternal Wisdom" in the Focus Text Section below (9.10.25).

After this experience, Monica said that "her hope in this world has been consumed" (9.10.26). She had seen her son baptized. She had had a climactic spiritual experience. Her work on earth was done.

Within five days, Monica fell ill with a fever and lost consciousness. With Augustine at her side, Monica regained consciousness (note the parallel to Augustine's unnamed friend in Chapter Four) and requested that she be buried at Ostia. Monica's last request was for Augustine to remember her "at the Lord's altar" wherever he might be (9.11.27). We shouldn't miss that Monica's last request is prayers for her repose in death. Augustine presents Monica as one who believed that her spiritual development would continue in heaven and not be complete before her resurrection. From others, Augustine learned of Monica's "contempt of this life" and "the good of death" (9.11.28). She expressed no fear in the face of her immanent death. She passed away at age fifty-six.

Augustine then tried to fight back his "enormous grief" by maintaining characteristic Roman detachment (9.12.29). By contrast, Adeodatus starting wailing over his grandmother's passing and was quickly rebuked for doing so. At first, Augustine attributed his pangs of grief to the breaking of their bond of living together. His soul "was hurting" and his life was "torn to pieces" (9.12.30).

Evodius, ("*Ev-oh-dee-us*") who was one of the friends in Augustine's philosophical circle, started to chant Psalm 101.1 – "I will sing to you, o Lord, concerning your loyal love and justice" (9.12.31). Then, as word of Monica's passing spread, a greater crowd gathered to mourn. Augustine continued to fight back his tears.

The more Augustine tried to maintain an outward stoic demeanor, however, the more pain he felt inside. He confesses that he was annoyed by such human frailties. Augustine wanted God to take away his pain, but even this brought little relief (9.12.32).

Augustine went and took a bath (a parallel to the bath scene in Chapter Two where Patricius recounted Augustine's "unstable manhood"), which did little good. In fact, only sleep brought him some relief. Augustine was trying not to grieve and it was not working well.

Finally, after some time, Augustine dropped his stoic demeanor and wept openly for his mother. As Augustine poignantly puts it, "So I gave way to the tears which before were restrained. They overflowed as much as they desired. My heart was resting upon them" (9.12.33). In Augustine's day, there were some who would not have approved of his weeping over his mother's death, but it clearly did him some good.

Augustine admits that, looking back on it, his wound is now healed. Since Monica was "regenerated through baptism (*per baptismum regenerasti*)," he had no worries for her soul (9.13.34). But, in accordance with his mother's wishes, he still felt a need to pray for forgiveness for her sins, employing a mixture of texts from the Old and New Testaments to do so (9.13.35).

Monica did not desire an elaborate funeral, just that she "be commemorated at [the] altar at which she had labored without missing a day" (9.13.36). Augustine ends the Chapter reiterating his mother's request for prayer and encouraging his readers to join in the same, something which Christians have done across the centuries. Augustine concludes with these poignant words:

So in the end may that which she asked of me be fulfilled more richly in the prayers of many induced by my confessions than through my own petitions alone (9.13.37).

Focus Texts

As I mentioned above, Chapter Nine is a culmination of sorts in the book. Not only does it mark the end of the story, it also recapitulates many of the key themes we have been observing in the previous Chapters. Our focus in this section will be on Augustine's baptism and the culminating mystical experience he has with his mother.

One thing to keep in mind is that when we consider the *Confessions* as a whole (not just the nine Chapters we are handling in this Guide), Chapter Nine marks the midway point whether measured by pages, lines or words.[3] Thus, we observe that the theme of death and rebirth, so central to Chapter Nine, is also central to the argument of the *Confessions* as a whole.

Augustine's Baptism

We begin with Augustine's baptism, certainly one of the high-points of the *Confessions*, since it represents Augustine's entry into the Church. We should remember that Augustine had desired to be baptized all the way back in the first Chapter. When he unexpectedly got better from his sickness, Monica shelved the plans. I noted, at the time, that since Augustine had expressed belief, had been received by the Church as a Catechumen and had desired baptism, he had met all the criteria for one who had been baptized "by desire." For all intents and purposes, Augustine's first conversion was as a young boy. Of course, he had resisted God's on-going entreaties and spent years in rebellion. The journey we have been recounting is central to the story.

What Augustine wants us to see is that his baptism in Milan at the Easter Vigil on April 24th, 387 by Saint Ambrose is the ultimate conclusion to his rebellion.[4] Augustine has come into the Church and his sins have been washed away by the waters of baptism (Acts 24.16). His rebellion and restlessness, so pronounced in the early Chapters of the book, are over. Given its momentous importance both for Augustine and for the history of western Christianity, some have argued that his baptism is the real climax of the book. I'm certainly sympathetic to that idea. The only problem is that Augustine makes so little of it. Consider the following text:

Focus Text 9A

> Then when the right time arrived to hand in my name [for baptism], we left the country and returned to Milan. It pleased Alypius also to be born again (*renasci*) together with me in you, having already been clothed with the humility of your sacraments (Col 3.12), and having powerfully tamed his body by the courage to trample barefoot on the frozen ground of Italy, a rare undertaking. The boy Adeodatus, born of my flesh and by my sin, also joined with us. You fashioned him well. He was not quite fifteen years old, yet in cleverness he surpassed many serious and learned men. I acknowledge your gifts, O Lord, creator of all things. You are abundantly able to reform our deformities, for I donated nothing to that boy, save for sin. You, and no one else, inspired us to raise him in your teaching ...before long, you took his life from the earth. I remember him without anxiety. There was nothing to fear concerning his childhood, adolescence, nor anything about his person. We joined with him, sharing the same spiritual birthday, and by your grace catechized into your teaching. We were baptized and the anxiety of our past life fled away from us. (9.6.14).

If this is a climax, it's an odd one. I'll admit that my decision to attach that key last sentence in Focus Text 9A to the one preceding it is a bit misleading. In Latin, Augustine emphasizes a break in the flow of ideas, as he begins the sentence with an emphatic "et" ("and").[5] Augustine wants us to know that this baptism is a big deal.

If that's true, why doesn't he say more? Have you not had the feeling at certain points in the *Confessions* that Augustine could have benefitted from some more brevity at times. So why the absolute lack of information here when we might like some more detail?

I think the reason for his sparse descriptions of the baptism is that no one outside the Church was allowed to know about the sacramental mysteries. For the first few centuries of the Church, publically professing Christian faith could get you killed. This was by and large no longer the case as Augustine was writing. But there were people still alive who had known Christians who lived through Diocletian's persecutions earlier in the century.

Hence knowledge of the details of the Church's sacred rites was reserved only for those who had formally come into the Church, had undergone preparation during the Lenten season and had been taught what the significance of Baptism and the Eucharist were all about. In fact, one was not even taught about the significance of Baptism and the Eucharist until after one had actually had undergone these rituals. Usually, the newly baptized would wear their white garments for eight days and only then would be explained the mysteries.[6] Consider what Ambrose says in his lectures (*On the Mysteries*) which he would have delivered to the newly baptized:

> *Now the time reminds us to speak of the mysteries and to provide an account of the sacraments. For, before baptism, if we had tried to sneak something in before those not yet initiated, we should rather be reckoned betrayers rather than teachers. Moreover, it is better that the very light of the mysteries has been poured out upon the unaware rather than if some talk had preceded it. Therefore, open your ears and inhale the sweet savor of eternal life and grab hold of the gift of the sacraments (1.2-3).*

It's wise to remember that Augustine would have never seen the Eucharist or a Baptism before this point. This is the first time he's been allowed to witness the full majesty of the sacramental power of the Church. Fortunately, Ambrose's catechetical sermons have survived, which enable us to have a very good idea what Augustine would have experienced at his baptism. They survived because they are an essential source for the Church's teaching on the Sacraments.

Why teach the details of the mysteries only after having received them? The reason for this is Christians have always insisted that one start with faith and then move to understanding, not vice-versa. Ambrose says the following at the start of *On the Sacraments*: "to have provided an account of the sacraments beforehand is not proper, since to a Christian man, faith comes first" (1.1).

Ambrose wants the newly baptized to understand there was more than met the eye when they saw the water. Before approaching the baptismal font, Augustine would have been anointed with oil and asked several questions: "Do you renounce the Devil and his works?" "Do you renounce the world and its pleasures (2.5)?" Then he would have approached the water. Ambrose says, "Perhaps someone will ask, 'Is this all?' Yes, it is all. It is truly all, where all is innocence, all is piety, all is grace, all is sanctification" (3.10).

Ambrose would then have reviewed the "types" of baptism which were in Scripture, reminding Augustine of the story of Naaman the Syrian, who was healed after washing in the Jordan, the Israelites' crossing of the Red Sea through which they started their journey to the promised land, Noah and the flood wherein Noah and his family were saved from the disaster which hit the inhabited earth as well as the healing of the paralytic at the pool of Bethesda. In every case, these events pointed to the saving significance of baptism in the lives of the people. To Ambrose, this is why Jesus commands his disciples to go baptize in the name of "the Father and the Son and the Holy Spirit" (Matt 28.19).

Next, Augustine would have been lowered into an octagonal baptismal font, which was designed to provide a link between baptism and death.[7] In fact, Ambrose specifically taught in *On the Sacraments* that the font was in "the form of a sepulcher" (3.1.1). According to the Scriptures, baptism represented death wherein Augustine was dying to his flesh, the old man, and being raised to new life. To Ambrose, baptism was about being born again. He puts it this way:

> *A remedy was given [for sin] that man should die and rise again. Why? It happened so that the thing which previously yielded damnation might instead yield a benefit. What is that thing except death? How, you ask? Because the intervention of death brings an end to sin. For when we die, we certainly stop sinning....therefore, death is the end of sin and the resurrection is the reformation of our nature (2.6.17).*

Augustine would then have been asked three questions: "Do you believe in God the Father Almighty?" "Do you believe in our Lord Jesus Christ and in his cross?" And "Do you believe in the Holy Spirit" (2.7.20)? After affirmative answers, Augustine would have been lowered into the font, thus signifying his being buried with Christ. The priest who had lowered Augustine then would have said to him, "God the Father Almighty who has regenerated you by water and the Holy Ghost and has forgiven your sins, himself anoint you unto eternal life."[8] For Ambrose, it was clear the sacrament of baptism transforms those who undertake it. He puts it this way:

> *You went, you washed, you came to the altar. You began to see what before you had not seen. That is, through the font of the Lord and*

through the preaching of the passion of the Lord, your eyes were then opened. You who before seemed to be blinded in heart, you began to see the light of the sacraments (3.2.15).

Ambrose's understanding of the sacraments would be a significant influence on the Church's theology all throughout the Middle Ages and even into modern times. To Ambrose and the Church, there are two essential elements in baptism – water and the triune name. The invoking of the name of the Trinity by a duly-consecrated authority transforms simple water into something which saves by the power of the Holy Spirit.

When Jesus tells Nicodemus that "unless one is born of water and the Spirit, he cannot enter the kingdom of God" (John 3.5), Augustine understands this text to be speaking of baptism. Augustine describes his understanding of John 3.5 in a letter to Boniface, dealing specifically with the baptism of infants:

Therefore, water, outwardly exhibiting the mystery of grace, and Spirit, inwardly conferring the benefit of grace, releases the bond of blame, and restores good to our nature. Having been begotten out of Adam alone, He regenerates man in Christ alone (98.2).

For Augustine, as for most early Christians, there is saving significance to baptism. Baptism wipes away original sin, restores corrupted wills and enables us to come into the Church and partake of the Eucharist. Both Baptism and the Eucharist impart grace to believers and are essential to salvation. They're powerful and efficacious. Augustine's Baptism represents a significant milestone in his process of conversion. The Prodigal Son has come home.

Questions for Reflection
1. Do you come from a tradition which denies the sacraments "do" something? What do you make of Ambrose's and Augustine's insistence that they do?
2. Why are the sacraments called "mysteries?" What does it connote?
3. Baptism is a significant milestone in Augustine's conversion. How do you understand salvation?

The Vision at Ostia

I've saved the best for last. Augustine's final mystical vision is the climax of the autobiographical portion of the *Confessions*. While many aspects of the vision are similar to what Augustine described in Chapter Seven, there are some marked differences between the two experiences. I intend to point out both the similarities and the differences in this section.

Before we get there, however, I think it's important to address a long-running disagreement on how to understand this experience. I referenced this briefly in Chapter Seven, but want to expand my comments a bit more here. There are some who insist the mystical vision in Chapter Seven wasn't really valid at all since it ended in failure. To these readers, Augustine experienced "that which is" in Chapter Seven, but the experience was fleeting and ultimately unsuccessful because it couldn't be sustained. According to these readers, after Augustine's so-called conversion in Chapter Eight and his baptism in Chapter Nine, he had a "successful" vision here.

While I certainly believe there are differences between these two visions, I have a different perspective. I want to keep emphasizing that Augustine does not conceive of conversion in terms of a single point in time. Conversion, to Augustine, is mostly about turning away from temporal realities to participate in eternal realities.

Those who insist that Augustine becomes "converted" in Chapter Eight's garden scene are usually reading a particular theology into this work. As we've discussed, Augustine is not converted at a single moment in Chapter Eight's garden scene. In fact, Augustine is also not finally converted after this mystical vision in Chapter Nine.

This is so because Augustine perceives salvation as a process in which the grace of God works to transform our wills, resulting in a turn (literally, a conversion) towards Christ. As we've seen, much of this turning can seem frustratingly slow. This is because we have the ability to resist God's invitations to join with him. In other words, we often miss God's quiet work of grace.

Thus we should not read the following Text as the final step in Augustine's conversion. Rather, we should read it as yet another important milestone. As we'll see, Augustine believes perfection is not possible in this life. But experiencing the presence of God is.

Focus Text 9B

> Now, the day was upon us when Monica was to depart out of this life (of that day, you knew, but we were ignorant). It happened that I might believe in the administration of your secret ways. She and I stood alone, gazing out a certain window which looked out onto the garden (*hortus*) at the house where we were staying at Ostia on the Tiber. We were far from the crowds. After the labor of a long journey, we were restoring our strength for our voyage. We were alone conversing with each other with sweet intensity. 'Forgetting what lies behind and reaching forward to those things which are before us,' (Phil 3.13), we were searching with each other in the presence of the Truth, which you are, for what sort of eternal life is in store for the saints, a life which 'no eye has seen, nor ear heard, nor has it gone up (*ascendit*) into the heart of man' (1 Cor 2.9). But with the mouth of our hearts gaping open with astonishment, we panted after the source of your celestial streams (Gen 2.10), the source of life, which is with you. Having been sprinkled according to our ability, this happened that we might reflect on such a remarkable matter (9.10.23).

Ostia is a suburb of Rome, about thirty-five miles to the southwest of the city (just a few miles south of the airport). It was an important launching point for those who wanted to travel to North Africa from Rome since it sits on the Mediterranean Sea.

Augustine and Monica were headed back to North Africa, but their journey was delayed because of the outbreak of civil war. One of Rome's main generals was blockading the port cities to take control of Italy.[9] His blockade and his campaign against Rome was eventually crushed, after which travel became more manageable.[10] In the interim, however, Monica died.

By now, you'll not find it a coincidence that this scene takes place overlooking a garden. This creates an obvious link back to the Garden Scene of Chapter Eight, but also farther back to Chapter Two when Augustine stole the pears and fell from grace. Said differently, Augustine wants us to see that his turn toward continence in Chapter Eight leads directly to his baptism and then to this mystical vision. The events are related.

On the surface, the voyage Augustine mentions is his impending return to North Africa. In hindsight, however, Augustine spoke better than he knew. He was really referencing Monica's impending death and her subsequent voyage which would take her to a new place, a place where she would see God face to face.

We should notice that the focus is on Monica in this scene.[11] Augustine upends the mystical literature of the period by putting a woman front and center at the climax of the story. Monica is the guide for this vision, the one about to witness the glories of the beatific vision. This has led some to see a tie between this scene and Virgil's trip through Hades, led by his father.[12] In both stories, a parent serves as a guide to the afterlife.[13]

However, we're also supposed to catch how Aeneas is not really the best model for this story. The Biblical text is. When Augustine quotes Philippians Three, he is returning to the Scriptures to put his experience in context. It might be helpful to quote from the immediately preceding verses of Paul's letter to the Philippians:

> [8]*Indeed I count everything as loss because of the surpassing worth of knowing Christ Jesus my Lord. For his sake I have suffered the loss of all things, and count them as refuse, in order that I may gain Christ,* [9]*and be found in him, not having a righteousness of my own, based on law but that which is through faith in Christ, the righteousness from God that depends on faith;* [10]*that I may know him and the power of his resurrection, and may share his sufferings, becoming like him in death,* [11]*that if possible I may attain the resurrection from the dead.* [12]*Not that I have already obtained it, or have already become perfect, but I press on in order that I may lay hold of that for which also I was laid hold of by Christ Jesus (Phil 3.13).*

In this text, Paul counts all things as loss in order that he might gain Christ. I hope I don't offend you by pointing out how strong Paul's language is in this text. When Paul says that he counts all things as "refuse," the translators are being polite. The Greek word he employs – *skubala* – is actually employed in several early extra-biblical sources to refer to "human excrement."[14] In other words, Paul is employing a really strong word – something akin to "shit" in English – to show how little regard he has for the gains of this life.

Paul doesn't leave us there since he wants to orient us to a different reality. That different reality is the ultimate end of our Christian lives, which is resurrection. Notice how much emphasis resurrection receives in the above text. Paul says that he is pressing on so that he might lay hold of Christ. By sharing in the sufferings of Jesus, he hopes ultimately to be raised from the dead. Augustine is showing us that right before Monica's death, resurrection is what their ultimate hope was. In resurrection, they would ultimately find the rest they had been wanting.

This is an example of how Augustine's vision in Chapter Nine differs from Plotinus' concept of what a mystical vision entails. To Plotinus, the fall was all about the descent of souls into bodies. The whole problem with the world was its physicality. As a result, for Paul to emphasize bodily resurrection, he is making a strongly anti-Platonist statement. Augustine may be influenced by the Platonic tradition in many things, but he departs from elements which are not Christian. His focus on resurrection demonstrates this vividly.

In fact, Augustine's use of 1 Cor 2.9 continues this theme of resurrection as the ultimate hope of the Christian life. The text says, "but as it is written, what no eye has seen, nor ear heard, nor the heart of man conceived, what God has prepared for those who love him." This is a loose quotation of Isa 64.4 which is referencing God's Wisdom (which, as we've seen, Augustine takes as a reference to Christ) and its place in salvation. Isaiah was looking forward to God's future intervention on behalf of the nation of Israel, which gives this text a future sense.[15] Paul employs this eschatological perspective to discuss resurrection – the goal of the spiritual life – as something which will finally be accomplished in the future.

The idea of resurrection is ridiculous, even offensive, for most outside the Church. But, for Augustine, this is where the big change occurs in his conception of the spiritual life. In Chapter Seven, before he had been initiated into the mysteries of the Church, there was very little talk of resurrection. But, now, it is front and center.

As such, there is a distinct contrast between pagan and divine wisdom to Augustine.[16] Like Paul, he presses on to find Christ, thus setting up the experience which follows. Let's consider this next step:

Focus Text 9C

Our discussion led us to the conclusion that the carnal senses, however pleasurable and however illuminating for this material world are not worthy of comparison, not even of mention, to the sweetness of that life. We were raising ourselves up with burning emotion (*affectu*) toward 'That Which Is' (*idipsum*). Step by step we passed through physical bodies and then onto the heavens themselves, where the sun and moon and stars shine above the earth. Then we soared (*ascendebamus*) higher by internal contemplation, as well as conversation and amazement at your works. Then we came to our own minds and transcended them that we might attain to that region of unfailing fruitfulness where you let Israel graze forever on the food of truth and where the life of Wisdom is, who makes all things, both the things which have been and the things which shall be. But Wisdom herself is not created, but is Herself that which has always been and that which will be forever. On the contrary, there is no "has been" and no future "to be" in Her. But there is only being, since She is eternal, since, to have been or to be in the future, is not an attribute of the eternal. So while we were discoursing and panting after That Which Is, we achieved it for a short time by a total thrust (*ictu*) of the heart. Then, we sighed, and relinquished 'the first fruits of the Spirit' (Rom 8.23) and we returned to the racket of our mouths, where the spoken word has both a beginning and an end. Who is like your Word, our God, who abides in Himself without growing old and restores all things (9.10.24)?

Wow. First, notice first what's not here. There are no strange voices. There are no bright lights or colors. There are no hallucinations. There is no pain. There is no time.

One of the reasons I am arguing against those who say that this vision is a "successful" Christian version of the failed pagan attempt to ascend to God in Chapter Seven is because some of the same interpreters use this perspective to deny any Neoplatonic influence in this experience. We've already seen that Augustine is perfectly capable of rejecting the parts of Neoplatonism he finds objectionable. But, to say that Augustine has completely rejected the Platonic tradition in favor of the Christian God, goes too far. While it's true that there are marked differences with the vision from

Chapter Seven (I've already mentioned several), both visions occur within a broadly Neoplatonic framework, even if Augustine has reinterpreted several of its key features.

The key Neoplatonic influences on Augustine are the interiority of the vision and the idea of ascent. Consider what the Plotinus writes concerning mystical ascent in one of the most famous and beloved passages ever written on the subject:

> *Therefore, we must ascend again to the good, which is the yearning of every soul. Now, if anyone has seen it, he knows what I am talking about when I say it is beautiful. For, as the good, it is desired. Even the desire for it is good. Now the acquisition of it happens by ascending to the upper regions and by being converted (epistrapheisa), having peeled off that which we put on when descending (this is similar to those who go up to the holy sacred offerings – they have cleansings and peel off their garments to ascend unclothed). As they ascend, they bypass all which is unsuitable to God, observing alone that which is solely unmixed, simple and pure, and from which all things derive and for which all things long and exist and live and think. For, it is the cause of life and intelligence and being (1.6.7).*

To Plotinus, the soul desires to rise up and see God. We do this through contemplation of the unchangeable divine forms, which Augustine understands to be located in the divine mind. Our minds unite with the mind of God and thus gain a perception of God beyond space and time. Augustine has abandoned the parts of the Platonic tradition that do not accord with Scripture or the Rule of Faith (particularly the idea that the world is one giant emanation from God). But in no way has he abandoned the notion of ascent which Plotinus and the whole Platonic tradition passed down to him.

In the *Confessions,* Augustine describes this mystical ascent as "a total thrust (*ictu*) of the heart" which happens for just a short time. When Augustine says "heart," he does not merely mean the emotional center of our being. Rather, by heart, Augustine is employing it as the "intellectual *and* spiritual center" of a person.[17] The heart is where the emotional, spiritual and intellectual faculties all become united.

The Latin word which I have translated "thrust" (*ictu*) in the Focus Text is an important one. I say this because in Latin, "*ictus*" has a broad semantic range of meaning. Depending on its usage, it can mean "blow, stab, stroke, beat, thrust, stress or stream."[18]

Would it surprise you to learn that the same Latin word figured prominently in Chapter Seven's mystical vision as well? There, Augustine described his vision of "That Which Is" as a "thrust of trembling contemplation (*in ictu trepidantis aspectus*)." Hence there is a textual link between the two visions, a rather odd occurrence if Augustine is trying to separate them, one as pagan and the other as Christian.

Next, what does Augustine mean by having to leave behind the "first-fruits of the Spirit?" This is a reference to Rom 8.23. Let's review what Paul says in this text:

> *For we know that the whole creation has been groaning in travail together until now; and not only the creation, but we ourselves, who have the first fruits of the Spirit, groan inwardly as we wait for adoption as sons, the redemption of our bodies (Rom 8.22-23).*

The important thing is this text points forward to a reality which is not yet complete. Augustine and Monica have both received the Spirit at their baptisms, but they are not fully redeemed. They await their respective resurrections for the redemption of their bodies.

This is a clear expression of what Augustine has been telling us all along in the *Confessions*: conversion is a process that culminates ultimately in resurrection and the beatific vision, but has a present reality. To Augustine, the first-fruits of the Spirit refer not to the Holy Spirit here, which he received at his baptism, but to the anticipation of the beatific vision. Augustine can rest assured that his mother's impending death is not ultimately a death sentence. It is simply a stage that we pass through on our journeys which will ultimately culminate in our resurrection from the dead.

Once again, the vision is fleeting and does not sustain. Augustine puts a very positive spin on the vision as he recounts it. Why does he do that if he could not keep the vision going? Consider what he says in the final paragraph of this scene:

Focus Text 9D

> Therefore we said, if for someone the commotion of the flesh were silent (*sileant*), if the phenomena of the earth, water and air were silent, if the heavens themselves were silent and if the soul itself were silent that it might go beyond itself by not thinking about itself, and if all dreams and imaginary revelations were silent, and if whatever was transient were silent, since if any could hear, they would all say, 'we did not make ourselves' (Ps 100.3), but 'he who abides forever' made us (Isa 40.8). These, having spoken, if they would stay silent (*taceant*), having only roused the discriminating ears of Him who made them, if he alone were to speak not by them, but by himself, so that we might hear his word not by the tongue of flesh, nor by calling upon angels, nor by the sound of thunder, nor by the murky sound of an obscure parable, but that we might hear Him in these things we love, let us listen without such things (such is now what happened when we extended ourselves and in swift contemplation, we arrived at eternal Wisdom who abides beyond all things). Oh that this could continue! Then other visions, so far inferior, could be taken away. This vision alone would ravish, engulf and hide the beholder in interior blessedness. Hence, the eternal life is like that single moment of understanding which we sighed after. Is this not what is written: 'Enter into the joy of your Lord' (Matt 25.21)? When will this be? 'When we all will rise again, but we will not all be changed' (1 Cor 15.51) (9.10.25).

Once again, wow. I have to admit to being surprised here. At the apex of the *Confessions* – the final mystical vision – it turns out to be quiet, even silent. There are no words to describe it. There is not even a "real" vision at all. What we hear is silence. Is this what you would expect from a "peak" spiritual experience? Augustine gives us something much more profound.

Indeed Augustine gives us silence. Notice how often the words like hearing and silence are used in the above text. Augustine gets this from Plotinus. Notice how Plotinus describes the movement of the soul as it contemplates the One, Plotinus' name for God:

> *Let the soul scrutinize the great soul, distinct, but not lowly, having become worthy of observation by being released from that which deceives and has enticed others, as well as by its silent constitution. Let not only the body which surrounds it, but also the surging waves of the*

corporate body be silent, even that which is beside it, let it be silent – let the earth be silent, the sea and the air be silent, even heaven itself let it be at rest (5.1.2).

Could it be that the quiet which Plotinus foresees and the quiet which Augustine and Monica experience is the fleeting experience of rest in this world? Yes, rest, the very thing we've been searching for since the first pages of the *Confessions*.

What Augustine has come to understand is that perfect rest is not available now. Of course, this is quite a bit different than the understanding of the Platonic tradition which taught that by contemplation one could transcend the physical world and spiritually attain perfect peace today. Here's where the traditions part.

For Augustine, we're still weighed down by sin. He has caught a fleeting glance of what is to come – the beatific vision — and it's beyond words. All we can do is sit in silence, sit in awe of what awaits us after our deaths. More than any other passage in the *Confessions*, Focus Text 9D is poetry, not prose. Words simply can't do justice to what Augustine experienced.

But we must not forget that this scene represents the fulfillment of Monica's vision from Chapter Three. Do you remember when Monica dreamt of Augustine standing on a rule (*regula*) which we interpreted as the Rule of Faith? We discovered that Monica's original vision foretold Augustine's coming to faith in his baptism.

Now we see even more is involved. We see that Augustine and Monica are united together in their faith, representative of the community which is united together with Christ in baptism. Augustine was ultimately pointing to this moment when he wrote in Chapter Three, "The joy which would come to that pious woman was predicted long ahead of time by the dream which would be fulfilled so long after" (3.11.20).

Monica's vision, which foretold what was to come, was fulfilled when both she and her son had a foretaste of the beatific vision together. By experiencing it together, Augustine once again upends the Platonic tradition. Consider the most famous thing which Plotinus ever wrote, the words which end the *Enneads*:

Now such is the life of gods and of divinely flourishing humans, release from foreign things in the here and now, a life without pleasure in the here and now, a flight of solitary to the solitary (6.9.11).

For Augustine, this experience isn't solitary at all. It's about community, togetherness. It's about Christ's calling his Church to himself. To Augustine (who, as usual, is following Paul), it's all about resurrection. Resurrection – and the beatific vision – is what Christians have to look forward to. This is where ultimate rest is to be found, in the union of the redeemed body and soul.

For Augustine, resurrection was the center of his hope. His hope was for redemption, the union of body and soul with Christ. From the beginning of the *Confessions,* his hope has been to be united with God in blessed union with him. His hope was for lasting rest.

Questions for Reflection

1. This scene happens right before Monica's death. Have you had a death in your family affect you in a significant way?
2. To Augustine, mysticism was something concrete, but fleeting. How do you sense God's presence in your own life?
3. Our world is noisy. Does silence play a role in your spiritual life?
4. Augustine makes a big deal out of the idea that resurrection is the ultimate goal of our spiritual lives. What does this mean to you?
5. Has Augustine's teaching in the *Confessions* changed how you approach the reading of the Scriptures or how your pray?

ENDNOTES

1   Henry Chadwick, *Augustine of Hippo: A Life* (Oxford: Oxford University Press, 2010), 4.

2   James O'Donnell, *Augustine: A New Biography* (New York: Harper Perennial, 2006), 9.

3   John O'Meara, *The Young Augustine: The Growth of St. Augustine's Mind Up to His Conversion*, 2nd ed. (New York: Alba House, 2001), 5.

4   Aristeas, *The Letter of Aristeas*, ed. H. St. J. Thackeray (London: Macmillan and Company, 1904), 7.

5   Maria Gaetti, "Plotinus: The Platonic Tradition and the Foundation of Neoplatonism," in *The Cambridge Companion to Plotinus*, ed. Lloyd P Gerson (Cambridge: Cambridge University Press, 1996), 12.

6   Chadwick, *Augustine of Hippo*, 5.

7   D. P. Simpson, "Curialis," *Cassell's New Compact Latin- English Dictionary* (New York: Macmillan, 1987), 57.

8   Gerald Bonner, *St Augustine of Hippo* (Norwich: Canterbury Press, 1986), 17.

9   Peter Brown, *Through the Eye Of A Needle: Wealth, the Fall of Rome, and the Making of Christianity in the West, 350-550 AD* (Princeton: Princeton University Press, 2012), 63–65.

10 New Advent, "Augustine of Hippo," *The Catholic Encyclopedia* (Denver: New Advent, 2003).

11 Eugene TeSelle, "Augustine," in *The Encyclopedia of Christianity*, ed. Erwin Fahlbusch and Geoffrey William Bromiley, vol. 1 (Grand Rapids: Wm. B. Eerdmans, 1999), 159–160.

12 Everett Ferguson, *Baptism in the Early Church: History, Theology, and Liturgy in the First Five Centuries* (Grand Rapids: Eerdmans Publishing, 2009), 854.

13 Ibid., 776–777.

14 O'Meara, *The Young Augustine*, 10.

15 Chadwick, *Augustine of Hippo*, 98.

16 Charles Quarles, "Rhetoric," ed. Chad Owen Brand, Holman *Illustrated Bible Dictionary* (Nashville, TN: Holman Bible Publishers, 2003), 1397.

17 Plato, "Apology," in *Plato: Complete Works*, ed. John M. Cooper and D. S. Hutchinson (Indianapolis, IN: Hackett Publishing, 1997), 20.a–c, P. 20.

18 Nello Cipriani, "Rhetoric," ed. Allan Fitzgerald and John C. Cavadini, *Augustine Through the Ages: An Encyclopedia* (Grand Rapids.: W.B. Eerdmans, 1999), 725–726.

19 Possidius, *The Life of Saint Augustine*, ed. Herbert T. Weiskotten (Merchantville, NJ: Evolution Publishing, 2008), chap. 3–4. pp. 6–7.

20 Saint Augustine, *Sermons (341-400) on Various Subjects* (New York: New City Press, 1995), 355.2, P. 165.

21 Chadwick, *Augustine of Hippo*, 50.

22 Augustine, *Sermons (341-400) on Various Subjects*, 355.2, P. 165.

23 Possidius, *The Life of Saint Augustine*, chap. 19–20, pp. 28–29.

24 Ibid., chap. 5, P. 8.

25 Peter Brown, *Augustine of Hippo: A Biography* (Berkeley: University of California Press, 2000), x.

26 O'Donnell, *Augustine*, 5.

27 Hannis Taylor and Mary Hunt, *Cicero: A Sketch of His Life and Works* (Chicago: A.C. McClurg & Co., 1916), 14.

28 Jaroslav Pelikan, *The Emergence of the Catholic Tradition*, vol. 1, The Christian Tradition: A History of the Development of Doctrine (Chicago: University of Chicago Press, 1974), 330.

29 Alan Ryan, *On Politics: A History of Political Thought*, vol. 2 (New York: Liveright Publishing, 2012), 411–412.

30 John Freccero, *Dante: The Poetics of Conversion* (Cambridge, MA: Harvard University Press, 1986), 24.

31 Donald Beecher, "Petrarch's 'Conversion' on Mont Ventoux and the Patterns of Religious Experience," Renaissance and Reformation / Renaissance et Réforme 28, no. 3 (January 1, 2004): 55–56.

32 Ludwig Wittgenstein, *Philosophical Investigations*, 4th ed. (Oxford: Blackwell Publishing, 2009), xxxiii.

33 Bertrand Russell, *A History of Western Philosophy* (New York: Simon and Schuster, 1945), 354.

34 Chadwick, *Augustine of Hippo*, 73.

35 Muḥammad Haykal, *The Life of Muḥammad*, 3rd ed. (Selangor, Malaysia: Islamic Book Trust, 2008), 52.

36 Robert Louis Wilken, *The First Thousand Years: A Global History of Christianity* (New Haven: Yale University Press, 2012), 130.

37 J. N. D. Kelly, *Jerome: His Life, Writings, and Controversies* (Peabody, MA: Hendrickson, 1975), 219–220.

38 Chadwick, *Augustine of Hippo*, 3.

39 Ibid., xxix.Note that there is scholarly disagreement over the exact dating of the Confessions. Brown puts its writing in 401, for example, almost six years after Augustine's consecration as Bishop. Cf. Brown, Augustine of Hippo, 64.

40 James O'Donnell, *Augustine Confessions*, vol. 1 (Oxford: Oxford University Press, 2012), xxxii.

41 Mark Vessey and Catherine Conybeare, "Reading the Confessions," in *A Companion to Augustine* (Malden, MA: Wiley-Blackwell, 2012), 101.

42 Michael Cameron, *Christ Meets Me Everywhere: Augustine's Early Figurative Exegesis* (New York: Oxford University Press, 2012), 209.

43 For a perspective that sees more continuity with his Manichaean past, see Jason BeDuhn, *Augustine's Manichaean Dilemma*, vol. 1 (Philadelphia: University of Pennsylvania Press, 2010).

44 Brown, *Through the Eye of a Needle*, 185.

45 Serge Lancel, *Saint Augustine* (London: SCM Press, 2002), 206.

46 Chadwick, Augustine of Hippo, 89.

47 Ibid., 90.

48 Paula Fredriksen, "The Confessions as Autobiography," in *A Companion to Augustine*, ed. Mark Vessey (Malden, MA: Wiley-Blackwell, 2012), 85.

49 O'Donnell, *Augustine Confessions*, 2012, 1:9.

50 Kim Paffenroth and Robert Peter Kennedy, *A Reader's Companion to Augustine's Confessions* (Louisville, KY.: John Knox Press, 2003), 10.

51 Robert McMahon, *Augustine's Prayerful Ascent: An Essay on the Literary Form of the Confessions* (Athens, GA: University of Georgia Press, 1989), 1.

52 O'Donnell, *Augustine Confessions*, 2012.

53 Augustine, *Confessions*, ed. Henry Chadwick (Oxford: Oxford University Press, 2008), 10.30, P. 203.

54 I am grateful to Frederick Crosson's essay on Chapter Five of the Confessions for pointing out many of the structural markers I cite in this introduction. Cf. Frederick Crosson, "Book Five: The Disclosure of Hidden Providence," in *A Reader's Companion to Augustine's Confessions*, ed. Kim Paffenroth and Robert Peter Kennedy (Louisville, KY: Westminster John Knox Press, 2003).

55 Cf. Augustine, *City of God*, trans. Bettenson, Henry (New York: Penguin Books, 2003), 2.14, pp. 63–64. Here Augustine demonstrates specific knowledge about Plato's pessimistic teaching on poets from the Republic.

56 Cf. Ibid., 13.16, P. 526. Here, Augustine quotes directly from Cicero's Latin translation of Plato's Timaeus.

57 Plato, *The Republic*, ed. H. D. P. Lee and M. S. Lane (London: Penguin, 2007), 440e, 5.2.

58 Walter C. Kaiser and Moises Silva, *Introduction to Biblical Hermeneutics: The Search for Meaning* (Grand Rapids, MI: Zondervan, 2009), 76.

59 Robert McMahon, "Book Thirteen: *The Creation of the Church as the Paradigm for the Confessions*," in A Reader's Companion to Augustine's Confessions, ed. Kim Paffenroth and Robert Peter Kennedy (Louisville, KY: Westminster John Knox Press, 2003), 217.

60 James Wetzel, *Augustine: A Guide for the Perplexed* (New York: Bloomsbury Academic, 2012), 44.

61 Merriam-Webster, "Confession," *Merriam-Webster's Ninth Collegiate Dictionary* (Springfield, MA: Merriam-Webster, 1988), 275.

62 Leo F. Stelten, "Confessio," *Dictionary of Ecclesiastical Latin* (Peabody, MA: Hendrickson, 1995), 299.

Notes to Chapter One

1   Augustine, *Confessions*, 1.3.3, P. 4.

2   Ibid., 1.5.5, P. 5.

3   Augustine, "On Forgiveness of Sins and Baptism," in *Nicene and Post-Nicene Fathers*, ed. Philip Schaff, vol. 5, 1.5 (New York: Christian Literature Company, 1887), 23–24, P. 24.

4   Augustine, *On the Usefulness of Belief*, ed. John H. S. Burleigh, Library of Christian Classics: Ichtus Edition (Philadelphia: Westminster Press, 1953), 1.2, P. 292.

5   Ibid.

6   Catholic Church, *Catechism of the Catholic Church*, 2nd ed. (New York: Doubleday, 1997), 1259, P. 352.

7   Vessey and Conybeare, "Reading the Confessions," 99.

Notes to Chapter Two

1   Brown, *Augustine of Hippo*, 3.

2   Augustine, *Confessions*, 2.5, P. 26.

3   http://www.reference.com/motif/society/an-idle-mind-is-the-devil's-workshop, Accessed 10-21-2013

4   Leo F. Stelten, "Dispersio," *Dictionary of Ecclesiastical Latin* (Peabody, MA: Hendrickson Publishers, 1995), 77.

5 Garry Wills, *Saint Augustine* (New York: Viking, 1999), 13.

6 R. S. O. Tomlin, "Augustine's Worldly Ambition and Career," in *A Companion to Augustine*, ed. Mark Vessey (Malden, MA: Wiley-Blackwell, 2012), 58.

7 Kate Kooper, "Love and Belonging, Loss and Betrayal in the Confessions," in *A Companion to Augustine*, ed. Mark Vessey (Malden, MA: Wiley-Blackwell, 2012), 72.

8 Robert J O'Connell, *St. Augustine's Confessions: The Odyssey of Soul* (New York: Fordham University Press, 1989), 48.

9 Bonner, *St Augustine of Hippo*, 54.

10 Augustine, *Confessions*, 2.10.18, P. 34.

11 Augustine, "The Punishment and the Forgiveness of Sins and the Baptism of Little Ones," in *Answer to the Pelagians*, ed. Roland Teske, vol. 1 (Hyde Park, NY: New City Press, 1997), 2.7.8, pp. 85–86.

12 John Burnaby, Amor Dei: *A Study of the Religion of St. Augustine* (Eugene, OR: Wipf & Stock, 2007), 187.

13 James O'Donnell, *Augustine Confessions*, vol. 2 (Oxford: Oxford University Press, 2012), 2.207, P. 207.

14 http://www.wikipaintings.org/en/albrecht-durer/mary-with-a-pear, Accessed 11-8-13

15 Homer, *The Odyssey*, trans. Robert Fitzgerald (New York: Farrar, Straus, and Giroux, 1998), 7.120, P. 114.

16 Cameron, *Christ Meets Me Everywhere*, 290.

17 Eugene TeSelle, "Serpent, Eve and Adam: Augustine and the Exegetical Tradition," in *Augustine: Presbyter Factus Sum*, ed. Joseph T. Lienhard, Earl C. Muller, and Roland J. Teske (New York: Peter Lang, 1993), 351.

18 Augustine, *Confessions*, 2.4.9, P. 29.

19 Ibid., 9.6.14, P. 164.

20 Wills, *Saint Augustine*, 17.

21 Marcus Quintilianus, *Institutes of Oratory*, ed. J. S. Watson (London: Henry G. Bohn, 1856), 9.2–3, P. 75.

Notes to Chapter Three

1 Leo F. Stelten, ed., "Conversio," *Dictionary of Ecclesiastical Latin* (Peabody, MA: Hendrickson, 1995), 59.

2 Walter Bauer and Frederick W Danker, *A Greek-English Lexicon of the New Testament and Other Early Christian Literature*, 3rd ed. (Chicago: University of Chicago Press, 2000), 382.

3   Jose Reta, "Conversion," ed. Allan Fitzgerald and John C. Cavadini, trans. Augustine Esposito, *Augustine Through the Ages: An Encyclopedia* (Grand Rapids, MI: W.B. Eerdmans, 1999), 239–240.

4   Lancel, *Saint Augustine*, 27.

5   Wills, *Saint Augustine*, 17.

6   Lancel, *Saint Augustine*, 36, note a.

7   Bonner, *St Augustine of Hippo*, 170.

8   Augustine, *On the Usefulness of Belief*, 1.2, P. 292.

9   Bonner, *St Augustine of Hippo*, 169.

10 O'Donnell, *Augustine Confessions*, 2012, 2:199.

11 Burnaby, *Amor Dei*, 247.

12 Kathryn Greene-McCreight, "Rule of Faith," ed. Kevin J. Vanhoozer, *Dictionary for Theological Interpretation of the Bible* (Grand Rapids, MI: Baker Academic, 2005), 703.

13 Ibid.

14 O'Donnell, *Augustine Confessions*, 2012, 2:199.

15 Ibid.

16 Willem VanGemeren, "The Law of the Perfection of Righteousness in Jesus Christ: A Reformed Perspective," in *Five Views on Law and Gospel*, ed. Greg L Bahnsen (Grand Rapids, MI: Zondervan, 1996), 30.

17 Elaine Pagels, *Adam, Eve, and the Serpent: Sex and Politics in Early Christianity* (New York: Random House, 2011), 122.

18 Miles Hollingworth, *Saint Augustine of Hippo: An Intellectual Biography* (Oxford: Oxford University Press, 2013), 127.

19 J. Kevin Coyle, "Mani, Manicheism," ed. Allan Fitzgerald and John C. Cavadini, *Augustine Through the Ages: An Encyclopedia* (Grand Rapids, MI: W.B. Eerdmans, 1999), 520.

20 Bonner, *St Augustine of Hippo*, 56.

21 Cameron, *Christ Meets Me Everywhere*, 101.

22 O'Meara, *The Young Augustine*, 48.

23 Ibid., 56.

24 Bonner, *St Augustine of Hippo*, 163.

25 Augustine, "Reply to Faustus the Manichaean," in Nicene and Post-Nicene Fathers Series 1, Volume 4 - Enhanced Version (Early Church Fathers), ed. Philip Schaff, vol. 4, *Nicene and Post-Nicene Fathers* 1 (Peabody, MA: Hendrickson Publishers, 2009), 13.6, P. 201.

26 Bonner, *St Augustine of Hippo*, 164.

27 Ibid., 165.

28 Ibid.

29 Ibid.

30 Fitzgerald and Cavadini, "*Augustine through the Ages*," 1999, 522.

31 Bonner, *St Augustine of Hippo*, 166.

32 Ibid., 167.

33 Ibid., 166.

34 Cameron, *Christ Meets Me Everywhere*, 103.

35 Bonner, *St Augustine of Hippo*, 168.

36 Coyle, "Augustine through the Ages," 522.

37 Bonner, *St Augustine of Hippo*, 169.

38 Ibid.

39 Hollingworth, *Saint Augustine of Hippo*, 136.

40 BeDuhn, *Augustine's Manichaean Dilemma*, 1:29.

41 O'Meara, *The Young Augustine*, 70.

Notes to Chapter Four

1   Walter A. Elwell and Barry J. Beitzel, "Pride," *Baker Encyclopedia of the Bible* (Grand Rapids, MI: Baker Book House, 1988), 1752.

2   James Wetzel, "The Trappings Of Woe and Confession of Grief," in *A Reader's Companion to Augustine's Confessions*, ed. Kim Paffenroth and Robert Kennedy (Louisville, KY: Westminster John Knox Press, 2003), 54.

3   Etienne Gilson, *The Christian Philosophy of Saint Augustine* (New York: Random House, 1960), 8.

4   Augustine, *Confessions*, 4.1.1, P. 52.

5   Ibid., 4.4.8, P. 57.

6   Carl G. Vaught, *The Journey Toward God in Augustine's Confessions: Books I-VI* (Albany: State University of New York Press, 2003), 94.

7   Ibid., 107.

8   Augustine, *Confessions*, n. 30, P. 68.

9   Robert Audi, "Aristotle," *The Cambridge Dictionary of Philosophy* (Cambridge: Cambridge University Press, 1999), 45.

10 Joseph Lienhard, "Friendship, Friends," ed. Allan Fitzgerald and John C. Cavadini, *Augustine Through the Ages: An Encyclopedia* (Grand Rapids, MI: W.B. Eerdmans, 1999), 372.

11 Ibid.

12 Plato, "Lysius," in *Complete Works*, ed. John M. Cooper and D. S. Hutchinson (Indianapolis, IN: Hackett Publishing, 1997), 698.

13 John Deigh, "Ethics, Goodness and the Question of Ends," ed. Robert Audi, *The Cambridge Dictionary of Philosophy* (Cambridge: Cambridge University Press, 1999), 285.

14 Aristotle, *Nicomachean Ethics*, ed. Terence Irwin, 2nd ed. (Indianapolis, IN: Hackett Publishing, 1999), 330.

15 Augustine, *Against the Academicians*, ed. Peter King (Indianapolis: Hackett Pub. Co., 1995), 3.6.23, P. 64.

16 Saint Augustine, *Letters 211-270, 1*-29** (Hyde Park, NY: New City Press, 2005), 258.2–3, P. 195.

17 Patout Burns, "Grace," ed. Allan Fitzgerald and John C. Cavadini, *Augustine Through the Ages: An Encyclopedia* (Grand Rapids, MI: W.B. Eerdmans, 1999), 391.

18 Hans Boersma, *Heavenly Participation: The Weaving of a Sacramental Tapestry* (Grand Rapids, MI: W.B. Eerdmans Pub. Co., 2011), 64–65.

19 Henri de Lubac, *Augustinianism and Modern Theology*, trans. Lancelot C. Sheppard (New York: Crossroad Publishing, 2000), 19.

20 Burnaby, *Amor Dei*, 257.

21 Wills, *Saint Augustine*, 31.

22 Ibid.

23 Ibid.

24 Augustine, City of God, viii.

25 Ibid., 15.7, P. 604.

26 Bauer and Danker, *A Greek-English Lexicon of the New Testament and Other Early Christian Literature*, 440.

27 Boersma, *Heavenly Participation*, 164.

28 I am grateful to Dr. Peter Kreeft for this point.

Notes to Chapter Five

1   Frederick Crosson, "Structure and Meaning in the Confessions," in *The Augustinian Tradition*, ed. Gareth B. Matthews (Berkeley: University of California Press, 1999), 30.

2   Crosson, "Book Five: The *Disclosure of Hidden Providence*," 83–84.

3   I am grateful to Frederick Crosson for this insight.

4   Crosson, "Book Five: The Disclosure of Hidden Providence," 78–79.

5   Augustine, *Confessions*, 5.3.5, P. 74.

6   Rebecca Weaver, "Prayer," ed. Allan Fitzgerald and John C. Cavadini, *Augustine Through the Ages: An Encyclopedia* (Grand Rapids, MI: W.B. Eerdmans, 1999), 674.

7   Ibid.

8   John Peter Kenney, *The Mysticism of Saint Augustine: Rereading The Confessions* (New York: Routledge, 2005), 65.

9   Crosson, "Book Five: The Disclosure of Hidden Providence," 75.

10 Eugene TeSelle, *Augustine the Theologian* (Eugene, Or.: Wipf and Stock, 2002), 89.

11 Gilson, *The Christian Philosophy of Saint Augustine*, 124.

12 Augustine, *The Augustine Catechism: The Enchiridion on Faith, Hope, and Charity*, ed. Bruce Harbert and Boniface Ramsey (Hyde Park, NY: New City Press, 2008), 18.

13 Fredriksen, "The Confessions as Autobiography," 97.

14 Augustine, *Letters 211-270, 1*-29**, 243.4–5, P. 166.

15 Virgil, *The Aeneid*, trans. Robert Fitzgerald (New York: Vintage Books, 1990), 4.499, P. 108.

16 Wills, *Saint Augustine*, 36.

Notes to Chapter Six

1   Prue Shaw, *Reading Dante: From Here to Eternity* (New York: Liveright, 2014), 93.

2   William A. Stephany, "Thematic Structure in Augustine's Confessions," ed. Allan D. Fitzgerald, O.S.A., Augustinian Studies 20 (1989): 137.

3   Pierre Courcelle, *Recherches Sur Les "Confessions" de Saint Augustin* (Paris: Edition E. de Boccard, 1950), 31–32.

4   O'Donnell, *Augustine Confessions*, 2012, 2:362.

5   Kooper, "Love and Belonging, Loss and Betrayal in the Confessions," 79–80.

6   Eric Plumer, "Book Six: Major Characters and Memorable Incidents," in *A Reader's Companion to Augustine's Confessions*, ed. Kim Paffenroth and Robert Peter Kennedy (Louisville, KY: Westminster John Knox Press, 2003), 89.

7   Hans Von Campenhausen, *Fathers of the Latin Church* (Peabody, MA: Hendrickson Publishers, 1998), 90.

8   Brown, *Through the Eye of a Needle*, 127.

9   Ibid., 518.

10 Cameron, *Christ Meets Me Everywhere*, 26.

11 Ibid., 37.

12 Ibid.

13 Plumer, "Book Six: Major Characters and Memorable Incidents," 100.

14 D. P. Simpson, "Curiositas, Curiosus," *Cassell's New Compact Latin-English Dictionary* (New York: Macmillan General Reference, 1987), 58.

15 Kenney, *The Mysticism of Saint Augustine*, 74.

16 Gilson, *The Christian Philosophy of Saint Augustine*, 135.

17 Kooper, "Love and Belonging, Loss and Betrayal in the Confessions," 77.

18 http://www.newadvent.org/cathen/04207a.htm, accessed 11-22-2013

19 http://www.bombaxo.com/hippolytus.html, accessed 11-22-2013

20 Ambrose, *On Virginity*, ed. Philip Schaff and Henry Wace, vol. 10, Nicene and Post-Nicene Fathers 2 (New York: The Christian Literature Company, 1896), 7.35, P. 369.

21 Ibid.

Notes to Chapter Seven

1 Quoted in Bernard McGinn, *The Foundations of Mysticism: Origins to the Fifth Century*, vol. 1 (New York: Crossroad, 1994), xiii. McGinn is quoting Teresa, *The Life of Saint Teresa of Jesus: The Autobiography of St. Teresa of Avila*, ed. Peers, Alison (Garden City, NY: Doubleday, 1960), 1.10, P. 119.

2 McGinn, *The Presence of God*, 1:xiii.

3 James O'Donnell, *Augustine Confessions*, vol. 3 (Oxford: Oxford University Press, 2012), 91.

4 As many have pointed out, the center of the *Confessions* is in Chapter Nine when measured by lines, words or pages. My assertion that Chapter Seven is the midway point in the *Confessions* only works by measuring Chapters or Sections.

5 Philip Cary, "Book Seven: Inner Vision and the Goal of Augustine's Life," in *A Reader's Companion to Augustine's Confessions*, ed. Kim Paffenroth and Robert Peter Kennedy (Louisville, KY: Westminster John Knox Press, 2003), 117.

6 J. N. D Kelly, *Early Christian Doctrines* (Peabody, MA: Hendrickson Publishers, 2004), 241–242.

7 Ibid., 292.

8 Kenney, *The Mysticism of Saint Augustine*, 23.

9 Thomas Aquinas, *Summa Theologica*, vol. 1 (Westminster, MD: Christian Classics, 1981), I.1, P. 1.

10 Gilson, *The Christian Philosophy of Saint Augustine*, 3.

11 Ambrose, *On the Sacraments and On the Mysteries*, ed. J. H. Srawley, trans. T. Thompson (London: SPCK, 1950), 4.19, P. 52.

12 Jose Reta, "Conversion," ed. Allan D. Fitzgerald, trans. Augustine Esposito, *Augustine Through the Ages: An Encyclopedia* (Grand Rapids, MI: Wm. B. Eerdmans Publishing Company, April 9, 2009), 243.
13 McGinn, *The Presence of God*, 1:233.
14 Kenney, *The Mysticism of Saint Augustine*, 56.
15 Ibid., 57.
16 Scott MacDonald, "The Divine Nature," in *Augustine's Confessions: Critical Essays*, ed. William E. Mann (Lanham, MD: Rowman & Littlefield Publishers, 2006), 98.

Notes to Chapter Eight
1 McMahon, "Book Thirteen: The Creation of the Church as the Paradigm for the Confessions," 217.
2 Mark Edwards, "Augustine and His Christian Predecessors," in *A Companion to Augustine*, ed. Mark Vessey (Malden, MA: Wiley-Blackwell, 2012), 218.
3 Augustine, *Confessions*, 8.2.3, P. 135.
4 Ferguson, *Baptism in the Early Church*, 784.
5 I am grateful to Dr. Guiseppe Mazzotta for this insight. Cf. Giuseppe Mazzotta, "Dante In Translation: Lecture V - Inferno IX, X, XI" (presented at the Open Yale Courses, New Haven, CT, September 18, 2008), http://oyc.yale.edu/italian-language-and-literature/ital-310/lecture-5#transcript.
6 Paul Henry, *The Path to Transcendence: From Philosophy to Mysticism in Saint Augustine* (Pittsburgh, PA: Pickwick Press, 1981), 81.
7 Lubac, *Augustinianism and Modern Theology*, 52.
8 Ibid., 173.
9 A. Sizoo, "Ad August. Conf. VIII, XII, 29," Vigiliae Christianae 12, no. 2 (July 1958): 105–106.
10 Garry Wills, *Augustine's Confessions: A Biography* (Princeton, NJ: Princeton University Press, 2011), 75.
11 Peter Brown, *The Body and Society*, 1st ed. (New York: Columbia University Press, 1988), 416.
12 Elizabeth A. Clark, "Asceticism," ed. Allan Fitzgerald and John C. Cavadini, *Augustine Through the Ages: An Encyclopedia* (Grand Rapids, MI: W.B. Eerdmans, 1999), 70.
13 Augustine, "On the Excellence of Marriage," in *Marriage and Virginity*, ed. David G Hunter, vol. 5, *The Works of St. Augustine* 1 (Hyde Park, NY: New City Press, 1999), 3, pp. 34–35.

14 Augustine, *City of God*, 14.23, P. 585.

15 Brown, *The Body and Society*, 402.

16 Ibid., 407.

Notes to Chapter Nine

1   Stephany, "Thematic Structure in Augustine's Confessions," 142.

2   Augustine, *The Confessions: Saint Augustine of Hippo*, ed. Fr David Meconi, trans. Maria Boulding (San Francisco: Ignatius Press, 2012), n. 19.22, P. 231.

3   O'Donnell, *Augustine Confessions*, 2012, 3:91.

4   Ibid., 3:106.

5   Ibid.

6   Augustine, *Saint Augustine: Select Letters*, ed. J. H. Baxter, The Loeb Classical Library (Cambridge, MA: Harvard University Press, 1930), 96.

7   O'Donnell, *Augustine Confessions*, 2012, 3:107.

8   Ambrose, *On the Sacraments and On the Mysteries*, 2.7.24, P. 68.

9   Brown, *Augustine of Hippo*, 121.

10 Spencer C. Tucker, *A Global Chronology of Conflict* (Santa Barbara: ABC-CLIO, 2009), 165.

11 Henry, *The Path to Transcendence*, 43.

12 C. Bennett, "The Conversion of Vergil : The Aeneid in Augustine's Confessions," *Revue Des Etudes Augustiniennes* 34, no. 1 (1988): 65.

13 O'Donnell, *Augustine Confessions*, 2012, 1:124.

14 Bauer and Danker, *A Greek-English Lexicon of the New Testament and Other Early Christian Literature*, 932.

15 G. K. Beale and D. A. Carson, *Commentary on the New Testament Use of the Old Testament* (Grand Rapids, MI: Baker Academic, 2007), 701.

16 Kenney, *The Mysticism of Saint Augustine*, 80.

17 T. Sorg, "Heart," ed. Colin Brown and David Townsley, *The New International Dictionary of New Testament Theology* (Grand Rapids, MI: Zondervan, 1986), 180.

18 Leo F. Stelten, "Ictus," *Dictionary of Ecclesiastical Latin* (Peabody, MA: Hendrickson, 1995), 119.

www.ingramcontent.com/pod-product-compliance
Lightning Source LLC
Chambersburg PA
CBHW081148090426
42736CB00017B/3227